"Bitter is the gatekeeper of adult taste."
—NAOMI DUGUID

Jennifer McLagan

Photography by Aya Brackett

Bitter

**A TASTE OF THE WORLD'S
MOST DANGEROUS FLAVOR,
WITH RECIPES**

TEN SPEED PRESS
Berkeley

"Alas! What various tastes in food
Divide the human brotherhood!"
—HILAIRE BELLOC

"A man's palate can, in time, become used to anything."
—NAPOLEON

"[Bitter] is a subdued edge, an acquired taste appreciated by adults."
—*KINFOLK MAGAZINE*

FOR H,

THANKS FOR TRYING TO MAKE ME LOVE RUTABAGA.

CONTENTS

INTRODUCTION

Now, how it is we see some food for some,
Others for others...
I will unfold, or wheretofore what to some
Is foul and bitter, yet the same to others
Can seem delectable to eat?
    —Lucretius

T his book began with a conversation about grapefruit, and how in the past they were bitter. My friend Laura, also a cookbook author, and I were lamenting the changes wrought to this wonderful fruit by marketing boards and the North American sweet tooth. When was the last time you tasted a proper bitter grapefruit with white flesh? For me, it has been years. The grapefruit of my childhood have been replaced with pink, sweet ones. Yes, today's grapefruit still has some acidity, but it has lost its bitterness and as a result is a fruit much less interesting to eat.

I grew up with bitter grapefruit. My mother conscientiously made me a three-course breakfast every morning before sending me off to school. This probably explains why today I avoid breakfast, drinking only a café au lait in the morning. However, I fondly remember the grapefruit halves she served, prepared with a grapefruit knife. This specialized knife, serrated on both sides, is gently curved, allowing you to separate the grapefruit flesh from its pith and skin. Once done, you cut between the membranes, making the segments easily accessible to a small spoon. The natural bitterness of the grapefruit's flesh was tempered with a light sprinkling of sugar and the ready-to-eat fruit was presented in a bowl.

"When it comes to food tastes, we all speak in different tongues .... People inhabit separate taste worlds." —LINDA BARTOSHUK

Later, when I began cooking, grilled grapefruit was a popular starter in hotel restaurants; it was prepared as my mother had done it, but with all the pips removed and a shot or two of sherry added. Topped with a mixture of brown sugar and a little butter, the fruit was slipped under the broiler until the sugar caramelized. The result was the perfect balance of bitter and sweet to stimulate the appetite.

My experience with grapefruit gave me a positive attitude to bitter, and it became an important part of my flavor palate. As I explored the world of bitter food, citrus zests, turnips, rapini (broccoli raab), chicories (endives), and cardoons became some of my favorite tastes, and I found myself craving them. They were for me, as Lucretius said, "delectable to eat," though other people found them "foul" and were unwilling to try them.

"Every culinary choice we make defines who we are—not just to ourselves, but also to others." —SYBIL KAPOOR

A reluctance to eat bitter foods is understandable, as we all have an innate aversion to bitter tastes. Our tongues are covered in taste buds that are very adept in detecting even the smallest traces of bitterness. This is a natural defense system to protect us: many poisons are bitter, so our response when tasting something very bitter is to grimace and often to spit it out. This reaction is strongest in babies, as small amounts of toxins can kill them. As we age, we lose taste buds, and we also learn that not all bitter foods will kill us. In fact, we realize that many bitter foods, like coffee, bitter alcohols, and chocolate, stimulate our nervous system in ways we enjoy, so we actively seek them out. Over time we have also discovered that many bitter foods contain compounds that can protect us against illness, and positively influence our health.

So does it matter if we avoid bitter? Absolutely yes! Bitterness is a double-edged sword: it signals toxic and dangerous, but it can also be pleasurable and beneficial. In the kitchen, eschewing bitter is like cooking without salt, or eating without looking. Without bitterness we lose a way to balance sweetness, and by rejecting it we limit our range of flavors. Food without bitterness lacks depth and complexity.

Looking around, I can see that interest in bitter is on the rise. It's returning to the drink world, with a growing interest in cocktails containing bitters; a good Manhattan is impossible without them, and bitter alcohols, like European aperitifs and Italian amaros, are becoming popular. Bitterness is slowly making its way into the North American culinary consciousness, too. The last decade or so has seen a huge increase in the popularity of bitter lettuces, beginning with mesclun mix; now bitter greens like arugula, dandelion, radicchio, and frisée are common in restaurants. Alongside these lettuces, vegetables like brussels sprouts, turnips, and white asparagus, all of which have a bitter edge, are appearing frequently on menus. Chefs are highlighting the bitter components of nuts and fruits like walnuts and citrus, and bitterness is an important part of the flavor profile of quality olive oils. The makers of craft beer exploit the bitterness of hops, while artisanal chocolate makers create bitter chocolate bars with higher and higher cacao content. Surely the time is right, I decided, to champion the use of bitter in the kitchen.

First I would have to define "bitter." I thought that would be easy until I actually tried to do it. When I discussed the taste of bitter with others, I realized that what I think of as bitter is not necessarily bitter for other people. Some even argued that grapefruit, which were the spark for this book, aren't even bitter: they're simply sour. Perhaps these people had never eaten a white grapefruit? Or was it a tougher problem than that? Was it possible to pin down the taste of bitter?

We can probably all agree that Fernet-Branca, rapini, citrus zests, and beer are bitter, but I became more aware of the diversity of what we think of as bitter when numerous friends, all working in the food world, sent me suggestions for foods to include in the book. While I agreed with most of their ideas, some surprised and even shocked me. Among them were Camembert, celery, cucumber, Campari, Belgian Chimay cheese, eggplant, lemons, pickled onions, rhubarb, Seville orange marmalade, sorrel, coffee, and white Châteauneuf-du-Pape wine. Aren't rhubarb and sorrel simply sour? Lemon is both sour—its juice—and bitter—its peel. Celery, cucumber, Seville orange marmalade, Campari, and white Châteauneuf-du-Pape wine all have bitter notes, but eggplant is rarely bitter today. The bitterness of Chimay cheese comes from its beer-washed rind, and I've discovered that cheeses made with cardoons have a touch of bitterness, but Camembert? Not in my experience. Perhaps my friend had a cheese that was a little sour and confused that with bitterness? How our food is prepared also influences our perception of bitterness.

TASTE AND FLAVOR

In everyday language we use the words *taste* and *flavor* interchangeably, and I will continue to do so here, apologizing to those who study taste and who make a very important distinction between taste and flavor. Technically, *taste* is a chemical sensation registered by the taste buds in our mouth and throat, and *flavor* is created in our brain with the information from our taste buds and our sense of smell (see page 240). Bitter is one of the original four basic tastes that also include sweet, sour, and salty. Now we know that we can taste savory, called umami, and recently science has discovered that we can discern fat. New research suggests that we should add metallic, calcium, and soapy to this list. For me, bitter is both a taste and a flavor.

Coffee gets only a small amount of its bitterness from the caffeine; most of it depends on how the beans are roasted and the method used for brewing it. Bitterness covers a wide span from aggressive to subtle; realizing that it is much more nuanced and difficult to pin down than the other tastes, I turned to science.

Specifically, I contacted Professor Russell Keast from Deakin University. Professor Keast works a stone's throw away from where I went to school in Melbourne, Australia. Not only is he a professor of food and sensory science, a member of the New Zealand Guild of Food Writers, but he was also a chef—so he's a man who can understand bitter from my perspective. He observed, "[Bitter] conveys a very simple hedonic message—if excessive, don't consume." That message, according to Keast, probably has something to do with why many of my foodie friends confused sour and bitter: this mix-up is common because both tastes can trigger a negative reaction in high doses. He also shone a light on the relative elusiveness and complexity of bitter: while only acids signal "sour," by contrast thousands of different compounds in foods elicit a "bitter" response.

And taste is only one of our senses that indicate bitterness. Smell, temperature, color, texture, and how the food feels in our mouth all relay a sense of bitterness to our brain. The pungency of arugula and horseradish can evoke a taste of bitter, as can the astringency that you find in celery, or the tannins in tea and cooked apricots. These sensations are delivered not through our taste buds, but via our somatosensory system, which includes touch, temperature, and texture. Beyond immediate sensory input are a whole range of cultural, environmental, experiential, and genetic factors that play a role in our perception of bitterness. The food's visual impact is very important, as is anything we have heard or read about it. These factors set up expectations about a food, so that we often dislike something even without tasting it because of how it looks, or how we think it will taste. What I find mildly bitter can be extremely bitter for others, just as the rutabaga that tastes bitter to me tastes sweet to many of my friends.

So when it comes to bitter, our understanding of it—even our experience of it—differs more widely than that of any of the other basic tastes. Bitter is not simply a reaction on our tongue—a taste in the strict sense—but also includes many different signals that register as bitterness in our brain. I was discovering that bitter was even more intriguing and perplexing than I had originally thought. To decipher bitter I would have to unravel the science of how our brain determines flavor. The research in this area is developing rapidly, and it encompasses everything from anatomy and genetics to culture.

The culinary history of why we keep bringing this taste into our kitchens despite our natural dislike of it gives another insight into bitter's persistent allure. As cooks, if we understand the role of bitter in the flavor spectrum, we can exploit and harness it in the kitchen. Cooking is about balancing tastes, and bitter often plays a vital role in a dish's harmony; it is crucial to the composition of a meal or menu. Without a touch of bitterness, your cooking will be lacking a dimension. Furthermore, bitter is both an appetite stimulant and a digestive—that is, it has the power to make you hungry as well as helping you digest your meal.

Here you'll find a mixture of recipes, culinary and physiological science, literary tidbits, and history. Like me, you'll probably be surprised by what you'll read here; it may make you rethink how you cook, serve, and savor a meal.

"How we think food and how we eat food are complex products of multiple histories. These cognitive, evolutionary, and cultural histories interact in unique ways in each individual, who brings to the table a personal history as well." —JOHN S. ALLEN

The complexity of bitter—and the individual variation we bring to experiencing it (see pages 24 and 35)—makes any exploration of the subject subjective. Mine, documented in this book and still unfolding (see page 247), reveals the prejudices of my palate and experience. I haven't included everything we eat that tastes bitter, and some of what I find bitter (pungent, harsh, tannic, astringent) you may not. My goal is to open up the possibilities in how you see bitter, so that while you may not become a lover of Fernet-Branca, you might cultivate a craving for a salad of bitter greens—to the benefit of your health and the delight of your palate.

It's worth trying to imagine bitter through the lens of the Japanese word *shibui*, which describes a tangy bitterness. According to *Kinfolk Magazine*, "When people are described as *shibui*, the image is of a silver-haired man in a tailored suit, with a hint of a bad-boy aura about him." So bitter is a cultured, intriguing, and sophisticated taste, with a dangerous side. Who could be more fun to cook or to dine with?

ONE

BORN TO BE BITTER

embers of the chicory genus, descendants of foraged wild greens and weeds, are loved for their bitterness—perhaps that's why so few of them have become mainstream in North America and, despite being widely cultivated, they have kept their bitterness. One of the best and easiest ways to explore the taste of bitter is through chicories. You'll find at least one member of this tribe to love. If you live in a part of the world where winter is a serious event, you'll discover that chicory and endive fill that craving for fresh vegetables when otherwise it's just flavorless winter lettuces or a never-ending diet of root vegetables.

Chicories come in a wide range of tastes, from mild to intensely bitter; textures, from soft to crunchy; and colors, from pale cream to vibrant burgundy. Most are interchangeable in recipes, and while we tend to eat chicory mainly as salad, many varieties are even better cooked. Raw chicories love dressings made with anchovies, lemon juice, and cheese. Cooked, their bitter taste complements rich meats like pork and duck. Chicory cooks quickly, so it can be added to soups or stews at the last minute to brighten the flavor.

The chicory genus is large and, in English, subject to some linguistic confusion—what you call *chicory* and what you call *endive* will likely depend on which country you come from. There are two main cultivated species; let's begin with the smaller one, *Cichorium endivia*, the endives, which includes curly and broad-leafed varieties.

> "It may come as no surprise to learn that I did actually come to enjoy these new tastes. I hadn't much choice. It is an adjustment of the palate that is necessary. Bitter is the taste of chicory—the French of yesteryear still miss it in their coffee—but the taste buds enjoy a 'pucker' from time to time."
> —SIMON HOPKINSON

Curly endive (pictured on pages 6 and 7) has lacy, dark green leaves on whites stems that form a floppy, unkempt head, and can be up to 12 inches / 30 cm across. It has an aggressively bitter taste and a chewy texture, especially the outer leaves. In the center of the head, the leaves are paler, softer, and less bitter. If you are trying curly endive for the first time, cook the dark green outside leaves to temper their bitterness and keep the inside ones for a salad. If you find even the inside leaves still too bitter, mix them with other lettuces, or break in your palate with frisée.

In France, *frisée* refers to large, pale green heads of curly endive that are up to 18 inches / 46 cm across and have been blanched (see below). On this side of the Atlantic, the blanched heart of curly endive is sold as frisée; it's gently bitter, and softer in texture than curly endive. It is best raw in a salad, either alone or mixed with other lettuces. It looks delicate but is robust enough to handle a hot dressing.

"Who wants to eat a good supper should eat a weed of every kind. This old Carrarese saying puts the matter in a nutshell, diversity is as important in weeds as it is in human beings." —PATIENCE GRAY

Broad-leafed endive (pictured on page 8) goes by several names: endive, escarole, Batavia endive, or simply chicory. Are you confused yet? I'm going to call it *escarole*, which is the common name in North American markets. On first glance, you might think it's a large Boston lettuce, with its flat, broad, green, gently ruffled leaves. On closer inspection, you'll see that the leaves are much more substantial, with firm, distinctly white stems. When you taste a leaf, you'll discover that familiar bitterness and crunch of chicory. Like curly endive, the inner leaves are paler and milder in taste. Both curly endive and escarole can be eaten raw in a salad, adding bitterness and texture; choose the pale creamy leaves from the center of the head. Try them with hot dressings like Hot Bacon and Mustard Dressing (page 41). Shred the outside green leaves and add them to soups or stews, stirring in just before serving to add a touch of bitterness.

BLANCHING

In cooking, *blanching* refers to cooking meat, fruit, or vegetables in boiling, often salted water for a short time, then refreshing them in cold water to stop further cooking. This method removes fat and blood from meat, sets the color of vegetables, and makes it easier to peel tomatoes and peaches. Blanching is also a horticultural technique applied to growing vegetables, like white asparagus, and chicories, like curly endive, Belgian endive, and radicchio. The method can be as simple as tying the plants up, or covering them with a box. Belgian endive's white leaves and pale white asparagus require more work and complete darkness. These plants are buried under the sand and are harvested before they emerge into the light. Preventing the light from reaching the plant's leaves stops chlorophyll from forming. This produces paler, more tender leaves, and with radicchio results in its brilliant color (see page 20).

The bitterness of chicory responds well to the mixture of salt from the miso and heat from the chile and ginger, making a vegetable side dish that is good hot or at room temperature. You can use either curly endive or escarole in this recipe, or a mixture of both. Whichever one you choose, use the darker outside leaves and keep the pale inside leaves for a salad. This recipe also works well with dandelion greens and members of the Brassica genus like rapini and brussels sprouts, with adjustments in cooking time.

CURLY ENDIVE WITH MISO AND CHILE DRESSING

SERVES 3 OR 4

17½ ounces / 500 g outside curly endive leaves

2 tablespoons lard or olive oil

1 red pepper, seeded and diced

1 shallot, diced

1 serrano chile, seeded and diced

1 tablespoon finely chopped fresh ginger

2 cloves garlic, germs removed, sliced

1 tablespoon red miso paste

Cut the endive leaves from the base and rinse and spin dry. Slice the leaves into 2-inch / 5-cm pieces.

Place the lard in a large saucepan over medium heat and, when it is hot, stir in the pepper, shallot, chile, and ginger. Cook, stirring, until the pepper softens. Add the garlic and continue to cook until it starts to color.

Add the endive leaves, cover, and cook for 5 minutes, giving the pan a shake from time to time. Uncover and stir in the miso until it is well mixed. Cover again and cook, stirring, for another 5 minutes. Uncover; the leaves should be wilted and dark green. Taste a piece of stem to see if it is tender and the seasoning is right, you should have enough salt from the miso and heat from the chile. Serve hot or at room temperature.

This recipe makes use of escarole's split personality by keeping its tender center raw and cooking the more robustly bitter outer leaves to reduce their bitterness and create a dressing. You could also make this with curly endive or a mixture of the two.

RAW AND COOKED ESCAROLE WITH GARLIC AND HERBS

SERVES 4

1 head escarole

6 tablespoons / 90 ml extra virgin olive oil

1 shallot, finely chopped

3 cloves garlic, germs removed, finely sliced

2 tablespoons red wine vinegar

Sea salt and freshly ground black pepper

1½ teaspoons fresh thyme leaves

3 tablespoons chopped fresh flat-leaf parsley

Cut the escarole leaves from the base and rinse and spin dry. Tear the small, pale yellow-green leaves into pieces and place in a salad bowl. Trim and discard any coarse areas from the dark green outer leaves, then slice them in half lengthwise and then crosswise into ¼-inch / 6-mm strips.

In a large frying pan, heat 2 tablespoons of the oil over medium heat, add the shallot, and cook until it becomes fragrant, stirring from time to time. Add the garlic and cook, stirring, until it colors lightly.

Pour in the vinegar and 2 tablespoons more of the oil. Add the sliced leaves and season well with salt and pepper. Cook, stirring, until they just wilt. Remove the pan from the heat, add the remaining oil and herbs, stir, and then pour over the pale escarole leaves in the salad bowl. Toss well and serve immediately.

BELGIAN ENDIVE

The other cultivated species of the chicory genus, *Cichorium intybus*, is a lot more color-ful and has some familiar members, starting with Belgian endive, the distinctive cigar-shaped chicory (you would think from its name it belonged in the other side of the family). *Belgian endive* is its North American name. It's called chicory, French chicory, or witloof in the United Kingdom, and just witloof in Australia. *Witloof* is a Flemish word meaning "white leaf," and while it is the most accurate moniker for this chicory, I'll call it Belgian endive here.

In the food world, new discoveries are often the result of lucky accidents, and Belgian endive falls into this category. It is a rather new vegetable developed in the mid-nineteenth century by M. Bresiers, the head gardener of the Brussels Botanical Gardens. This enterprising man didn't want to wait until spring to plant his chicory, so he decided to grow it inside. He dug up his plants, removed the leaves, and planted the roots in a dark, warm environment, covering them completely with mushroom compost. He was surprised to see that instead of the floppy-leafed plant he grew in his garden, the roots produced pale leaves in a compact torpedo shape. The following year, he tried it again and Belgian endive, or witloof as he called it, was born. In 1867 it was for sale in the Brussels market, and by 1883 you could buy it in Paris.

Belgian endive is still grown twice, first outside, where it produces green leaves that, while edible, are very bitter and usually fed to animals. The plant is dug up with its root intact, trimmed, then replanted inside and covered with sand or soil to prevent light from reaching it. After about a month, the root produces the tightly closed white head of Belgian endive. When the plant begins to push through the soil—you'll notice the tip of the Belgian endive is often the palest yellow-green—it's harvested. Heads of endive are carefully packed into boxes between layers of purple paper to prevent any exposure to light, which turns the edges of the leaves green and increases their bit-terness. Unfortunately, many markets dump the endive into a basket and leave them exposed, so look for endive with the palest yellow-tipped leaves. In North America the heads of endive I buy weigh in around 3½ ounces / 100 g each, while in France they can be double that size. If your heads are on the larger side you can cut them in half lengthwise. There is also a burgundy-tipped Belgian endive, the result of crossing it with radicchio. It is generally smaller in size and the leaves have a coarser texture, but it can be used in any of the recipes.

Often, recipes for endive begin by boiling them, but as British chef and food writer Simon Hopkinson points out, "When cooking endive it is absolutely essential that you do not use water. The endive itself is pretty well all H₂O." Cooking Belgian endive in water leaves you with a tasteless, waterlogged vegetable; it's probably why you think you don't like cooked endive. Here I've adapted Hopkinson's recipe, slowly caramelizing them in butter so they become meltingly soft. The butter enriches them and mellows their bitterness. You need a pan just big enough to hold the endives snugly, as they'll shrink as they cook. Serve them with a grilled veal or pork chop. Or try them in Belgian Endive Flemish Style (opposite).

BELGIAN ENDIVE BATHED IN BUTTER

SERVES 4

8 Belgian endives, about 1¾ pounds / 800 g

7 tablespoons / 3½ ounces / 100 g unsalted butter, diced

Sea salt and freshly ground pepper

3 tablespoons freshly squeezed lemon juice

Preheat the oven to 300°F / 150°C.

Wipe the endives with a damp cloth and trim their bases, if necessary. In an ovenproof frying pan with a lid, just large enough to hold the endives in a single layer, melt the butter over low heat. When the butter is melted, increase the heat to medium and cook the butter, shaking the pan from time to time, until the milk solids begin to brown and you can smell a nutty aroma.

Add the endives and lower the heat. Turn them to coat with the butter and season with salt and pepper. Cook the endives until they are lightly colored, then pour in the lemon juice. Cover the pan and place in the oven for 1 hour. Remove the pan and turn the endives carefully, cover, and return to the oven. Cook for another 45 minutes to 1 hour, until the endives are limp and very, very soft.

This is a classic from the Belgian kitchen. Belgian cuisine is known mainly for French fries, waffles, and chocolate; while all these are good, there is so much more. Nutmeg is a very popular spice in Belgium, and it's essential to this dish. The endives are cooked like the butter-roasted ones on the opposite page, but for a shorter time, and are turned halfway through the cooking time. This makes a satisfying lunch or a supper.

BELGIAN ENDIVE FLEMISH STYLE / SERVES 4

8 Belgian endives, about 1¾ pounds / 800 g, cooked for 1¼ hours (opposite)

2 cups / 500 ml whole milk

1 slice onion

5 black peppercorns

1 fresh bay leaf

A good pinch of freshly grated nutmeg

Butter for greasing

8 slices quality ham

1¾ ounces / 50 g flour

3½ ounces / 100 g Emmental cheese, grated

Sea salt and freshly ground black pepper

Transfer the cooked endives to a colander set over a bowl to drain. Leave the cooking liquid in the frying pan. Press gently on the endives to extract all the liquid and add it to the pan.

In a saucepan, bring the milk, onion slice, peppercorns, bay leaf, and nutmeg to a simmer over low heat. Remove the pan from the heat, cover, and leave to stand for 20 minutes.

Preheat the oven to 350°F / 180°C. Lightly butter a gratin dish. Strain the milk into a large measuring cup. Wrap the drained endives in the ham slices and place in the gratin dish.

Bring the liquid in the pan to a boil and reduce to about ¼ cup / 60 ml. Remove the pan from the heat. Whisk in the flour, then return the pan to a low heat and cook, stirring, for 3 minutes. Remove the pan from the heat again and slowly whisk in the milk, then return it to low heat and cook, whisking, until the sauce is thick and glossy, about 2 minutes. Continue to cook for another 3 minutes, whisking from time to time. Remove the pan from the heat. Whisk in the cheese and check the seasoning, adding more salt, pepper, and nutmeg if necessary.

Pour the sauce over the ham-wrapped endives. Bake for 30 minutes, or until golden and bubbling.

VARIATION The size of the ham slices will vary. Last time I made this dish in Paris, I discovered that my charcutier's idea of thin slices of ham was very different from mine; his were much thicker. So instead of wrapping each endive head, I lined the gratin dish with 1 ham slice, put the cooked endive on top, covered them with a second slice, then poured the cheese sauce over. To serve, I had to cut through the ham and, while less elegant, it tasted just as good.

CHICORY COFFEE

Coffee was a very expensive beverage when it arrived in Europe in the seventeenth century. People attempted to make it with cheaper substitutes, using everything from acorns to grains, figs to burnt toast, and the roasted roots of dandelion and chicory. When roasted and ground, chicory root looks like coffee, but it has none of coffee's taste, aroma, or caffeine. This didn't seem to bother some drinkers, and chicory was seen as the most tolerable substitute for coffee, as well as a good addition to extend ground beans. The Dutch developed a variety of chicory with an extra-large root, 2 inches / 5 cm in diameter and 12 inches / 30 cm long, just for making "coffee."

Frederick the Great, the ruler of Prussia in the mid-eighteenth century, became dismayed at the popularity of coffee drinking in his country. He thought it would be better for the local economy—and more patriotic—if his subjects drank beer like their ancestors instead of wasting their money on imported coffee. To encourage beer drinking he restricted coffee roasting to licensed establishments, increasing its cost. I don't know whether Prussians drank more beer, but they did turn to chicory coffee.

When coffee prices spiked during the Napoleonic wars, the French developed a preference for chicory coffee, which they took with them to Louisiana. Chicory coffee and blends of coffee with chicory remain popular today in parts of France and in New Orleans. Chicory was also added to coffee during the American Civil War. With the Confederate ports blockaded, Southerners quickly learned to make coffee with chicory and dandelion roots as well as acorns.

In the late nineteenth century, coffee essence, a mixture of water, sugar, and coffee, became popular. Simply mixed with boiling water it was useful on the battlefield, where soldiers didn't have the time or equipment to brew coffee. One of the popular brands, appropriately called Camp Coffee, was developed in Scotland in 1885. It is a liquid mixture of 26 percent chicory, 4 percent coffee, and the rest is water and sugar. The original Camp label showed a Scottish Gordon Highlander soldier sitting drinking a cup of coffee, while his Sikh servant stood by holding a tray with a bottle of Camp Coffee and a jug. The instructions on how to make the coffee were printed underneath. In time, this label led to allegations of glorifying imperialism, so the company changed it. They simply removed the tray, leaving the Sikh standing with his empty arm awkwardly crooked. Then, in 2006, the label was changed again to show the soldier and the Sikh seated side by side both enjoying a cup of Camp Coffee, with no indication as to which one of them had whipped up the beverage. Whether many people still use Camp Coffee I don't know, but at least they can rest assured that the label is now politically correct.

This dressing runs neck and neck with Hot Bacon and Mustard Dressing (page 41) as the best match with bitter greens, and is my first choice for Belgian endive. I love the soft crunch of the bitter leaves with the salty, garlicky dressing. This dressing is also good on a salad of frisée or radicchio. Try it warm on curly endive, escarole, or puntarella. There is only one proviso with this recipe: you must love anchovies and garlic.

BELGIAN ENDIVE SALAD WITH **ANCHOVY DRESSING**

SERVES 4

1 can (1¾ ounces / 50 g) anchovies in olive oil

2 large cloves garlic, germs removed, finely chopped

2 teaspoons freshly squeezed lemon juice

1 teaspoon Dijon mustard

Freshly ground black pepper

½ cup / 125 ml extra virgin olive oil

3 Belgian endives, about 10½ ounces / 300 g

Tip the anchovies and their oil into a saucepan and add the garlic. Place over very low heat and cook until the anchovies melt into a paste. Add the lemon juice and mustard and stir, then pour the mixture into the small bowl of a food processor. Blend until pureed, but with a little texture, and season well with black pepper. With the motor running, gradually add the olive oil. Taste the dressing for seasoning; I doubt you will need any salt, but you might want more lemon juice or pepper. Leave to cool. You will have about ¾ cup / 175 ml.

Wipe the endives with a damp cloth and trim their bases, if necessary. Quarter the endives lengthwise. If you are at all nervous about the bitterness, cut out the core: it is the bitterest part of the endive. Needless to say, I leave it in. Slice the endive wedges on an angle into ¼-inch / 6-mm strips. Place them in a bowl and toss with enough of the dressing to coat the leaves.

Any extra dressing can be kept in the refrigerator for a week or two. Put it in a jar with a lid, as it will not stay emulsified and you will have to give it a good shake before using.

VARIATION Use this dressing warm. Once it is pureed, return it to the pan and warm it gently.

RADICCHIO

Radicchio is the most colorful member of the chicory family. You might think that *radicchio* signifies "red" in Italian, but *radicchi* is actually an Italian name for the weeds that grow wild around the Mediterranean. Like the other members of *Cichorium intybus* species, radicchio is an offspring of those weeds. Thanks to its color, radicchio is popular—it's probably the best known of all the chicories.

Colorful radicchio is added to salads, and about half the radicchio grown in the United States ends up in salad mixes. This is a shame, because while cooking dulls radicchio's brilliant color, it develops its flavor. This chicory was originally a specialty of the region around Venice, Italy, and is protected by an Italian PGI (protected geographical indication). Each of the four varieties of radicchio bears the name of a local town. The most commonly available radicchio is Chioggia, which resembles a small red cabbage, round in shape with tightly packed, firm leaves with white spreading ribs. Verona is smaller, with maroon leaves and white central stems that form a loose oval shape. Castelfranco makes up for its lack of burgundy color with its beauty: it looks like a rose in bloom. It is so pretty you might even be tempted to put it in a vase rather than eat it. It has pale, creamy yellow leaves flecked and spotted with burgundy and pink; it is best in a salad. The most esteemed radicchio is Treviso, with its long, elegant burgundy spears, each with a thick white rib. There are two varieties of Treviso: the early (*precoce*) has narrow, burgundy leaves with wide, distinctive white stems that form a loose head; the late (*tardivo*) has wider, more tightly packed leaves that form a flamboyant chef's hat shape. Treviso has the most pronounced flavor and is preferred by bitter lovers. It is my favorite to cook with, although I do use Chioggia and Verona when it is not available. Treviso is sometimes sold with a piece of the root still attached, which can be boiled and eaten.

Radicchio, like Belgian endive, requires serious coddling during its cultivation. This chicory begins life as a leafy green and needs cold temperatures to change color. To fully develop its burgundy hue, radicchio also undergoes blanching (*imbianchimento* in Italian), just like Belgian endive. It was a Belgian gardener who introduced the technique to the Italians. At the end of the 1860s, Francis Van Den Borre traveled to the Veneto area to design fashionable villa gardens. He noticed the local farmers growing chicory and, familiar with the techniques of blanching Belgian endive, he explained the method to them. Growing radicchio in the dark prevents the chlorophyll from developing in the leaves, and results in brilliant-colored heads of leaves with bright white veins. Borre's descendants stayed in Italy, and today they run a plant and nursery business in Treviso, just outside of Venice.

I was wandering around Turin looking for a lunch spot, which can be a bit of a task for me: I had my heart set on eating cardoons, as it was peak season. The first place had them on the menu, but it was empty; the second one had no cardoons, and the third was closed. By the time I found my way back to the first one, it was full. So I found a seat in the window at my second choice and settled on a radicchio strudel. It was delicious: radicchio seasoned with prosciutto, mixed with Fontina cheese, and baked in a regular pastry, not the filo that is usually associated with strudel. I was almost happy that the restaurant serving cardoons had been full.

RADICCHIO PIE / SERVES 6

2½ ounces / 75 g fatty
prosciutto or pancetta,
diced

14 ounces / 400 g
radicchio

1 leek

1 tablespoon
balsamic vinegar

2 teaspoons finely grated
fresh ginger

1¼ teaspoons sea salt

Freshly ground
black pepper

4½ ounces / 125 g
Fontina cheese

Lard Pastry (opposite)

1 egg, beaten

2 tablespoons fresh
bread crumbs

Place the diced prosciutto in a large frying pan over low heat and cook slowly until the fat is rendered and the prosciutto is just beginning to crisp.

Meanwhile cut the radicchio and leek in half lengthwise, rinse well, and then slice into ½-inch / 1-cm strips, using just the white and pale green of the leek. Add the sliced radicchio and leek to the pan and increase the heat to high. Cook, stirring, for about 2 minutes, until the radicchio turns brown and wilts slightly. Remove from the heat and add the vinegar, ginger, and salt, and season with pepper. Let cool.

Preheat the oven to 375°F / 190°C. Line a rimmed baking sheet with parchment paper.

Cut the cheese into ¼-inch / 6-mm dice and then add to the radicchio mixture. Divide the pastry in half. Roll one piece into a 13 by 8-inch / 33 by 20-cm rectangle. Place the pastry on the baking sheet. Brush the edges of the pastry with the beaten egg. Sprinkle the breadcrumbs evenly, keeping them within the egg-washed border, then mound the radicchio mixture on top making sure the cheese is evenly distributed. Roll the second piece of pastry into a slightly bigger rectangle, about 14 by 9 inches / 36 by 23 cm. Place the second rectangle over the top of the radicchio mixture and press the pastry edges together. Trim the edges, then use a fork to seal them well.

Brush the pie with the remaining egg wash and cut 5 or 6 diagonal slits in the top. Bake for 35 to 40 minutes, or until the pastry is golden brown and the filling is beginning to bubble up through the slits. Transfer to a cooling rack and let sit for 10 minutes. Serve hot or at room temperature.

This is a good pastry for savory pies. The lard gives it a wonderful flakiness and lightness, especially if it is made with leaf lard, the fat from around the pig's kidneys. Good-quality lard is essential, so render your own or make sure of its source.

LARD PASTRY

2 cups / 8¾ ounces / 250 g flour

¾ teaspoon baking powder

½ teaspoon fine sea salt

⅔ cup / 4½ ounces / 125 g chilled lard (preferably leaf lard), diced

⅓ cup / 75 ml ice-cold water

Combine the flour, baking powder, and salt in a food processor and pulse to mix. Add the lard and pulse until it is reduced to pea-size pieces, about 15 seconds. Turn the mixture into a bowl.

Pour the water over the flour and lard mixture and mix with a fork. Squeeze a bit of the mixture between your fingers. If it holds together, transfer the dough to a lightly floured surface; if not, add another couple of teaspoons of ice water and test again. Gently knead the dough into a ball and flatten slightly. Wrap in plastic wrap and refrigerate for at least 30 minutes before using. This pastry keeps for several days refrigerated and it freezes well.

TASTE BUDS EXPLAINED

The Flemish painter Adriaen Brouwer was a friend of Rubens and contemporary of Rembrandt. In 1640, he painted *The Bitter Potion*, in which he captured the universal response to an extremely bitter taste. It's the expression of disgust on the subject's face that captures our attention. We know from our own experience that he has just drunk something very bitter. All of us close our eyes, wrinkle our nose, and screw up our face when we swallow something very bitter; we can't stop ourselves, it's an involuntary reaction. The subject of Brouwer's painting is holding a bottle and a cup, which art historians speculate contained a quinine mixture, taken to prevent malaria.

Our ability to taste is an essential trait that can determine whether we live or die. Should we swallow the food in our mouth or spit it out? We have about ten thousand taste buds in our mouth. Each is a cluster of fifty to one hundred receptor cells and each one of these cells can pick out all the tastes, though some respond more strongly to a specific taste. Our taste buds communicate with our brain and our organs, sending them vital information about the food we are consuming. These cells are replaced about every ten days; and while these cells are continually renewing themselves, they are also declining in number as we age, and the older we get the faster they decline.

To complicate matters, when it comes to taste buds we are not all equally endowed. Babies and young children have more taste buds, making them particularly sensitive to strong and bitter tastes. As adults our sensitivity to taste varies, too. However, unlike sight, hearing, or smell there is no simple, foolproof test to determine our responsiveness. You can determine whether you are a more sensitive taster by counting the number of taste buds on your tongue: the more you have, the more sensitive you will be. Another test is with the very bitter chemical 6-n-propylthiouracil (PROP), used to treat hyperthyroidism. People who find it unbearably bitter are described as supertasters, while normal tasters will find it mildly bitter and those that don't taste it are nontasters. While genetics play a part, generally a population breaks down into 25 percent supertasters and nontasters, while normal tasters make up the remaining 50 percent.

What does being a supertaster mean? Not that you have a superior palate or will be a great cook (most chefs fall into the mid-range). It simply means that you are highly sensitive to a particular bitter taste. This can be a curse, as supertasters often avoid all bitter foods, many of which are good for them, and become picky eaters who reject strong tasting foods. Both the PROP test and counting your taste buds are rather blunt instruments to assess bitter sensitivity. Bitter is a very nuanced taste, and each of our taste buds has around twenty-five bitter receptors. Some of them respond to only one bitter taste while others react to more than fifty different bitter chemicals. So grapefruit triggers one receptor and coffee another, sending different bitter signals to our brain.

Despite genetic factors and different sensitivities to bitterness, we all have the same basic anatomy, and there is no biological reason why we should like or dislike one food more than another. Culture, experience, peer pressure, and our environment create our food preferences. Every time we eat, all these factors come into play. Food is botany overlaid with history, family, and identity. These all interact, giving us each a distinct sense of taste, and it begins even before we are born.

We understand the influence of alcohol and tobacco on the unborn child, and now studies show that if a mother eats a lot of a particular food during pregnancy—blue cheese, fennel, carrot, mint, and vanilla are among those that have been tested—her child will have a preference for that food. During our very early years we are dependent on others for our food, so our family unit, our social group, and even our religion shape food preferences. Food preferences bind us together and unite us in a social network by building a common flavor palate and cuisine from which we judge the food of others. Food is a basic building block of culture just like poetry and music are. Our taste preferences are often the last to be relinquished. Immigrants may learn the language and habits of their adopted country, but they cling to their familiar foods.

If our early food experiences exposed us to bitter tastes we are more likely to appreciate them. This explains why the use of bitterness varies widely across culinary cultures. Italians and Asians have a long tradition of enjoying bitterness and incorporating bitter foods into their cuisine, while in North America sweetness rules. If bitter is not part of our food culture, or has a negative cultural connotation, we are more likely to avoid it. Although the influences of our family, culture, and past experience are strong, we are not condemned to live and die in the taste world we were raised in. Our palate is malleable and exposure to new foods can help us overcome old prejudices. We can travel and experience new and different foods. Or, if we live in a city with a large immigrant population, we can do this without even stepping on a plane. Simply seeing other people eating and enjoying a certain food will encourage us to try it.

Taste and how we create flavor in our brain is currently being studied at the molecular level. MRIs reveal which parts of our brain react when we eat certain foods. What we don't yet really understand is how our brain transforms the detection of taste into a perception of taste and then into flavor. Taste remains the least understood of our senses.

I love the winey hue that radicchio gives the rice in this dish, and the way its bitterness balances the pumpkin's sweetness. Now I know that using the word *pumpkin* reveals my birthplace, but I just can't get my head around "squash." However, so I don't confuse you, use a firm, dry pumpkin (or squash) like Hubbard or kabocha, which has a mild chestnut flavor.

I prefer to make risotto in small batches. This will stretch to serve four as a starter, depending on the rest of your meal; you can also double the recipe. Do use homemade stock, as it will make all the difference to the final result. You could also use a well-flavored vegetable stock to make this dish vegetarian. You'll probably only need 2 cups / 500 ml of the stock, but it will depend on your rice, so it is better to have a little extra just in case.

RADICCHIO AND PUMPKIN RISOTTO

SERVES 2

2½ cups / 625 ml chicken stock, preferably homemade

¼ cup / 2 ounces / 60 g unsalted butter

1 shallot, finely chopped

6 ounces / 170 g pumpkin, cut into ½-inch / 1-cm dice, about 1¼ cups

Sea salt

5¼ ounces / 150 g radicchio leaves, rinsed and trimmed

½ cup / 3½ ounces / 100 g risotto rice (Vialone nano, Arborio, or Carnaroli)

2 tablespoons white wine or dry vermouth

Freshly ground black pepper

Parmesan cheese

Pour the stock into a saucepan and bring to a boil. Lower the heat so the stock barely simmers.

In another saucepan, melt half the butter over medium heat. Add the shallot and cook until translucent. Add the diced pumpkin and stir to coat the pieces with the butter. Season with salt, and cook until the pumpkin starts to soften slightly at the edges, about 5 minutes.

Meanwhile, cut the radicchio leaves in half lengthwise, then crosswise into ¼-inch / 6-mm strips. You should have about 4 cups / 1 l.

Add the rice to the pan, stirring to warm the grains and coat them in butter. Stir in the radicchio and continue stirring until it wilts and changes color. Pour in the wine and cook, stirring until it evaporates; season with black pepper. Now add a ladleful of hot stock and keep stirring the simmering rice constantly until the liquid is almost completely absorbed. Continue adding the stock, one ladleful at a time, when the previous liquid is almost completely absorbed.

After 20 to 25 minutes, the pumpkin should be cooked and the rice should be creamy and cooked but still slightly al dente. Remove the saucepan from the heat and let sit for 2 minutes. Check the seasoning, stir in the remaining half of the butter, and serve in warm bowls. Grate Parmesan over the top.

This is a flexible recipe. Radicchio varies in size and weight, so grill what you have—and yes, you can use Chioggia or Verona radicchio, though I find it easier to grill Treviso, and I prefer its more intense bitterness. Any creamy cheese works as long as it's mild; you want it to balance, not overwhelm the bitterness of the radicchio. My choice would be a Normandy Camembert, a Pierre Robert, or a Brillat-Savarin.

GRILLED RADICCHIO
WITH CREAMY CHEESE

SERVES 4 AS A SIDE DISH

2 heads Treviso radicchio, about 7 ounces / 200 g each

Olive oil

Sea salt and freshly ground black pepper

2½ ounces / 75 g creamy cow's milk cheese

2 teaspoons balsamic vinegar

Cut the radicchio heads into quarters and drizzle with olive oil, turning to lightly coat the pieces. Season with salt and pepper.

Heat a gas grill to medium, or set a heavy cast-iron pan over medium heat. When it is hot, add the radicchio and cook, turning often, until it is soft, brown in color, and lightly charred, about 12 minutes. Cut the cheese into pieces.

Transfer the radicchio to a serving dish. Top with pieces of the cheese and sprinkle with the balsamic vinegar. The heat of the radicchio will melt the cheese.

VARIATIONS

Grill, drizzle with the balsamic vinegar and more olive oil, and serve with Serrano ham and fresh figs.

Try the recipe with Belgian endive, using lemon juice instead of balsamic vinegar.

Gorgonzola cream pasta sauce is often too rich, even for someone who loves animal fat like me. By adding radicchio, you offset the richness of the cheese and cream with a hit of bitterness. This lightens the sauce and makes it more complex and interesting. Generally speaking, adding finely shredded or chopped chicory to rich dishes is a great way to make them more digestible and more complex.

RADICCHIO AND GORGONZOLA PASTA SAUCE

SERVES 4
AS AN APPETIZER

Sea salt

10½ ounces / 300 g penne

1 cup / 250 ml whipping (35 percent fat) cream

3½ ounces / 100 g Gorgonzola dolce cheese, diced

3½ ounces / 100 g radicchio leaves

Freshly ground black pepper

Bring a large saucepan of salted water to a boil over high heat. Add the penne, stir, and return to a boil. Adjust the heat so the water boils gently and cook the penne until al dente.

While the penne is cooking, pour the whipping cream into a frying pan and bring to a boil over medium heat. Continue to boil until the cream thickens slightly and reduces to about ⅔ cup / 150 ml. Add the cheese, lower the heat, and stir until melted.

Rinse and dry the radicchio and chop finely. Add to the sauce and stir until the leaves soften and change color. Season with salt and pepper. Drain the penne and add to the pan, toss to coat with the sauce, and serve.

In winter I like to roast root vegetables in olive oil or pork or duck fat with a couple of rosemary branches. I serve them with roasted or grilled meat, or simply make a meal out of them. You can use whatever combination of root vegetables you want. Roasting vegetables caramelizes them, giving them a sweetness that is even more pronounced when you add a member of the chicory family—escarole, dandelion chicory, radicchio, sugarloaf or endive—for contrast. I start the vegetables in very hot fat, but if you're cooking them with a roast, you can cook them at a lower temperature for longer.

ROASTED CHICORY AND ROOT VEGETABLES

SERVES 6

1 large carrot

1 rutabaga

2 potatoes

1 pound / 450 g butternut squash

2 onions

¼ cup / 60 ml duck fat

2 large branches rosemary

Sea salt and freshly ground black pepper

1 pound / 450 g shredded chicory

Preheat the oven to 450°F / 230°C.

Cut all the vegetables except the onions into similar sized chunks, making the rutabaga a touch smaller, as it usually takes the longest time to cook. Cut the onion into wedges.

Put the duck fat in a roasting pan just large enough to hold the vegetables snugly in a single layer and place in the oven for 5 minutes. Remove the pan and carefully toss the vegetables into the hot fat, stirring to coat. Add the rosemary and season well with salt and pepper.

Roast for 15 minutes, then stir and lower the oven to 375°F / 190°C and roast for another 30 minutes, stirring halfway through. Check to see whether all the vegetables are tender; if not, roast until they are. Once the vegetables are cooked, scatter the shredded chicory on top, stir, and cook for a final 10 minutes or until the chicory wilts, softens, and changes color. Stir again, check the seasoning, and serve.

MORE CHICORY

Sugarloaf chicory could be mistaken for a sweetheart (pointed) cabbage, or romaine lettuce. It is about the same size and shape as the latter, with tightly overlapping leaves that have a cabbage-like texture. As its name suggests, it does have a touch of sweetness, but then as you chew on the leaves its bitterness kicks in. You can use it in salad, coarsely chopping the leaves and tossing with Haralds's Vinaigrette (page 192), or try cooking it (page 34). Even more interesting members of the chicory tribe are the *Catalogna chicories* with their dark green saw-toothed leaves that resemble dandelion leaves. In fact, most of the dandelion bunches we buy are really Catalogna chicory, not true dandelions. Their leaves come in various lengths, and one variety even has red stems. They are bitter. The most bizarre-looking member of the Catalogna family is the asparagus chicory, or, as the Italian call it, *puntarella*.

What I love about being interested in food is that there is always something new to discover: a technique, a spice, a vegetable. Puntarella was a discovery for me. It was my husband who first noticed it at our local market (we're lucky enough to live in a very mixed ethnic neighborhood with an independent grocery store). Looking for some dandelion greens, my husband grabbed what he thought was an extra-large bunch. Not until we paid did we realize he'd bagged something else: most puntarella comes from Italy and is sold by weight, making it a lot more expensive than a bunch of dandelions.

At first glance it does look like a large bunch of dandelion leaves; however, on closer inspection you see that they are attached to a cauliflower-like base. In the center of the leaves protruding from the base are numerous hollow, pale green or white shoots tipped with green. They look like short, fat asparagus. Both the bitter leaves and the shoots of this chicory are edible. It requires more preparation than just rinsing (see page 36), but it is worth the effort. In a salad it has a mildly bitter crunch, while cooking develops its bitter taste.

While sugarloaf chicory makes a great salad, it is also delicious quickly sautéed. I like the richness of duck fat to balance the initial sweetness then bitterness of this slightly schizophrenic vegetable. Serve it with a rich meat or a cream-sauced dish.

SUGARLOAF CHICORY SAUTÉED IN DUCK FAT

SERVES 6 AS A SIDE DISH

1 head sugarloaf chicory, about 1¾ pounds / 800 g

¼ cup / 1¾ ounces / 50 g duck fat

3 shallots, diced

3 cloves garlic, germs removed, finely sliced

Sea salt and freshly ground black pepper

Freshly squeezed lemon juice

Cut the sugarloaf chicory in half lengthwise, rinse, and remove the base and any browned spots. Coarsely shred, and set aside.

In a large frying pan melt the duck fat over medium-low heat. Add the shallots and garlic and lower the heat. Cook gently, stirring, until the shallots and garlic soften and caramelize slightly, about 5 minutes.

Add as much of the sliced chicory as you can, stirring to wilt. As it wilts, add the rest of the chicory and continue to cook until it softens and just begins to release liquid; do not over-cook. Season with salt and pepper, then add a good squeeze of lemon juice. Serve hot or at room temperature.

I'LL HAVE THAT ON A ROUND PLATE, PLEASE

There is a current trend in restaurants for serving food on odd-shaped plates: large squares, long rectangles, triangles, and shapes better suited to a hospital room than a dinner table. Many times I've found myself seated at a table that was not big enough to hold the plates of food. What is wrong with round plates? Too boring?

We assess the flavor of what we eat with so much more than just our sense of taste and smell. Many subtle things that we are unaware of affect how our food tastes. Research is revealing how sound, our environment, color, and the shapes on the wrapping—and yes, even the form of the plate—can influence how food tastes. Much of this work is undertaken by packaging and marketing companies, in order to discover ways to subconsciously attract us to their products. However, it is important that we as cooks understand them. It is already well documented that the larger the plate we choose the more we will eat.

In Western culture there is a strong tendency to associate sweet foods with soft, rounded shapes and circles, while bitter and carbonated tastes are linked to sharp-edged designs like stars and pyramids. This could be the result of cultural conditioning. For example, many beers and sparkling waters use stars and triangles on their labeling that were probably first incorporated into the packaging to represent awards (the star) or purity (the triangle, a stylized mountain). These sharp shapes on foods that we know are bitter and/or sparkling come to represent bitter or sparkling tastes in general.

Experiments were conducted using a range of chocolates and beers. They were tasted and then ranked on a visual scale that had a rounded shape at one end and an angular shape at the other. Dark, high-cocoa-content chocolates landed at the angular end of the scale while milk chocolate was at the rounded end. The same results were recorded with beer: the more bitter the beer, the closer it was to the angular end. Food aromas were also rated, with the more pleasant ones at the rounded, smoother end of the scale and the nasty, harsher ones at the angular end. Shape symbolism is subconscious and it is probably culturally specific. The chocolate test was carried out with the Himba people in Namibia and the results were opposite: they matched bitter chocolate with rounded shapes.

So while the design of a package and the shape of our plate might be a small factor in the taste of our food, it is still worth considering. Culture, experience, and our subconscious all play a role in our perception of the bitterness of a food; even the plate we serve it on will subtly prejudice us. So when you make a dish or a meal with something bitter, you might try putting it on a round plate.

The classic way to serve puntarella chicory is raw in a salad with a strong anchovy-garlic dressing (see page 19). However, I find that this chicory is only mildly bitter when raw and that the dressing can overwhelm it. A simple dressing of blood oranges is a better match, and they are in season together.

PUNTARELLA CHICORY
WITH **BLOOD ORANGES**

SERVES 6

1 puntarella chicory, about 1½ to 1⅔ pounds / 700 to 750 g

4 blood oranges

2 tablespoons freshly squeezed lemon juice

Sea salt and freshly ground black pepper

6 tablespoons / 90 ml extra virgin olive oil

Fill a sink with cold water. Begin by removing the dark green outer leaves with their stems from the base of the puntarella, discarding any brown ones, and drop them into the water. Next, cut the spears from the core: it is just like removing cauliflower florets. Trim any larger green leaves from the spears and drop everything into the sink. Rinse well.

Drain the spears and slice thinly lengthwise. Place them in a large bowl and add ice and cold water, then refrigerate for a couple of hours. They will crisp up and curl.

Drain the leaves and then drop them into a large saucepan of boiling salted water. Cook for 2 minutes, counting from when they hit the water. Drain and refresh in cold water. Place them in a towel and squeeze dry, then chop them coarsely. Place them in a salad bowl. Drain the spears, dry well, and add to the leaves.

Finely grate the zest from one orange and set aside. Then cut a thick slice off the top and bottom of each orange to reveal the flesh. Stand the fruit upright on a cutting board and, cutting from the top down to the bottom, remove the skin and pith. Holding the fruit over a bowl to catch the juice, use a small knife to cut along either side of each segment to the center to free it from the membranes.

Place the segments in the salad bowl and transfer 2 tablespoons of the juice to a small bowl (set aside the remaining juice for another use). Whisk the orange juice with the grated zest and lemon juice, then season with salt and pepper. Gradually whisk in the olive oil, then pour over the chicory, toss, and serve.

Instead of serving the dressing on raw puntarella, I prefer this classic combination when the chicory is steamed or braised and served warm. The result is a more balanced dish. However, you—like many Italians—might disagree, so try it both ways.

PUNTARELLA CHICORY AND **ANCHOVY DRESSING**

SERVES 4

1 puntarella chicory, about 1½ to 1⅔ pounds / 700 to 750 g

2 tablespoons olive oil

Anchovy Dressing (page 19)

Fill a sink with cold water. Begin by removing the dark green outer leaves with their stems from the base of the puntarella, discarding any brown ones, and drop them into the sink. Rinse very well. Drain and cut into 1-inch / 2.5-cm pieces.

In a large frying pan with a lid, heat the oil over medium heat. When hot, stir in the leaves, then cover and cook, stirring from time to time, for about 15 minutes. The leaves are cooked when they are tender but still have some texture.

Meanwhile, cut the spears from the core of the puntarella and rinse well. Cut any thicker spears in half lengthwise, and then cut into about 1-inch / 2.5-cm pieces (cutting each spear into 2 or 3 pieces).

When the leaves are cooked, add the sliced spears and anchovy dressing, stirring to mix. Cover and cook until the spears are just tender. This will take about 12 minutes; test often—they should have the texture of cooked asparagus. Serve hot or warm.

Raw puntarella is only mildly bitter. To enhance its bitterness you must cook it. This dish was developed from one by Elizabeth Schneider, an expert on all vegetables, common and uncommon. Similar-size heads of puntarella often vary in weight depending on how many shoots they have in the center. I've made this recipe with heads ranging from 1 to 1⅔ pounds / 450 to 750 g.

BRAISED PUNTARELLA CHICORY | SERVES 4

1 puntarella chicory, about 1½ to 1⅔ pounds / 700 to 750 g

3 tablespoons olive oil

2 onions, halved and sliced

Sea salt

2 tablespoons tomato paste

1 cup / 250 ml water

1 tablespoon small capers

1 tablespoon currants

Freshly ground black pepper

Freshly squeezed lemon juice

Fill a sink with cold water. Begin by removing the dark green outer leaves with their stems from the base of the puntarella, discarding any brown leaves, and drop them into the sink. Rinse very well. Drain and cut into 1-inch / 2.5-cm pieces.

In a large frying pan with a lid, heat the oil over medium heat. Add the onions, season with salt, and cook, stirring often, until the onions soften and begin to turn golden. Meanwhile, mix the tomato paste with the water. Rinse the capers and add them with the currants to the tomato mixture. Cut the spears from the core of the puntarella and rinse well. Cut any thicker spears in half lengthwise, and then cut into about 1-inch / 2.5-cm pieces, cutting each spear into 2 or 3 pieces.

When the onions are golden, add the tomato mixture and the sliced puntarella leaves. Stir to mix well, then cover and cook over low heat, stirring from time to time, for about 15 minutes, or until the leaves are just tender but still have some texture. Now add the sliced spears, stir, cover, and cook until they are just tender. This will take about 12 minutes; test often—they should have the texture of cooked asparagus.

Season with freshly ground black pepper, more salt if necessary, and a good squeeze of lemon juice. Serve hot, warm, or at room temperature.

DANDELIONS

Dandelions grow wild throughout the temperate zones of the world. A weed to some, the dandelion is also a tasty, chewy, bitter green, rich in vitamins A and C and iron. The name *dandelion* comes from a French expression, *dents de lion* or "lion's teeth," a reference to the shape of the plant's leaves. Curiously, the French have another name for the plant: *pissenlit,* which translates as "piss in the bed," and is a reference to the dandelion's diuretic quality. Though it's appreciated mainly for its leaves, the roots and flowers of the dandelion are also edible. In France, *cramaillotte,* often called "dandelion honey," is a jelly made with the flowers. Wild dandelions are rare in the marketplace; you may find some cultivated dandelions in specialized ethnic markets, but most likely the "dandelions" you'll find for sale are neither wild nor cultivated *Taraxacum officinale,* but Catalogna, or dandelion chicories (see page 33). The bitter leaves of these chicories resemble those of dandelions, but they are a touch more lemony than the real thing. You can use dandelion chicories in any dandelion recipe—and buying a bunch, even if it isn't really dandelion, is a lot less work than harvesting your lawn.

> "From a cook's perspective many bitter ingredients can add a fascinating complexity to the taste of food." —SYBIL KAPOOR

Eat dandelions raw with hot fatty dressing to mitigate their bitterness and soften their sturdy leaves. Braising softens them and mellows their bitterness, unlike dandelion chicories that become more bitter with cooking, and you can always mix them other greens. Try them in Arugula with Orecchiette (page 104) or Arugula Pizza (page 101).

Preparing dandelions is simple: just rinse well and trim the thick stems. If the stems are very pronounced, as often happens with dandelion chicory, trim the leaves from the stems with a sharp knife.

The secret to this recipe is good fatty bacon or pancetta, so that you have enough fat to dress the leaves. The hot fat softens the leaves and tempers their bitterness. While this dressing is usually paired with dandelion greens, it works well with curly endive, escarole, and frisée and even a brassica like brussels sprouts.

DANDELION SALAD WITH HOT BACON AND MUSTARD DRESSING

SERVES 4

3 slices bacon, about 2¾ ounces / 80 g

Up to 3 tablespoons lard

1 bunch dandelions, about 1 pound / 450 g, prepared (opposite)

1½ tablespoons red wine vinegar

1 tablespoon Dijon mustard

Sea salt and freshly ground black pepper

2 tablespoons dry vermouth or white wine

Cut the bacon into 1 by ¼-inch / 2.5-cm by 6-mm pieces. In a heavy frying pan, add 2 tablespoons of the lard and bacon and cook over medium-low heat for about 15 minutes or until the bacon has rendered all its fat and is crisp.

While the bacon is cooking, rinse and dry the dandelions and tear them into pieces; you should have about 10 cups / 2.5 l. Warm the salad bowl by placing it in a low oven or rinsing it with hot water. Place the dandelions in the warmed salad bowl and add the bacon.

Check the amount of fat you have in the pan; you'll need ¼ cup / 60 ml, so add the remaining lard as necessary. Whisk together the vinegar and mustard and season with salt and pepper. Heat the fat until hot and then whisk into the vinegar and mustard.

Pour the vermouth into the pan and stir to deglaze the pan, then whisk the contents of the pan into the dressing. Pour over the salad, tossing well to coat the greens with fat, and serve immediately.

A HISTORY OF BASIC TASTES

The question of taste has occupied philosophers, scientists, psychologists, and epicures throughout history. For the last century or so there have been only four tastes: bitter, sweet, salty, and sour, but it wasn't always so. In the past, taste was a philosophical question and there were some very interesting answers. The Chinese distinguished five tastes, adding pungent to our four and relating them to the essential five elements of Chinese philosophy: water, fire, wood, metal, and earth. In Western philosophy taste was the least important of all the senses. Ancient Greek philosophers believed that indulging our sense of taste led to desire, passion, and even gluttony, all of which were baser instincts and definitely not to be encouraged. Did those philosophers ever have any fun? For them, sight, which allowed us to appreciate art, and hearing, which gave us language, were the superior senses.

Plato proposed six basic food tastes: bitter, sweet, sour, salty, astringent, and pungent. Aristotle came up with seven and postulated that sweet and bitter were the two poles of taste and between them lay salty, pungent, harsh, astringent, and acidic. Theophrastus, who studied with both Plato and Aristotle, added oily to make eight. Eight tastes came to be accepted by most philosophers, although some amalgamated harsh and astringent while acidic and sour were used to describe the same taste, leaving bitter, sweet, sour, salty, sharp, pungent, harsh, and fatty. By the end of the sixteenth century insipid had been added, even though it describes a lack of taste rather than an actual taste.

In eighteenth-century Europe, the Enlightenment brought in new ways of thinking, and old beliefs and philosophies were challenged and reevaluated. Carl Linnaeus, a Swedish doctor and the father of animal and plant classification, who also named the source of quinine (see page 80), turned his attention to taste. He created a list of eleven basic tastes: bitter, fatty, sour, astringent, sweet, salty, sharp, viscous, insipid, aqueous, and nauseous. The Frenchman Père Polycarpe Poncelet in his book *Chimie du goût et de l'odorat* (1755) postulated that our sense of taste was like music on our palate. The harmony could be broken down into seven musical notes, or tastes: bitter (*amer*), acid (*acide*), sweet (*doux*), peppery (*piquant*), astringent (*austère*), sweet and sour (*aigre/doux*), and weak or tasteless (*fade*). *Fade* is the French for lack of taste, which is another way of saying insipid. He oddly described sweet and sour taste as distinct from acid or sweet, and interestingly overlooked salty. There was a desire to reduce all flavors into a few tastes. It was thought that they could be mixed like primary colors or musical notes to make different colors or harmonies of taste. Not everyone agreed; Brillat-Savarin, the French epicure, thought taste was limitless:

"The number of tastes is infinite, since every soluble body has a special flavor, which does not wholly resemble any other."

Yet the attempts continued to reduce food to a few basic tastes. Simplicity was appealing, and when Adolf Fick, a German doctor, narrowed them to just four in 1864, the idea stuck. In 1916, another German, psychologist Hans Henning, created his taste pyramid that allowed you to map any taste. His taste tetrahedron, a pyramid with a triangular base, had bitter, sweet, salty, and sour located at its points. Any combinations of two tastes would lie along edges of the pyramid while mixtures of three tastes were found on its surfaces. The theory was that any taste was a mixture of these basic ones and could be plotted on the taste pyramid.

"We are quite close to throwing out the theory of five tastes."
—HESTON BLUMENTHAL

While simplifying the number of tastes was appealing, it created problems by limiting our thinking about and our research into taste. If there are only four tastes, we only looked and tested for four. Yet this magic number persisted until relatively recently. Umami, a savory taste, has long been recognized in Japan as an important "basic" taste. The Japanese scientist Kikunae Ikeda isolated umami in 1909, but it took until the end of the century for Western scientists to accept his work and admit that the theory of four basic tastes was not really adequate. More tastes have since been considered: fat, a taste close to my heart, is on most lists thanks to work by researchers in France and Australia. Others up for inclusion are alkaline, astringent, rancid, metallic, pungent, soapy, and menthol.

The theory of "basic tastes" no longer appears the best way to think about taste. French researcher Annick Faurion suggests it would be more useful to imagine taste in at least ten dimensions. Perhaps we should return to the list proposed by Linnaeus. It is now understood that bitter is not one taste but a collection of many different bitter tastes. The bitterness of grapefruit is not the same as the bitterness of coffee or brussels sprouts. *Harsh, pungent,* and *tannic* are all words we use to describe bitterness, but are they enough? We need to increase our vocabulary to describe bitter. Bitter is a complicated and vexing taste—sometimes blatant and tongue-curling, yet also subtle and often elusive, so that not until we remove it do we realize that we have lost a vital taste.

My first restaurant job was in a bistro in the suburbs of Melbourne. There were three of us in the small kitchen: Maria, the dishwasher, an older, generously proportioned Italian woman; myself, working on appetizers, vegetables, and desserts; and the chef, Hans, a thin young man from Switzerland. He was not much to look at, but he did have large, deep brown eyes, which Maria called "bedroom eyes." I was much more interested in his rösti, which he served with veal, Zurich style—quickly cooked slices of veal in a cream and mushroom sauce. That was pretty exotic cooking for Australia in the mid-1970s. Every day I would cook potatoes for the next evening's rösti. They would rest overnight in the refrigerator before being grated and cooked in hot fat. I'm sure Hans would never have put dandelions in his rösti, but I like the bitter note with the starchy, fat-infused potatoes.

DANDELION POTATO RÖSTI | SERVES 2 TO 4

2 large boiling potatoes, about 14 ounces / 400 g

1 fresh bay leaf

Sea salt

¼ cup / 1¾ ounces / 50 g duck fat

1 small shallot, finely chopped

1 bunch dandelions, about 1 pound / 450 g, prepared (see page 40)

Freshly ground black pepper

Put the rinsed, unpeeled potatoes in a saucepan and cover with water. Add the bay leaf and some salt, and bring to a boil over medium-high heat. Lower the heat, cover, and simmer for 15 to 18 minutes, or until the potatoes can just be pierced with a skewer. Drain and let cool, then refrigerate for at least 4 hours, or overnight.

In a heavy frying pan over medium-low heat, melt 1 tablespoon of the duck fat and add the shallot. Cook the shallot, stirring, until softened but not colored. Add the rinsed dandelions and increase the heat. Stir until the dandelions wilt and begin to stick to the pan. Remove the pan from the heat and let cool. Chop the dandelion mixture coarsely.

Using a box grater, grate the potatoes on the coarse side. (You can peel the potatoes if you wish; I leave the skin on.) Place them in a large bowl with the chopped dandelion mixture. Season generously with salt and lots of freshly ground pepper and then mix well.

In a heavy frying pan about 9 inches / 23 cm in diameter, heat 1 tablespoon of the fat over medium-high heat. When the fat is hot, add the potato and dandelion mixture and cook for 2 minutes. Using a spatula, gently pat the mixture into a fat pancake; don't press too hard. Continue to cook for 5 minutes. Give the pan a shake to loosen the rösti and cook for another 5 minutes. If you think the rösti is sticking, loosen the base with a spatula and add some more duck fat.

Loosen the edges with a spatula and shake the pan again to detach the bottom of the rösti. Place a flat baking sheet over the pan, and using oven mitts, hold the baking sheet and pan together and flip them over in one quick movement so the rösti falls onto the baking sheet. Don't worry if the rösti breaks a little; you can patch it back together when you slide it back into the pan.

Add another tablespoon of fat to the pan and when it is hot, slide the pancake back into the pan, browned side up, doing any necessary repairs, and cook for another 10 minutes.

Slide the cooked pancake onto a board. Wait a few minutes, then cut it into 4 wedges and serve.

VARIATION Radicchio, curly endive, or escarole could all replace the dandelions.

The filling for these ravioli can be made with any mixture of bitter greens you want. Using a combination of greens makes for a more complex flavor. Make sure you use some escarole so you have the pale inside leaves to add to the dish just before serving—they'll add another layer of bitterness and texture. If you want to make the filling a little less bitter you can add Swiss chard or spinach leaves. You can also use arugula or even methi, which are fresh fenugreek leaves (see page 235). Make the filling ahead of time so it can drain in the refrigerator. I always use square wonton wrappers to make ravioli, and every time I buy them they seem to be a slightly different size. It doesn't matter: just adjust the amount of filling. These ravioli freeze well: place them on wax paper–lined baking sheets in a single layer and pop them in the freezer. When frozen, pack the ravioli into freezer bags; always cook them from frozen (don't thaw first).

BITTER GREENS RAVIOLI

MAKES ABOUT 30 RAVIOLI, ENOUGH FOR 6 SERVINGS

6 packed cups / 7 ounces / 200 g trimmed bitter green leaves

3 tablespoons olive oil

½ cup / 22 g finely chopped chives

¼ cup / 55 g ricotta cheese

Sea salt and freshly ground black pepper

1 egg white

1 teaspoon water

One 7½-ounce / 215-g package square wonton wrappers

¾ cup / 6 ounces / 170 g unsalted butter

1½ tablespoons freshly squeezed lemon juice

1½ cups / 1¾ ounces / 50 g shredded pale escarole leaves, optional

3 tablespoons chopped flat-leaf parsley

Pecorino cheese

Rinse the leaves; remove and discard any thick stems, then slice the leaves thinly. In a frying pan with a lid, heat the oil over low heat. Add the leaves, stir, cover, and cook very gently, stirring from time to time, until soft. Tip the mixture into a sieve and allow to cool. Put the sieve over a bowl, cover the mixture with plastic wrap, place a weight on top, and refrigerate overnight.

Next morning, place the drained greens mixture in a food processor and puree. Transfer to a bowl and mix in the chives and ricotta cheese, until blended. Season with ¼ teaspoon of the salt and lots of freshly ground pepper. You should have about 1 cup / 230 g of mixture.

Whisk the egg white with the water. Put a wonton wrapper, floured side down, on the counter, and place a heaped teaspoon of the bitter greens mixture in the center. Brush the visible surface of the wonton wrapper with the egg white mixture, then top with a second wrapper, floured side up. Press well to expel all the air trapped in the ravioli and seal. Then, using a cookie cutter centered on the mound of filling, trim the ravioli into a round; press the edges again to make sure the ravioli is well sealed, and place on a parchment-lined baking sheet. Repeat with the remaining wrappers and mixture, placing them slightly overlapping on the baking sheet. Cover the ravioli with a clean dish towel and refrigerate until ready to cook (up to 4 hours), or freeze.

CONTINUED

To cook, bring a large saucepan of water to a boil. Meanwhile, cut the butter into small pieces and place in a large frying pan over low heat. When the butter is melted, increase the heat to medium and cook until the milk solids just start to brown and you can smell a nutty aroma. Remove the pan from the heat and pour in the lemon juice; the butter will bubble and spit.

When the water is boiling, add some salt, and drop in the ravioli in batches; don't crowd them. Simmer until the ravioli float to the surface of the water and the wonton wrappers become slightly transparent, about 3 minutes. Drain the ravioli and add to the pan with the butter. When all the ravioli are cooked, return the pan to the heat and carefully turn the ravioli to coat with the sauce. Add the shredded escarole and parsley and some grated Pecorino, then serve immediately with more Pecorino.

MEMORABLE TASTE

What makes a meal memorable? And how well do we recall the details? One of my most memorable meals was a black truffle dinner at Jamin, chef Joël Robuchon's Paris restaurant, in 1993. We began with a cauliflower puree garnished with black truffles, which was followed by a black truffle tart, and the main course of *poulet de Bresse* with more black truffles. I know we had cheese followed by dessert, but I have no recollection of either. According to Paul Rozin, a professor of psychology at the University of Pennsylvania, the average American rarely remembers more than two dishes from any meal. What they do remember is the ambience, how they felt, and their dinner companions. His research shows that the French are much better than Americans at remembering their meals because they have a long tradition of spending time around the table and sharing their food experiences with their dining companions.

Perhaps my time in France has helped my memory? But as a food person, shouldn't I have done better? Rozin would not be surprised that I'd forgotten dessert. At the MAD2 conference in Copenhagen, Denmark, he gave a lecture on what makes a meal memorable. He compared eating a meal with attending a classical music concert, as they last a similar length of time. He is, of course, referring to an upscale restaurant meal like mine at Jamin, which lasts two hours or more. We can't recall everyday meals unless they were special in some sense. Rozin explained that meals are hard to remember because, unlike a classical concert, they don't usually have any repetition. Pieces of classical music are written around a musical theme that is repeated and reinterpreted throughout the work. They often begin and end with a bang, so most of us can recall the overtures and endings of classical works, but we do not remember what was played in between.

The first course sets the mood for the whole meal, so we remember it. If there is a new or surprising food, we will recall that, too. Dessert suffers by being at the end of the meal and, unlike the bang of a grand finale at the end of a concert, it is often more of a whimper. So I remember the unusual pairing of cauliflower with truffle at the start of my meal, and the tart topped with equal-sized truffle slices that was surprising and different. The chicken dish was a French classic and it included truffles. My meal, like classical music, had a theme—black truffles—making it easy for me to remember each dish. It was my birthday, so I know the date and recall my dinner companions, I can even describe the dining room. As for dessert, I'm sure it was delicious, but not unusual or surprising. If it had been blood ice cream or Tobacco Panna Cotta (page 234) I would have remembered it.

TWO

LIQUID BITTER

For most of us, our first encounter with bitter was as a liquid, stealing a sip of beer or a taste of coffee as children. The experience was usually negative, because babies and young children have more taste buds in their mouths, making them very sensitive to bitter tastes. It's a protective mechanism, as many bitter-tasting foods and liquids can be toxic, and even small doses are dangerous for them. As we age, we learn that not all bitter things are poisonous, and we come to appreciate a glass of beer, a gin and tonic, and coffee and tea. It also helps that bitter liquids tend to contain stimulants, giving us a very strong reason to consume them. For cooks, bitter liquids are one of the easiest ways to add bitterness to a dish.

"We overcome our natural dislike of all things bitter if what we are putting in our mouths has a psychoactive effect." —RUSSELL KEAST

Beer can add bitterness to everything from stews to jelly, as can coffee and tea. Too often we restrict coffee and tea to dessert and mask their bitter taste with too much sugar. It is better to balance them with the sweetness of fruit and don't be afraid to add them to savory dishes.

For a real dose of bitterness try bitter alcohols in your cooking. While we willing mix them into cocktails we overlook the fact that they are also excellent with meat, and in desserts. They are the best way to introduce bitterness to a dish without adding too much liquid. Bitter liquids are an easy way for a cook to begin experimenting with bitterness.

BEER: THE OLDEST BEVERAGE

Humans have been making alcohol for a very, very long time. Probably the oldest beverage (aside from water) is beer, which can be dated to Neolithic times and may be even older. Unlike animal bones, plant material is rarely preserved, which makes it impossible to know with certainty who brewed the first beer. In all likelihood it came about by accident—a grain gruel left to ferment. Some scholars argue that our taste for alcohol encouraged us to settle down and domesticate grasses so we could have a supply of grain to make it.

The earliest written records of brewing are Sumerian dating from the third millennium BCE. The Sumerians, as it happens, also developed cuneiform, one of the oldest forms of writing, to record economic activity. Their accounts reveal that 40 percent of their grain harvest was used to brew beer. They brewed at least nineteen different beers but they left behind no precise recipes. However, the Egyptians, who were also skilled beer brewers, left detailed information about their brewing methods in tomb paintings. They made a range of beers from mildly alcoholic ones to sweet, aromatic ones that reached 12 percent alcohol. These early beers were flavored with various herbs and spices, like bog myrtle, rosemary, yarrow, coriander, and juniper. None of them was very bitter, and they went bad quickly.

It is hops that give more modern beer its characteristic bitterness—and, most importantly, preserve it. Brewing spread from the Middle East into Europe, where hops grew wild, and were used for dying cloth and making rope. Their first documented addition to beer was in 822 CE in the statutes of a Benedictine monastery near Amiens in northern France, but it is not clear whether they were added simply for their bitter flavoring or also to preserve the beer. Not until much later, in 1150, when Hildegard of Bingen, abbess of a Benedictine convent on the Rhine, wrote about the ability of hops to preserve liquids, do we know for sure that brewers understood the preservative power of hops. Today very few beers are made without them, as hopped beers can last years, while unhopped ones spoil in a few weeks.

Hops have antibacterial acids, and a mere 7 ounces / 200 g of hops is enough to flavor and preserve 26 gallons / 100 l of beer. The bitterness and flavor profile of beer change with the hop variety and where it is grown. Hops are not only grown for brewing beer; their shoots are edible, too (see page 62).

Cooking with beer is as simple as using wine or stock. In Belgium and Britain, where little wine is produced, beer is often used for cooking. When braising with beer, think about balancing its bitterness with fat, salt, and something sweet like caramelized onions or carrots. It really doesn't matter which beer you use—as long as it is bitter.

My fascination with jelly (or, as you may know it, gelatin dessert) began as a child. My mother made wobbly sweet jellies for dessert. They were fruit flavored and came from a package; it was one of the only packaged foods we ate. Jelly is glimmering, transparent, and fleeting—perfect out of the mold, then resembling a train wreck the moment it's cut.

When I started to cook I eschewed the packaged jellies. I jellied coffee, Champagne, and even milk using sheets of gelatin that looked like old glass windows. Then I went one step further (or one step too far, depending on your opinion) and made my gelatin from scratch, using calf's feet and a lot of patience. Still, despite making everything from fruit jelly to headcheese, I had never thought of jellying beer.

This beer jelly isn't dessert; it's distinctively savory, and that's what makes it interesting. I discovered it at Semilla restaurant in Paris, where it accompanies their house-smoked salmon. The salmon was delicious, but the beer jelly grabbed my attention. I serve it with fatty smoked fish, beer-poached shrimp, country ham, or a plate of Cheddar cheese, smoked sausage, and pickles. Or serve it as a palate cleanser between courses. You only need a small amount of this jelly, 1 or 2 cubes; set it in ice cube trays so you can avoid cutting it. Each ice cube mold in a tray usually holds about 1 tablespoon, so you'll need two trays. The jelly will keep for a couple of days in the refrigerator.

BEER JELLY | MAKES 2 CUPS / 500 ML

2 cups / 500 ml cold wheat beer

1 package / ¼ ounce / 7 g powdered gelatin

½ teaspoon sea salt

¼ cup / 1¾ ounces / 50 g superfine (caster) sugar

2 teaspoons freshly squeezed lemon juice

Pour ¼ cup / 60 ml of the beer into a small saucepan, sprinkle over the gelatin, and let stand for 5 minutes. Add the salt.

Pour the remaining beer into a bowl and add the sugar and lemon juice, then stir to mix. Stir the beer a few times to get rid of the foam. Rinse the ice cube trays with water; it will make the jelly cubes easier to unmold.

Place the saucepan over low heat and stir to dissolve the gelatin. When it is dissolved, pour it into the beer-sugar-lemon mixture, stirring to mix, then pour into the rinsed trays and refrigerate until set.

When ready to serve, turn out the jelly cubes onto a damp surface. Wet your hands and a thin spatula to make it easy to transfer them to a serving plate.

A while ago, I was reading *Le goût transmis*, a book about families involved in the world of food. One chapter described a family-run brewery in northern France and how the passion for their craft had been passed down through four generations. We think of France being a wine country, but in the north, close to the Belgian border, beer is the drink of choice. The area is not good for growing grapes, but hops thrive. Included in the book were some family recipes using beer. When I read this one, I thought it was too simple and would need something else to make it tasty. I was wrong. I've altered it slightly, but it's a good example of the fact that often the simplest dishes are the best—and though this soup is simple, its flavors are surprisingly complex. The beer and the well-toasted bread add bitterness, while the cream balances them. Don't forget freshly grated nutmeg, which is probably a Flemish influence; it adds to the flavor. Followed by cheese (a good Cheddar, perhaps) and a salad, it makes a light dinner.

BEER SOUP | SERVES 4 GENEROUSLY

4 cups / 1 l beef stock, preferably homemade

1 cup / 250 ml amber beer

⅔ cup / 150 ml whipping (35 percent fat) cream

1 tablespoon dark rye flour

Sea salt and freshly ground black pepper

Freshly ground nutmeg

4 slices country-style sourdough bread, well toasted (see page 221)

Pour the beef stock, beer, and cream into a saucepan. Place over medium-low heat and bring to a gentle simmer. Sprinkle over the rye flour and then whisk it in. Season the soup well with salt, pepper, and a little nutmeg. Continue to simmer, uncovered, for 20 minutes, whisking occasionally. Do not allow the soup to boil.

Place a slice of toasted bread in each soup bowl, check the seasoning of the soup, then ladle the soup over the toast and finish with a touch more nutmeg.

When I was at cooking school, we cooked carrots in a little water with butter and sugar, reducing the cooking liquid to make a sweet glaze, a classic dish called *Carottes Vichy*. The choice for the cooking water was of course Vichy; however, in 1970s Australia, there was no bottled water, let alone French Vichy water. Carrots are naturally sweet and really don't need any more sugar, so instead of bottled water and sugar, I cook them in beer—still with the butter, of course. The beer and the butter reduce to form a lightly bitter glaze that contrasts with the sweetness of the carrots.

I cut the carrots thickly so that all the beer is reduced by the time the carrots are cooked; however, you can cut the carrots into sticks. If your carrots cook before the beer forms a glaze, simply remove them from the pan and keep warm while you boil down the liquid until it's syrupy.

BEER-GLAZED CARROTS | SERVES 4

17½ ounces / 500 g carrots

3 tablespoons / 1½ ounces / 45 g unsalted butter

½ teaspoon sea salt

1 cup / 250 ml beer

Freshly ground black pepper

Peel the carrots and cut into ½-inch / 1-cm rounds. Over medium heat, melt the butter in a saucepan large enough to fit the carrots in a single layer. Add the carrots and salt and cook for 5 minutes, stirring to coat the carrots with the butter. The carrots will release liquid.

Pour in the beer and bring to a boil. Reduce the heat so the beer bubbles gently, and cook for about 25 minutes, stirring occasionally, until the carrots are cooked and the liquid is reduced to a couple of tablespoons. Season with black pepper and more salt, if necessary.

Mussels steamed in white wine is a classic dish, but beer is a good alternative. The natural sweetness of mussels is balanced by a lager or an ale, and the chile adds a touch of heat. You can just add the coriander seeds to the beer, but as it is not strained they'll end up in your teeth; that's why I wrap them in cheesecloth or put them in a tea ball.

Mussels are usually sold already cleaned and only require a rinse under cold water before cooking. If they still have their "beard" attached, pull the beard and cut it off with a small knife. Scrape off any barnacles attached to the shell, then rinse. Check the mussels after rinsing to make sure they are all firmly closed. Discard any that do not close after a tap on the counter, or that have broken shells.

MUSSELS IN BEER / SERVES 2 AS A MAIN COURSE OR 4 AS A STARTER

2 tablespoons / 1 ounce / 30 g unsalted butter

1 onion, finely chopped

½ small fennel bulb, finely chopped, fronds set aside

½ serrano chile with seeds

1 cup / 250 ml lager or pale ale

1 tablespoon coriander seeds, crushed and placed in a tea ball or wrapped in cheesecloth

1 fresh bay leaf

2¼ pounds / 1 kg cleaned mussels (see headnote)

½ teaspoon sea salt

Freshly ground black pepper

Crusty bread, to serve

In a large saucepan, melt the butter over medium heat. When melted, add the onion, fennel, and chile. Cook, stirring from time to time, until the vegetables soften and begin to caramelize.

Add the beer, coriander, and bay leaf. Bring to a boil and boil for 2 minutes, then add the cleaned mussels. Stir, then cover and cook for about 5 minutes, giving the pan a couple of shakes, until the mussels open; discard any that don't open. While the mussels are cooking, chop the fennel fronds.

Remove the coriander seeds and bay leaf from the pan. Season the mussels with salt and pepper. Ladle the mussels and liquid into warm bowls, sprinkle with the chopped fronds, and serve with crusty bread.

THE WORLD'S MOST EXPENSIVE VEGETABLE

Humulus lupulus, or hops (pictured on page 50–51), is a flowering plant in the Cannabaceae family, which also includes cannabis. A climbing plant that, instead of using tendrils to climb, has stiff hairs on its stem that cling to whatever they can—so it is, technically speaking, a bine, not a vine. Hops need long days of summer sunshine to flourish, so the plants are trained onto wires to increase their exposure to the sun. They encircle the wires in a clockwise direction, growing some 26 feet / 8 m in only six weeks. The bine produces distinctive cone-shaped flowers that resemble soft green pinecones that are harvested and dried for brewing. Depending on the hop variety, and where it is grown, it will add different flavors and aromas to the beer as well as helping to preserve it.

"A hop-garden was one of the sights connected with Philip's boyhood and the oast-houses to him the most typical feature of the Kentish scene. It was with no sense of strangeness, but as though he were at home, that Philip followed Sally through the long lines of the hops. The sun was bright now and cast a sharp shadow. Philip feasted his eyes on the richness of the green leaves. The hops were yellowing, and to him they had the beauty and the passion, which poets in Sicily have found in the purple grape. As they walked along Philip felt himself overwhelmed by the rich luxuriance. A sweet scent arose from the fat Kentish soil, and the fitful September breeze was heavy with the goodly perfume of the hops." —W. SOMERSET MAUGHAM

While Germany is the major producer of hops, it is the Flemish who really appreciate them. Not only do they make great beers, but they also eat hops—the shoots, that is. Hop flowers are harvested at the end of the summer, but their shoots are a spring vegetable, traditionally available from mid-April to early May. However, such is their popularity in Belgium that growers now force the plants in heated greenhouses so the shoots can be ready for market at Christmas. Forced hop shoots sell for up to 1,000 euros a kilo, making them one of the world's most expensive vegetables. These forced hop shoots are grown like Belgian endive (see page 15). The plant roots are transplanted into greenhouses and kept well covered with a blanket of soil to keep them white. Hop shoots resemble small, thin, white asparagus, and the most valuable are the smallest and whitest. Like white asparagus, they are harvested by hand, with most of the production going directly to restaurants. Chefs sauté or blanch them quickly in boiling salted water to keep their crisp texture. They add them to salads, pair them with eggs, or mix them with those two stalwarts of Belgian cuisine, cream and nutmeg. The hop shoot growers prefer to eat them raw with a glass of beer. In the spring they are picked in the fields before they break through the soil, but they are still expensive—around 100 euros a kilo—thanks to their short season and labor-intensive harvesting.

> "Turkeys, heresies, hops, and beer,
> All came to England in one year."
> —OLD ENGLISH PROVERB

At the beginning of the sixteenth century, Flemish migrants took their love of hops with them across the Channel to Kent. This area soon became known as the hop-garden of England, and by the end of the nineteenth century, many Londoners spent their summers in Kent picking hops. This gave them the opportunity to holiday in the countryside and earn some extra money. Somerset Maugham, who grew up in Kent, wrote nostalgically about the local hop fields and oast houses, where the hops are dried, in his novel *Of Human Bondage*. While he paints an idyllic view of the experience, hop picking was piecework and very weather dependent, so often the workers earned very little. George Orwell gave a more realistic account in his essay *Hop-picking* (1931) and novel *A Clergyman's Daughter* (1935).

The English also adopted the Flemish habit of eating hop shoots. Dorothy Hartley, that renowned chronicler of English food, noted that boiled hop sprouts with buttered toast was a popular spring dish in Kent. In her book *Food in England*, she gives a recipe for buttered hop tops, explaining that the shoots must be harvested by early May and only up to the fourth leaf. After soaking them in cold water, she boils them until tender. She suggests a hop sauce for fish, chicken, or mutton, and adds finely chopped hops to her thick pea soup. From her description, it is clear that English hops were harvested after they emerged from the ground, and so were green and tougher than the blanched Flemish ones. Perhaps that is why they never became a gourmet vegetable in England. The renewed interest in foraged foods is making British hop shoots—or hop asparagus, as they are called—popular again. Green hop shoots are popular in Italy, too, where *risotto di bruscandoli*, or hop risotto, is a specialty of Veneto. In hop-growing areas of North America, pickled green hop shoots are available.

And how do they taste? Alas, I haven't tried them, so I can only quote others. The green ones have a grassy, green asparagus-like taste, while the white ones are crunchy with a fresh walnut taste. I know I will like the white ones better, so a trip to Belgium with a lot of euros is on the horizon.

Caramelizing onions with bacon, browning beef, and then slowly braising it all in beer makes a great winter dish, but it takes time. Sausages cooked in beer make a quicker, delicious alternative. Beer is a great liquid to cook with, especially when the other ingredients are fatty, rich, sweet, or, as here, all three. The beer balances the fatty sausages and the sweet onions and carrots. This simple dish is flexible: use whatever beer you like, and you can change the sausages. Mashed potatoes are the perfect accompaniment.

BRATWURST IN BEER | SERVES 3 OR 4

4 bratwurst sausages, about 1⅓ pounds / 600 g

2 tablespoons lard or duck fat

3 carrots, peeled and thickly sliced

2 onions, halved and sliced

1 teaspoon sea salt

Freshly ground black pepper

2 cloves garlic, germs removed, sliced

1 fresh bay leaf

2 cups / 500 ml beer

Pat the sausages dry and with a sharp knife prick them twice on both sides. In a heavy flameproof casserole or Dutch oven over high heat, melt 1 tablespoon of the fat. When the fat is hot, brown the sausages quickly, then transfer them to a plate.

Lower the heat to medium and add the remaining fat. When it has melted, add the carrots, onions, and salt and season well with pepper. Cook, stirring, until the onions soften and color lightly.

Add the garlic and bay leaf, then pour in the beer and bring to a boil over high heat, stirring to deglaze the pan. Boil for about 10 minutes; the carrots should be slightly tender, but not completely cooked.

Cut the sausages in half crosswise and add them to the pan. Lower the heat to a simmer and cook, uncovered, for 10 minutes. Turn the sausages and cook another 10 minutes. Check the seasoning and serve.

COFFEE AND TEA

Despite being bitter and tannic, coffee and tea are among the top five most popular beverages in the world. Few of us enjoyed them on our first encounter, yet billions of us have learned to like them. The bitterness of both comes from the bitter alkaloid caffeine and is reinforced by astringent, phenol-rich compounds like tannins. Easily soluble in water, tannins manifest as dry and puckery sensations via our trigeminal nerve, and their effects are persistent and long lasting. Caffeine, as well as being bitter, is a stimulant that affects our nervous system. Most of us know that a cup can kick-start us in the morning and that too much caffeine can leave us jittery and wide awake in the middle of the night. While tea leaves contain more caffeine than coffee beans, the extraction of caffeine is more efficient when making coffee: an average cup contains about 100 mg of caffeine as compared with 50 mg in black tea. It takes about 30 minutes for the caffeine from a cup of coffee or tea to work its way to a peak level in our blood. Depending on our metabolism, this level will drop by half within four to five hours. Both coffee and tea have been by turns vilified and praised for their effects on our health; the current opinion is that, in moderation, they are good for us—mostly because they are both excellent sources of antioxidants.

While it's the stimulant effect of caffeine that has helped us accept the bitterness of these beverages, the bitter, complex nature of well-brewed coffee and tea makes them interesting additions to a cook's palate of flavors. I like to balance tea with sweetness, especially fruit; the tannins in tea intensify the flavors of the fruit. I may be alone in my dislike of coffee desserts; I prefer adding a small amount of coffee to a sauce for rich meats, or when deglazing a roasting pan, for a wonderful balancing note of bitter. Think of coffee as a seasoning; adding a small amount gives a hint of bitter to a dish. It works with meat, vegetables, and even seafood.

Tea's bitterness is altered by the brewing time: the longer you leave it, the more caffeine and tannin you will extract. The bitterness of coffee depends not only on the bean, but also on how it is roasted and brewed. There is a vast array of coffee roasts to choose from, many of which result in less bitter coffee. I have a preference for darker roasts, which tend to be more bitter. However, for these recipes I used a medium-roast coffee made in a plunger pot.

This started off as one recipe and ended up as two. I wanted to make Tea Ice Cream (page 68) and began with a traditional custard base. When I took the mixture out of the refrigerator to churn it, I thought, why not just serve it as tea custard with poached fruit? Now, the choice of fruit is important. The tannins in the tea are strong and for that reason I think you should stay away from berries. I like to play up the tannins and match it with poached pears or apricots. When you cook apricots, they develop a tannic taste. Serving the custard cold with warm poached fruit also stimulates the trigeminal nerve, which senses the temperature of food. Poached peaches would also be a good match.

TEA CUSTARD WITH POACHED FRUIT

MAKES 2 CUPS / 500 ML

2 cups / 500 ml whole milk

2 tablespoons / ⅓ ounce / 10 g orange pekoe tea leaves

5 egg yolks

⅓ cup plus 1 tablespoon / 2½ ounces / 75 g sugar

A pinch of fine sea salt

1 recipe Simple Syrup (page 83)

12 apricots, halved and pits removed, or 2 pears, halved

Pour the milk into a saucepan and place over medium heat. Heat until small bubbles form around the edge of the milk; remove the pan from the heat and stir in the tea leaves. Cover and leave to brew for 20 minutes. Strain the milk into a measuring cup, pressing on the leaves to extract all the liquid. Discard the tea leaves.

In a large bowl, whisk the egg yolks, sugar, and salt until light in color and thick, about 5 minutes. Slowly whisk in the milk. Pour the mixture into a clean pan and cook over medium heat, stirring constantly, until the mixture thickens and coats the back of a spoon. Strain the mixture into a bowl and cool quickly by placing it in a larger bowl or a sink filled with cold water and ice. Stir the mixture often. When it is cool, cover and refrigerate.

Pour the syrup into a saucepan and bring to a boil over medium heat. Add the fruit, lower the heat so the syrup barely simmers, and cook the apricots until they are just tender. Allow the fruit to cool just slightly. Serve them warm with the cold tea custard.

In France, prunes are often marinated in Armagnac with delicious results; I always keep a few in my cupboard. Prunes, with their slight tannic taste, are a perfect match with tea. Earl Grey tea has bergamot oil added to it, and the bitter orange flavor also works well with the prunes. If you happen to live in Italy, you could add fresh bergamot zest, but regular orange zest is just fine. Don't be tempted to add sugar; too many recipes do, and prunes, which are dried plums, are quite sweet enough. They need the bitter tea to make them sing. You must wait at least two days before eating them, as this allows the sugar from the prunes to mix with the tea. These keep well in the refrigerator and make a pick-me-up that isn't alcoholic.

TEA-INFUSED PRUNES / SERVES 6

1 tablespoon / 5 g
Earl Grey tea leaves

2 cups / 500 ml water

1 pound / 450 g prunes

A large strip of
orange zest,
4 by 1 inch / 10 by 2.5 cm

Place the tea leaves in a teapot or glass measuring cup. Bring the water to a boil, then remove it from the heat and wait 1 minute. Pour the water over the tea and stir. Cover and let stand for 10 minutes.

Put the prunes in a large bowl, strain over the tea, and add the orange zest. Leave to cool, stirring from time to time. Cover and refrigerate for at least 2 days before serving.

This brings a whole new meaning to iced tea! The vodka is added to make the ice cream scoop more easily. You can serve this ice cream by itself, with a shortbread cookie, or with the poached fruit (page 67).

TEA ICE CREAM / MAKES 2 CUPS / 500 ML

Tea Custard (page 67)

2 tablespoons / 1 ounce /
30 ml vodka

Make the tea custard and refrigerate overnight. Also, place a container for the ice cream in the freezer to get cold. The next day, remove the ice cream mixture from the refrigerator, stir in the vodka, and then churn in an ice cream machine following the manufacturer's instructions. Transfer to the cold container and freeze until ready to serve.

DRINKING BITTER

A glass or two of alcohol relaxes you, making you feel more at ease and loquacious: no wonder it is a popular choice in social situations. It also has other virtues, which humans discovered in our history. Alcohol is a result of fermentation, and, as well as making one more social, it kills harmful bacteria, making alcoholic liquids often safer to drink than the local water supply. Alcohol halts infection, and larger amounts help relieve pain. Was the love of alcohol the reason humans settled down to grow grains and grapes? Our ancestors were very adept at turning grains into alcohol: the Sumerians made beer (see page 55) from barley and wheat, and in other parts of the world people used rice and corn.

Like fat, alcohol is also good at capturing flavors and essences from organic matter. Early humans were not only brewing beer and other alcohols to drink, but they were also using these beverages to extract beneficial compounds from plants, making medicines to treat illness and disease. While they didn't understand the science of what they were doing, observation and experience gave them a wealth of practical knowledge and led to effective medicines.

The earliest evidence of an alcoholic beverage that may have been medicinal has been found at Jiahu, a Neolithic site in China, which dates from around 7000 BCE. Using biomolecular archaeological techniques that can analyze minute traces of organic liquids in ancient receptacles and break them down into their component parts, researchers from the University of Pennsylvania discovered that this early drink was made from rice, honey, grapes, and the fruit from hawthorn trees. They intend to investigate further to learn whether it also contained any medicinal herbs or spices. This group of scientists is especially interested in discovering compounds that fight cancer. One candidate is wormwood (see page 84), which has a long history of use in traditional Chinese medicine and is employed today to fight cancer. Wormwood has already been found in a Chinese rice wine dating from 1050 BCE. Ancient Egyptian papyri, circa 1850 BCE, describe combinations of herbs and plants infused in wine and beer to treat specific ailments. These reveal that bitter alcoholic liquids were ingested not simply for their mood-changing effects but also as medicines.

The bitter alcohols we drink today, including Fernet-Branca and Campari, have their origins in these herbal medicines and have developed into what we know as bitters, aperitifs, and digestives. Bitter plants have always been regarded as a digestive aid. They have a double effect, first stimulating our appetite and then keeping our digestive system working at the end of the meal. Steeping the herbs in wine or other alcohol was a way to preserve them as well as extract their volatile compounds. In Europe, bitter alcohols were often made by religious orders that maintained large herb gardens or lived in remote areas with an abundance of wild herbs. The next step after infusing herbs into alcohol was to distill these herbal liquids. Trapping the vapor released from heating the alcohol and herbs, then cooling it, yields a liquid purer and higher in alcohol than the original. The origins of distilling are hard to pin down, but by the early twelfth-century apothecaries in Salerno, Italy, were producing large quantities of distilled alcohol to make medicinal drinks. In the fourteenth century, teacher and scholar Arnaud Villanova wrote about distilling herbs and the power of the resulting liquid, which he called *aqua vitae*, the water of life, a term still used today in many languages. These aqua vitae were considered medicinal, and for a long time they remained in the hands of doctors, monks, and apothecaries. Royalty and the wealthy nobility eager to obtain them directly employed distillers in their households so that they could make medicines when they needed them. By the early eighteenth century distilling had become an important domestic skill, with people making their own herbal remedies.

"... a bitters influenced aperitif is just about the most delicious drink around. Its indomitable perkiness as a drink marks it as a winner on so many levels. The bitterness makes your mouth work overtime—invigorating and quenching. ..." —CLAIRE THOMSON

Distilling is a lot of work, and it was increasingly taken over by commercial enterprises that could distill large quantities with better quality control. From the middle of the eighteenth century to the end of the nineteenth, numerous bitter alcohols entered the marketplace. In 1752 Latvian pharmacist Abraham Kunze created Riga Black Balsam. Part of this beverage's mythology revolves around its claim to have restored the health of Catherine the Great of Russia when she fell ill while visiting Riga. Its dark black color and very bitter taste instantly make you think of medicine rather than a pleasant drink to warm the heart. The formulas for most herbal bitters are closely guarded secrets, but they usually include the same bitter ingredients: gentian, wormwood, bitter oranges, bitter almonds, cinchona bark, and angostura.

The nineteenth century saw an explosion of bitter concoctions; Angostura bitters (1824), which contains no angostura (see page 90), and Peychaud bitters (1830) were initially developed as medicines that were not to be drunk straight, but first mixed with water. You only needed to add a drop or two, so these bitter, highly alcoholic concoctions were sold in small bottles.

Soon they were being added to other drinks. Peychaud, a French apothecary who settled in New Orleans, mixed his bitters with cognac and in 1838 began serving it in an egg cup, *coquetier* in French; this may be the origin of the word *cocktail*. Drinks with the addition of bitters became popular in America throughout the nineteenth century. Prohibition boosted the use of bitters, as the government classified them as medicinal and so they were not banned. They also helped mask the unpleasant taste of illegally distilled alcohol. With the current renaissance in cocktail culture, there is a resurgence of interest in adding bitterness to mixed drinks. A large range of cocktail bitters with flavors from orange and rhubarb to the more exotic celery are available, and they are all designed to enhance a drink, not to be drunk straight.

The Italians naturally extended their strong culture of eating bitter plants into drinking them. Bitters, called *amari* in Italian, are alcohols designed originally to be drunk straight in very small quantities. There are numerous regional specialties, and almost every town has its own amaro, among the more well known (and the year of their creation) are: Ramazzotti (1815), Fernet-Branca (1845), Campari (1860), and Averna (1868). Newer additions include Aperol (1919) and Cynar (1952). The Italians also use the bitter plants gentian, chicory, and tobacco to flavor aqua vitae or grappa; for example, in the region around Venice they make a radicchio grappa.

"Bitters are the ultimate matchmaker: just a dash or two can bring a perfect balance to two seemingly incompatible spirits." —BRAD THOMAS PARSONS

Across the Alps in France, bitter aperitifs and digestives like Suze (1885), Salers (1885), and Gentiane (1900), all based on the root of the alpine plant gentian (see page 90), became popular. Almost every European country has its own preferred bitter alcohol, like Germany's Jägermeister (1935), which includes bitter orange, and Hungarian Unicum (1790), which is made with various herbs and spices. Distilling was mainly for making medicinal drinks, but gradually sugar was added, creating drinks enjoyed for pleasure rather than to cure an illness.

Bitter drinks don't need to be alcoholic to have health benefits, as in the case of tea and coffee. Today we mix tonic water with gin or vodka, but originally it was drunk straight as a bitter medicine to ward off malaria. It was so bitter that the English cut it with gin to make it palatable (see page 80). While commercially produced tonic waters still contain quinine, it is just a token amount and adds little of either bitterness or health benefit to the beverage.

In 1876, Dr. Augustin Thompson created a drink he called Moxie. It was, according to the good doctor, a cure for "paralysis, softening of the brain, nervousness and insomnia." Its power came, so Thompson said, from a South American plant discovered by his friend Lieutenant Moxie, after whom he named the beverage. The plant was probably the very bitter gentian, which was well known in the nineteenth century and which grows throughout the world's temperate regions. The drink was bitter and very medicinal tasting; in 1884 soda was added to the formula, making Moxie the first mass-produced soft drink. It outsold Coca-Cola, but only for a short time. The other company produced a sweeter drink, which people preferred, and supported it with advertising, and Moxie quickly fell out of favor. However, Moxie fans still exist, and they have kept the beverage alive in the northeastern United States. In 2005 they convinced the state of Maine to declare it their official soft drink. A festival in Lisbon Falls, Maine, celebrates everything Moxie, and includes a drinking competition and a tasting of recipes made using Moxie, ranging from muffins to pizza—all proving that Moxie still has moxie.

This is a surprising combination that reveals the ability of bitter to heighten other flavors: the tea makes these peaches more intensely peachy. Reducing the poaching liquid makes a dark caramel that is barely sweet and also tricks the eye. You think that the dish will be very sweet, so your palate is surprised by slight bitterness. Don't put the syrup on the peaches until just before serving; otherwise, it will become too liquid.

TEA-POACHED PEACHES / SERVES 4

2 cups / 500 ml water

⅓ cup plus 1 tablespoon / 2½ ounces / 75 g sugar

2 tablespoons / ⅓ ounce / 10 g orange pekoe tea leaves

4 just-ripe peaches

Bring the water and sugar to a boil in a saucepan over medium-low heat, stirring to dissolve the sugar. Boil for 1 minute, then remove the pan from the heat and wait 1 minute. Now stir in the tea leaves, then cover and let stand for 20 minutes. Strain the liquid into a saucepan, pressing on the leaves to extract all the liquid. Discard the tea leaves.

Bring another pan of water to a boil, add the peaches, and simmer for 1 minute, then transfer to a bowl of cold water and ice. Peel the peaches, then cut them in half and remove the pits. Place the halves in the saucepan with the tea syrup and bring to a simmer. Simmer gently until the peaches are just cooked, about 12 minutes, turning them once.

Transfer the peaches to a dish and let cool. Bring the cooking liquid to a boil and boil until syrupy and reduced to ⅓ cup / 75 ml, about 10 minutes. Pour the syrup into a small bowl and let cool. Spoon a little syrup over the peaches just before serving.

This liquid is very useful for poaching everything from sweetbreads and brains to fish and seafood. Simmer the bouillon for 20 minutes before straining and using it; this will infuse the flavors of the spices and aromatics into the cooking liquid.

COURT BOUILLON | MAKES 4 CUPS / 1 L

5 cups / 1.25 l water

1 carrot, peeled and sliced

1 shallot, sliced

1 stalk celery

Large strip of lemon zest

2 tablespoons freshly squeezed lemon juice

2 star anise

A 5-inch / 13-cm piece of cinnamon (see page 117)

1 large branch fresh thyme

1 fresh bay leaf

10 black peppercorns

4 cloves

1 teaspoon coarse sea salt

Place the water, carrot, shallot, celery, lemon zest and juice, star anise, cinnamon, thyme, and bay leaf in a saucepan. Bring to a boil over medium heat, skim, and add the peppercorns and cloves. Lower the heat, cover, and simmer for 20 minutes. Remove from the heat, let cool, and strain, discarding the solids. Add the salt. Use immediately, or store in the refrigerator for up to 4 days. The court bouillon can also be frozen.

This recipe began with one by Pierre Gagnaire, called "Grilled 'Coffee and Cardamom' Veal Sweetbreads," from his book *Reinventing French Cuisine*. I liked the idea of coffee, cardamom, and sweetbreads together, but alas the Gagnaire recipe was a disaster. A fault of translation or transcription? As my husband and I love sweetbreads, we were happy to keep trying the combination in different ratios, but there comes a point when you just need to move on. I was about to give up when I came up with this recipe. All that it has in common with the Gagnaire one is the three main ingredients. Cardamom mellows coffee's bitterness, and it is a popular addition to coffee in many cultures; it's often ground with the coffee beans. What is most interesting here is that the creamy, bitter coffee sauce makes the sweetbreads taste sweet. Keep the sweetbreads whole or in large pieces so you can slice them at the end of cooking.

COFFEE CARDAMOM SWEETBREADS | SERVES 2

11½ ounces / 325 g
sweetbreads

Coarse sea salt

Court Bouillon (page 75)

Sea salt and freshly
ground black pepper

Lemon wedge, optional

½ cup / 125 ml
brewed coffee

3 green cardamom pods,
crushed

2 tablespoons flour

2 tablespoons olive oil

2 teaspoons whipping
(35 percent) fat cream

3 tablespoons /
1½ ounces / 45 g cold
unsalted butter

To prepare sweetbreads, place the sweetbreads in a bowl and cover with cold water, adding about 1 teaspoon of coarse sea salt per 1 cup / 250 ml of water. Soak for 4 to 6 hours, changing several times, to remove any blood.

Drain the sweetbreads and place them in a saucepan, noting their soft, wobbly texture. Cover the sweetbreads with the court bouillon and bring them slowly to a simmer over medium-low heat. If you have no court bouillon, you can cover them with cold water and add a teaspoon of sea salt and a lemon wedge. Check the sweetbreads from time to time; depending on their size, they may be ready even before the water simmers. While they cook, fill a bowl with cold water and add some ice cubes. The sweetbreads are ready when they are just firm to the touch but still have some springiness to them (at this point they are only partially cooked).

Slide them into the ice water to stop the cooking, then drain them and place them on a board. Remove any fat and gristly, sinewy bits or blood vessels, and then peel off as much of the membrane as you can without breaking up the sweetbreads. This is much easier to do while the sweetbreads are still warm.

Line a pie plate with a clean kitchen towel and place the peeled sweetbreads on top. Fold the cloth over the sweetbreads and top with another pie plate. Place a weight, like 2 cans of beans, on the second pie plate and refrigerate for 3 to 4 hours, or until the sweetbreads are firm. Now the sweetbreads are ready to use in a recipe; they can be kept covered in the refrigerator for up to 2 days. You will notice that a little pink liquid will seep out of the sweetbreads; this is normal.

In a small saucepan, bring the coffee to a simmer over medium heat. Add the cardamom pods, remove from the heat, cover, and let stand. Season the flour with salt and pepper, and then toss the sweetbreads in the flour to coat, shaking off the excess. In a small frying pan, heat the olive oil over medium heat. When hot, add the sweetbreads and cook, turning often, until they are golden and crispy on all sides, about 15 minutes.

Transfer the sweetbreads to a plate and keep warm. Strain the coffee into the pan and bring to a boil, using a wooden spoon to deglaze the pan by scraping up the browned bits from the bottom. Boil until the coffee is reduced to 3 tablespoons. Reduce the heat to low, whisk in the cream, and season with salt and pepper.

Cut the butter into 4 pieces. Over very low heat, slowly whisk the butter into the sauce, thoroughly incorporating each piece before adding another. While you're whisking, you want to keep the sauce warm but not hot, so that the butter emulsifies rather than melts into the sauce. Cut the sweetbreads into thick slices and spoon over the sauce.

Coffee's bitterness is a perfect foil for a pork chop with a good layer of fat. The taste of black currant is complex, intense, and musky, with hints of chocolate, which ties the rich pork and bitter coffee together. It is important to use good-quality black currant preserves with whole fruit as its first ingredient, rather than a sweet black currant jelly. Depending on your preserves, you might want to add more or less to the sauce, but err on the side of caution: you want to maintain the bitterness of the coffee.

PORK CHOPS IN COFFEE BLACK CURRANT SAUCE

SERVES 4

4 rib pork chops, about 1½ inches / 4 cm thick

Sea salt and freshly ground black pepper

2 tablespoons lard

1 shallot, finely chopped

1 large branch fresh thyme

1 cup / 250 ml brewed coffee

1 cup / 250 ml chicken stock, preferably homemade

1 heaping tablespoon black currant preserves

Twenty minutes before cooking, remove the pork chops from the refrigerator. Pat dry and season with salt and pepper. In a frying pan large enough to hold the chops, heat the lard over medium-high heat. When the fat is hot, add the chops and brown for 2 minutes on each side.

Transfer the chops to a plate, lower the heat, and add the shallot and thyme to the pan. Stir, and cook until the shallot begins to color. Pour in the coffee and chicken stock and bring to a boil, deglazing the pan by scraping up the browned bits from the bottom. Boil to reduce the sauce by about half.

Return the chops to the pan and lower the heat so the liquid is simmering. Cook the chops for 5 minutes, basting with the sauce from time to time. Turn the chops and cook for another 5 minutes, or until cooked.

Place the chops on a platter and keep warm loosely covered with aluminum foil. Remove the thyme from the pan and add the black currant preserves. Stir and cook the sauce until syrupy and reduced to about ⅓ cup / 75 ml. Return the chops to the pan with any juices, and turn to coat with the sauce. Check the seasoning of the sauce—remember it should be pleasantly bitter—and serve the chops, spooning over the sauce.

VARIATION Try this sauce with venison or wild boar chops, and replace the thyme with rosemary.

THE DRINK THAT BUILT AN EMPIRE

According to Winston Churchill, "It saved more Englishmen's lives, and minds, than all the doctors in the Empire." And what was "it"? A wonder drug? No, it was a gin and tonic.

The drink originated with enterprising businessman Erasmus Bond, who in 1858 patented his formula for "Improved Aerated Liquid." The English living in India had been mixing their dose of antimalarial quinine with sugar, water, and gin to make it palatable. Bond's aerated liquid was a bubbly mixture of water, sugar, and quinine, known as Indian or quinine tonic water. He promoted it as a medicine. However, it soon moved out of the medicine cabinet and onto the bar as the English discovered it was the perfect mixer for gin.

The first Europeans to understand the value of quinine were the Jesuits. They accompanied the Spanish conquistadors to Bolivia and Peru, where they saw the Quechua people using the bark of the native cinchona tree (pictured on page 52) as a muscle relaxant to control their shivering when it was very cold. (I may now change my opinion that tonic water is exclusively a summer beverage.) They returned with the bark to Europe in the mid-seventeenth century, where it became known as "Jesuit's bark." It first appears in medical literature in 1643, as a treatment for fevers and malaria. Despite its effectiveness, it was greeted with much suspicion and skepticism. Many believed its dramatic results were too good to be true, and there was also religious bias from the Protestants against this "Popish powder" because of its association with the Jesuits. The debate over the medicinal usefulness of cinchona bark continued well into the nineteenth century.

The name *cinchona* comes from a story told of the Countess of Chinchón, the wife of the Spanish viceroy of Peru. According to the account, she fell ill with malaria in 1630 and was cured by an infusion of the bark. Alas, it is not true, but it did provide Linnaeus (see page 42) with an idea for the plant's name when he classified it in the eighteenth century. (He used the countess's name, changing it to "cinchona" to improve its euphony and ease of pronunciation.)

There were many problems with cinchona bark as a medicine; its quality was uneven and it was often adulterated, reducing its effectiveness. In 1820, two French chemists, Pelletier and Caventou, discovered the beneficial antimalarial alkaloid in the bark, quinine. Cinchona bark also contains the alkaloids quinidine, cinchonie, and cinchonidine. The first two also fight malaria by stopping the reproduction of the malaria parasite, but they are not as effective as quinine. Now the quinine could be extracted from the bark, and the quality controlled. It was widely accepted as the treatment for malaria, and this had a profound effect on world history, making it possible for Europeans to colonize the tropics. Quinine became part of the daily ration of sailors on ships in tropical ports, and was also part of the daily regime of the English in India. By the 1850s imports of cinchona were costing the British government £53,000 a year. More than two million pounds of cinchona bark were exported in 1860 from the west coast of South America to Europe and America, providing an important source of income for the local economies of Peru, Ecuador, and Bolivia. These Andean republics tried to maintain a monopoly on the bark, banning the export of seeds and seedlings, and the price rose. The European powers, realizing they would need a secure source of quinine, decided to grow cinchona trees themselves, and the Dutch and English ignored the ban. In 1865, the Dutch planted seeds and saplings on the island of Java, where they flourished, while the British tried growing them in India and Ceylon (Sri Lanka) with less success. The Dutch became the leading suppliers of quinine, with 97 percent of the world's production by the end of the century, while the British managed a mere 2½ percent. During World War II, quinine supplies fell under German and Japanese control; this spurred the development of synthetic quinine.

In order to argue that the gin and tonic I sip on a hot summer's day is medicinal, I make my own tonic water. Today most tonic waters are just carbonated sugary drinks with a trace of quinine. I discovered just how good tonic water could taste when my friend Stephen Blackwood gave me a jar of his homemade brew. Despite its cloudy brown appearance it made a fabulous gin and tonic; I have included a recipe (page 82). My tonic water may not protect you against malaria, but it is half of the perfect tipple for a hot summer's day.

Tonic water has become a popular DIY project, and it is really quite simple to do. Recipes abound on the Internet, and they are mostly variations of the same formula. This recipe comes from my friend Stephen Blackwood, who began with a recipe from Jeffrey Morgenthaler. My recipe is yet another version, tweaking the ingredients to my taste. Once you get the basics down, you can add other spices and flavorings to suit your taste—and your favorite gin. Two things to remember: this tonic is not clear (it is amber colored from the cinchona bark), and you need to add sparkling water in equal amounts with the tonic. Its use isn't restricted to mixing with gin or vodka; it's excellent without alcohol, making a refreshing beverage perfect for a hot, steamy summer day.

HOMEMADE TONIC WATER | MAKES ABOUT 6 CUPS / 1.5 L

4 cups / 1 l filtered water

1 grapefruit

1 orange

1 lemon

1 lime

2½ ounces / 75 g chopped fresh lemongrass, about 2 stalks

3 tablespoons / 33 g citric acid

¼ cup / ¾ ounce / 22 g powdered cinchona bark

10 allspice berries, crushed

2 small star anise

1 teaspoon coarse sea salt

¼ teaspoon black peppercorns

1½ cups / 375 ml Simple Syrup (opposite)

Pour the water into a saucepan. Grate the zest of each fruit and add to the pan. Now squeeze the juice from all the fruit and pour into the pan. Add the lemongrass, citric acid, cinchona bark, allspice, star anise, salt, and black peppercorns. Place the pan over medium heat and bring to a boil, whisking from time to time. Reduce the heat, cover, and simmer for 30 minutes. Remove the pan from the heat and let stand, covered, for another 30 minutes.

Strain the liquid through a fine-mesh sieve into a large measuring cup, discarding the solids. Let stand for 8 hours or overnight so the powdered cinchona falls to the bottom of the measuring cup.

Now carefully strain the liquid again, this time through a coffee filter so as to leave all the solids behind. Straining the liquid can take a while. The strained tonic will be an opaque, amber color. Stir in the simple syrup and refrigerate.

I store the tonic in glass screw-top jars. As it sits in the refrigerator, the powdered cinchona continues to precipitate out of the liquid, forming a layer at the bottom of the jar. When you use the tonic, don't shake the jar; just carefully pour the liquid from the top, leaving the solids behind. The tonic will keep a couple of months refrigerated.

NOTE Thanks to the popularity of making your own bitters, cinchona bark is available powdered from most good spice and health food stores. You will probably find the citric acid in the same store.

It is always handy to have simple syrup in the refrigerator. Often I make four times the recipe, but this is the right amount for the tonic recipe. Sugar syrup can also be infused with herbs and spices and used for poaching fruit.

SIMPLE SYRUP / MAKES ABOUT 1½ CUPS / 375 ML

1 cup / 7 ounces /
200 g sugar

1 cup / 250 ml water

Bring the sugar and water to a boil in a saucepan over medium-low heat, stirring to dissolve the sugar. Boil for 1 minute, then cover and let cool.

I know you don't need a recipe for a gin and tonic, but with homemade tonic you need to add sparkling water. These proportions are what I prefer and will give you a place to start; my husband prefers more gin, but he is the martini drinker in the family. You'll find your own perfect mix.

GIN AND TONIC / MAKES 1 DRINK

1½ ounces / 45 ml gin

3 ounces / 90 ml
Homemade Tonic Water
(opposite)

3 ounces / 90 ml
sparkling water

Lime

Pour the gin into a tall glass over ice. Add the tonic and sparkling water, then a squeeze of lime juice, and garnish with a slice of lime.

WORMWOOD

Wormwood has silvery green leaves and grows easily in temperate zones, making it a popular ornamental plant. It is a member of the Asteraceae family, which includes dandelion and chicory. This very bitter and aromatic plant (of which there are three types, the most notorious being *Artemisia absinthium*) contains thujone, a compound that kills both insects and intestinal parasites, which explains the plant's name. However, in very high doses it can be toxic to humans. Wormwood has a long history of medicinal use as a digestive aid, anti-inflammatory, and anti-malarial. Traces of wormwood were discovered in a medicinal liquid in a Chinese tomb dating from 1050 BCE, and it was an ingredient in medical prescriptions recorded in ancient Egyptian papyri. Today wormwood is being studied at the University of Pennsylvania for its ability to treat lung and colon cancers.

> "After the first glass of absinthe you see things as you wish they were. After the second you see them as they are not. Finally you see things as they really are, and that is the most horrible thing in the world . . . That is the effect absinthe has, and that is why it drives men mad."
> —ATTRIBUTED TO OSCAR WILDE

Wormwood is an ingredient in the liqueur Chartreuse and in vermouth (the name *vermouth* comes from the German word for the plant, *wermut*). It is also the main ingredient in the infamous drink absinthe, a fashionable libation in nineteenth-century France. Originally Swiss, the recipe for this alcohol was perfected by a young distiller named Henri-Louis Pernod in 1798; its success allowed him to found his own distilling company. Several things led to absinthe's popularity, its vivid green color, the belief that it inspired creativity, and the ritual that arose around drinking it. Absinthe wasn't simply drunk; rather, a measure was poured into a glass, and then a sugar cube was set on a special flat, perforated spoon balanced over the glass. Next, cold water was slowly dripped over the sugar into the glass. The water dissolved the sugar, sweetening the absinthe and turning it a cloudy green. Nicknamed "the green fairy," the drink became popular with artists, poets, and writers in the nineteenth and early twentieth centuries; Edgar Allan Poe, Paul Verlaine, Oscar Wilde, Pablo Picasso, and Vincent van Gogh were some famous absinthe drinkers. While it's true that high amounts of thujone are toxic and can adversely affect the human nervous system, absinthe's reputation as an addictive, hallucinogenic drink that caused convulsions and insanity was grossly overstated. Some drinkers did suffer harmful effects and even died, but their deaths were most likely related to alcoholism; it must be remembered that absinthe is 68 percent alcohol. The French author and playwright Alexandre Dumas *père* lists absinthe in his *Dictionary of Cuisine*, where he states that it killed more French soldiers in Africa than all the Arab weapons. Dumas also claims it was responsible for the death of French poet Alfred de Musset, who died at the age of forty-six from a heart condition complicated by alcoholism. Despite his indictment of absinthe, Dumas proceeds to give us a recipe for making a *crème d'absinthe*.

> "The third angel sounds his trumpet. And a great star, blazing like a torch, called Wormwood, falls on a third of the rivers and springs of water. A third of the waters turn bitter and many people die from the waters that had become bitter." —BOOK OF REVELATION 8:10-11

The outcry against absinthe was so strong that in 1915 it was banned. This caused the Pernod distillery to close, but five years later it reopened with a wormwood-free anise-flavored drink. Today absinthe is no longer illegal, and many companies, including Pernod, are now producing it again using wormwood—and still with 68 percent alcohol.

Wormwood's bitterness is often used metaphorically to represent the wages of sin. In Deuteronomy, we are told not to turn against God, and in Proverbs, Solomon counsels against lust and adultery. In both passages the Bible tells us that if we commit these sins, the result will be as bitter as wormwood. The most dramatic depiction of wormwood as a consequence of sin is, naturally enough, in the book of Revelation, where it is foretold that a star, named Wormwood, will fall to earth, turning some of the rivers and streams bitter. This event is dramatically and colorfully depicted in one of the stained glass windows of the Sainte-Chapelle at the Château of Vincennes in Paris.

Campari and orange juice is an excellent aperitif, and a good introduction to bitter. The same combination, though in different proportions to the cocktail, can be frozen into a granita. The advantage of this kind of ice is that you don't need any fancy machines; you simply need to stir the mixture during the freezing process to break up the ice crystals. The result is a granular ice. If you prefer more bitterness, try the grapefruit variation below.

CAMPARI GRANITA / SERVES 4 TO 6

1 cup / 250 ml strained freshly squeezed orange juice

½ cup / 125 ml Campari

½ teaspoon freshly squeezed lemon juice

Stir the orange juice, Campari, and lemon juice together, then pour into an 8-inch / 20-cm square metal pan. Place in the freezer. Stir the mixture with a spoon every hour or so, to break it up into large ice crystals. If you forget to stir the mixture and it freezes solid, don't panic. To return the granita it to its granular texture, break it into chunks and pulse briefly in the food processor. To serve, spoon the granita into chilled glasses.

VARIATION Replace the orange juice with freshly squeezed grapefruit juice and add 2 tablespoons / 25 g superfine (caster) sugar.

Stock and butter make a rich sauce for a veal chop, and a splash of Campari adds a touch of bitter that makes it more interesting. Campari, while bitter, is not aggressively so. If you want to try this with another bitter alcohol, you will probably need even less. Veal is seasonal and at its best in the spring—in France they promote *veau de la Pentecôte* (Pentecost or Whitsunday veal) at butcher shops and in restaurants. With the slightly bitter glaze you will want to match this chop with sweet green peas and new potatoes. Veal chops are best cooked medium-rare to medium.

CAMPARI-GLAZED VEAL CHOPS

SERVES 2

2 veal rib chops, 1½ inches / 4 cm thick, frenched

Sea salt and freshly ground black pepper

1 tablespoon extra virgin olive oil

¾ cup / 175 ml veal or chicken stock, preferably homemade

2 tablespoons Campari

1 tablespoon cold unsalted butter

One hour before cooking, remove the chops from the refrigerator. Preheat the oven to 425°F / 220°C.

Pat the veal chops dry and season with salt and pepper. Place a large ovenproof frying pan over medium-high heat and add the olive oil. When the oil is hot, brown the chops on both sides, about 2 minutes per side. Transfer the chops to a plate.

Pour in ½ cup / 125 ml of the stock and bring to a boil, stirring to deglaze the pan by scraping up the browned bits from the bottom. Return the chops with any juices to the pan, and place in the oven. Cook for 10 minutes, and then remove the pan from the oven, remembering the handle of the pan will be very hot.

Transfer the chops to a plate and let them rest, loosely covered with aluminum foil. Add the remaining stock to the pan and bring to a boil, stirring and scraping to deglaze the pan again. Add the Campari and boil to reduce slightly; you want about ¼ cup / 60 ml of sauce. Whisk in the butter, and season with salt and pepper. Serve the chops with the sauce.

There is no middle ground with Fernet-Branca: you either love it or you hate it. It's one of Fergus Henderson's preferred tipples; he was drinking it when I met him in Toronto. Created in 1845, it is made from numerous herbs and spices, including gentian, bitter orange, and cinchona bark, and it rivals Riga Black Balsam for bitterness. It is also high in alcohol, at 31 percent. I doubt anyone has ever enjoyed Fernet-Branca on the first or even second tasting; like all bitter drinks, you have to learn to like it, and then all of a sudden you find yourself craving it. Many swear that it is the perfect hangover cure; I'm not sure that drinking more alcohol after already consuming too much is a good idea. Others find it indispensible after overindulging in rich food, and that makes more sense.

If you buy a bottle to channel your inner Fergus Henderson and hate it, don't despair. You can use it like cocktail bitters in mixed drinks, or hang on to it for a hangover that's so bad you'll drink anything to feel better. If that fails, follow the German example and mix it with Red Bull to kick-start your day, or sweeten it up by adding cola, as they do in Argentina. Or you can try this recipe.

FERNET-BRANCA CHICKEN LIVERS | SERVES 2

3 tablespoons chicken or duck fat

½ red onion, thinly sliced

1 large sprig rosemary

Coarse sea salt and freshly ground black pepper

8 ounces / 225 g chicken livers

1 tablespoon currants

1½ tablespoons Fernet-Branca

1 tablespoon small capers, rinsed and dried

¼ cup / 60 ml chicken stock, preferably homemade

2 pieces thick toast (page 221)

Place a small frying pan over medium-low heat and add 2 tablespoons of the fat. When it's melted, add the onion and the rosemary sprig and season with salt and pepper. Cook, stirring from time to time, until the onion softens and begins to caramelize; this will take 15 to 20 minutes.

Meanwhile, trim away the connecting threads and separate the chicken livers into two lobes. Cut away any traces of green on the livers, and set aside. Put the currants in a small bowl and pour over the Fernet-Branca; set aside.

When the onion is cooked, transfer it to a bowl and discard the rosemary sprig. Add the capers with the Fernet-Branca and currants to the onion. Wipe out the pan.

Pat dry the chicken livers and season with salt and pepper. Melt the remaining 1 tablespoon fat in the pan over high heat. When it is hot, add the chicken livers and lower the heat to medium-low. Cook, stirring, until the livers are just pink in the center, about 3 minutes per side; cut a liver in half to check doneness. Add the onion mixture and chicken stock to the pan and stir to heat through. Check the seasoning and serve on the toast, allowing the sauce to seep into the toast.

THE BITTEREST PLANT IN THE WORLD

Gentian belongs to a large genus of plants (Gentiana) and is loved by many gardeners for its intensely blue, trumpet-shaped flowers. Less familiar is the yellow-flowered gentian native to alpine areas of central and southern Europe. This plant is prized not for its flowers but for its root, and even if you have never heard of yellow gentian, you've probably tasted it. It is an ingredient in many bitter alcohols and the soft drink Moxie (see page 73).

The plant, according to Pliny the Elder in his *Natural History*, was named after Gentius, king of Illyria, who was the first to discover its medicinal powers. The plant flourished in his Balkan kingdom and he used it as a digestive, analgesic, and anti-inflammatory as well as a beverage to warm the body. While Pliny may not be the most reliable source, the Greek doctor Pedanios Dioscorides, author of the pharmacopoeia *De materia medica*, backs up his tale.

While all parts of the gentian plant are bitter, it is the very bitter root that has a long history of medicinal use. It contains two bitter compounds: gentiopicroside, which has analgesic properties, and amarogentin, a very bitter and powerful digestive. How bitter is it? A single gram of amarogentin dissolved in 15,322 gallons (58,000 liters) of water will turn the water bitter. This makes gentian probably the bitterest plant on the planet; it is used to rank the bitterness of other plants.

In France and Switzerland, there are a number of alcohols made from gentian. One of the best known is Suze, which was the subject of Picasso's *Glass and Bottle of Suze*, a collage made from of scraps of paper, newspaper clippings, and charcoal. Picasso even placed a genuine Suze label on his illustrated Cubist bottle. The piece was created in 1912 during the Balkan War, and art historians have speculated that Picasso was making a political statement: the clippings in the collage are from the French newspaper *Le Journal* and describe the atrocities that were taking place in the Balkans. And Suze, of course, is distilled from gentian root, named after an ancient Balkan king.

Take a look at that bottle of Angostura bitters that you probably have somewhere in the back of your liquor cabinet. On that oversized label, despite the fact that the formula is secret, you will see gentian is listed as an ingredient. Angostura is not named after the bitter angostura plant, a relative of the citrus family that grows in South America, but the town of Angostura on the Orinoco River in Venezuela. It was there that German physician Dr. Johann Gottlieb Benjamin Siegert developed the bitters in 1824. Siegert was the surgeon general in Simón Bolívar's army and needed a medicine to treat the soldiers' intestinal problems. His concoction became famous after winning numerous medals at world fairs. Today Angostura bitters is no longer promoted as a health tonic but it is an essential ingredient for cocktails.

If you are familiar with Suze and think you won't like this, you may be happily surprised by how it works in combination with the grapefruit juice. Finding a bottle of Suze may well be the hardest part of this recipe; if you can't get Suze, use another alcohol based on gentian—just make sure whichever one you choose is around 15 percent alcohol; otherwise, it will affect the sorbet's texture. My friend Lesley Chesterman gave me this recipe, and of course I've tinkered with it. Lesley suggested pink grapefruit, because it gives the ice a pretty color, but my feelings about pink grapefruit are strong. White grapefruit not only makes the ice less sweet, but it also lets the yellow color of the Suze dominate.

SUZE SORBET | MAKES ABOUT 2 CUPS / 500 ML

1½ cups / 375 ml freshly squeezed and strained grapefruit juice, from about 3 medium grapefruit

2 tablespoons freshly squeezed and strained lemon juice, from about ½ lemon

3½ ounces / ½ cup / 100 g superfine (caster) sugar

⅓ cup / 75 ml Suze

Stir the grapefruit and lemon juices together with the sugar and Suze until the sugar is dissolved. Cover and refrigerate the mixture overnight. Also, place a container for the sorbet in the freezer to get cold.

The next day, remove the sorbet mixture from the refrigerator, stir again, then churn in an ice cream machine following the manufacturer's instructions. Transfer the sorbet to the cold container and freeze until ready to serve.

Since I convinced you to buy a bottle of Suze to make the sorbet (on page 91), I feel obligated to give you a couple more recipes that include Suze. Perhaps you'll acquire the habit of sipping Suze on the rocks before dinner to stimulate your appetite and appear sophisticatedly continental. For those who find straight Suze too bitter, following are two cocktails to ease you into the Suze habit. You can of course use any bitter alcohol based on gentian; there are some good artisanal products made in the Auvergne region of France like the one from Louis Couderc distillery in Aurillac.

My friend Maryse Lalanne told me she learned to love Suze with this drink. Crème de cassis is sweet and modifies Suze's bitterness; the secret is not to add too much.

BLACK CURRANT SUZE | MAKES 1 DRINK

1½ ounces / 45 ml Suze

½ ounce / 15 ml
crème de cassis

Stir the Suze and crème de cassis together over ice and serve.

Grapefruit and Suze make a great sorbet, and the combination is also refreshing as a cocktail. Use freshly squeezed juice or nothing; remember, there is no bitterness left in commercial grapefruit products. And you know I am going to say white grapefruit juice, please.

GRAPEFRUIT SUZE | MAKES 1 DRINK

1½ ounces / 45 ml Suze

4 ounces / 125 ml
freshly squeezed
grapefruit juice

Pour the Suze into a tall glass filled with ice; stir, then top with the grapefruit juice.

Unlike my husband, most of us find Riga Black Balsam (see page 71) just too bitter and alcoholic to drink straight even if we are feeling poorly. The Russians like this tipple and traditionally mix it one to one with vodka. My husband picks up his supply of Riga Black Balsam at the Russian grocery store down the street from our Paris apartment as we rarely see it in Toronto. While grapefruit juice is bitter, too, it does mellow out the strength of the Riga Black Balsam, but it is still not a drink for the faint of heart. To keep with the Russian tradition I've added vodka, and it also helps abate the bitterness.

BLACK LATVIAN | MAKES 1 DRINK

3 ounces / 90 ml freshly squeezed grapefruit juice

1 ounce / 30 ml Riga Black Balsam

1 ounce / 30 ml vodka

½ teaspoon freshly squeezed lemon juice

Shake all the ingredients in a cocktail shaker over ice. Strain into a glass filled with ice.

THREE

PUNGENTLY BITTER

**D**oes bitter have a smell? I would argue yes (see page 240). There are vegetables with pervasive, powerful odors that signal bitterness. They are strong tasting and strong smelling—pungently bitter. Yet despite their peppery heat and bitterness, they can seem tame on first encounter. Their pungency is only exposed when they are cut and their cells' structure is broken, releasing a combination of nitrogen and sulfur compounds. This is their defense against being eaten and it often works: brussels sprouts are one of the most widely disliked vegetables. And like brussels sprouts, these powerfully pungent vegetables are all members of the Brassica genus.

The brassica family includes brussels sprouts, cabbage, kale, rutabaga, turnip, broccoli, mustard, horseradish, and arugula. All these plants contain glucosinolates, which are bitter and pungent and are responsible for that unpleasant sulfur smell we associate with cooking cabbage. However, pungent, bitter, and even smelly are, in this case, good for us. Glucosinolates help detoxify the body and fight cancer, making them an important addition to our diet—we should all learn to love brassicas. Luckily their levels of bitterness and pungency vary, so you should be able to find one that suits your palate—there's no excuse for avoiding these healthy bitter vegetables. They will also be more intensely flavored in the summer and less so in the winter: many of these vegetables are picked after a frost, as the cold weather reduces their bitterness.

There are members of this family that I don't find bitter (broccoli, kale, and cabbage), while others, like rapini and turnip, delight me with their bitterness. My choices for inclusion in this chapter reflect my personal tastes, but such is the versatility of brassicas that you can often substitute one for another in a recipe.

ARUGULA

Arugula, also called rocket, grows wild around the Mediterranean and has been cultivated since Roman times. It may be the most fashionable brassica at the moment, appearing in upscale salads and mesclun mix, where it adds a bitter note, and as a topping on high-end pizza. A few leaves often garnish rich dishes in smart restaurants. Two varieties are generally available in markets: the larger leaf variety sold in bunches with the roots attached and the small leaf one sold by weight. Worth looking out for is wild arugula, which is slimmer and sharper in flavor and has a more feathery leaf. It makes a good substitute in recipes that call for wild greens.

Arugula is delicious cooked. The heat softens its texture and dulls its pepperiness, but develops its bitterness. This brassica is very versatile and can be used in many recipes that call for chicories.

"Bitterness is a crucial piece of the taste spectrum that when presented in balance rounds out our flavor experience." —MELISSA PASANEN

Arugula is one of only three foods regarded by both first-century BCE naturalist Pliny and physician Dioscorides, as an aphrodisiac. The hot pungent bitterness of the leaf was probably the reason for this conclusion, but there is no evidence that backs up the claim. Some cultures use arugula medicinally, to treat eye infections, digestive and kidney ailments, and fight scurvy. It is full of vitamins A and C, with good amounts of iron and calcium and like most bitter foods is an appetite stimulant. Eating arugula will improve your general health and perhaps that might positively affect your sex life.

Often arugula is just scattered on pizza at the end of cooking, the heat of the pizza being enough to wilt it. In this recipe most of the arugula is added at the beginning, giving a touch of bitter pungency to the sweet roasted tomato sauce. Then the rest is added for a quick final cooking. This pizza can be made with any bitter greens: try turnip or dandelion greens. Of course you can buy the dough and the tomato sauce, but they are easy to make; just start the day before.

ARUGULA PIZZA | SERVES 3 OR 4

⅔ cup / 150 ml warm water

1½ teaspoons / 6 g active dry yeast

1 teaspoon sugar

2 cups / 8¾ ounces / 250 g flour

½ teaspoon fine sea salt

¼ cup / 60 ml plus 1 tablespoon extra virgin olive oil

1 pound / 450 g ripe tomatoes

1 onion, halved and thinly sliced

3 cloves garlic

Basil leaves

Sea salt and freshly ground black pepper

½ red onion, thinly sliced

Cornmeal

½ bunch arugula

1 tablespoon dried oregano (Greek), crumbled

3 large slices prosciutto

1 cup / 1 ounce / 30 g freshly grated Parmesan cheese

Mix ⅓ cup of the warm water with the yeast and sugar in a measuring cup and leave to proof in a warm place for about 10 minutes.

Stir the flour and salt together. Add the remaining ⅓ cup water and 1 tablespoon of the olive oil to the yeast mixture, then stir into the flour and mix to form a dough. Turn the dough out onto a floured surface and knead for 10 minutes, until smooth and supple. You can do this in a stand mixer with a dough hook.

Place the dough in a lightly greased bowl, cover, and leave in a warm place until the dough has doubled in size, about 1 hour. Punch the dough down and, if not using straight away, cover and refrigerate for up to 1 day. Let the dough rise again. If you refrigerate the dough, take it out at least 1½ hours before baking the pizza.

While the dough is rising, make the tomato sauce. Preheat the oven to 400°F / 200°C. Cut the tomatoes in half. Place the sliced onion in an ovenproof dish just large enough to hold the tomato halves. Place the tomatoes on top of the onion, cut side down. Add the garlic and pour over the remaining olive oil. Add some basil leaves and season with salt and pepper.

Bake for 1 hour, or until the tomatoes are browned and the onion is soft. Let cool slightly, then pass everything through the coarse disk of a food mill. You will have 1 to 1½ cups / 250 to 375 ml of sauce, depending on your tomatoes; you'll need 1 cup / 250 ml. If necessary, pour the sauce into a saucepan

CONTINUED

ARUGULA PIZZA
CONTINUED

and bring to a boil, then lower the heat and simmer, stirring from time to time, until the sauce is reduced to 1 cup / 250 ml. Season with salt and pepper and set aside; refrigerate if not using straight away.

Place the sliced red onion in a bowl of ice-cold water and leave it for 1 hour. If you refrigerated your pizza dough, take it out now. Place a pizza stone (or unglazed ceramic tiles) in your oven.

Preheat your oven to the highest temperature you can. Lightly grease a 12-inch / 30-cm pizza pan and sprinkle with cornmeal. Roll out the pizza dough and place on the pan. Rinse and dry the arugula. Remove any thick stems, then slice the leaves thinly; you should have about 3 cups / 2½ ounces / 70 g.

Drain the red onion and squeeze it in a towel to remove all the moisture. Scatter over the base of the pizza and top with three-quarters of the arugula, then the tomato sauce. Sprinkle with the oregano and season with salt and pepper. Bake in the oven for 15 minutes, or until the crust is puffed and golden. Remove from the oven and top with the prosciutto, Parmesan cheese, and remaining arugula. Slide the pizza off the pan and directly onto the pizza stone and bake for another 2 to 3 minutes to melt the cheese and wilt the arugula.

I remember clearly the first time I ate an arugula salad. It was in London at the top of the Oxo tower in the 1990s. Called rocket in the United Kingdom, arugula was new and exotic. The leaves were tossed with a lemony dressing that highlighted their peppery taste and topped with shaved Parmesan cheese. I loved the combination.

Although you can make this with any variety of arugula, the more pungent, feathery ones are the best. Now that arugula is so popular, often not enough care is taken in preparing it. These leaves have long, thin stems that must be removed, as they are tough and unpleasant to eat.

ARUGULA SALAD / SERVES 4

6 cups / 5 ounces / 140 g small feathery arugula leaves

1 tablespoon freshly squeezed lemon juice

Sea salt and freshly ground black pepper

3 tablespoons extra virgin olive oil

Wedge of Parmesan cheese

Remove the stems from the arugula leaves and discard; rinse the leaves, then spin them dry.

In a salad bowl, mix the lemon juice and salt and pepper. Slowly whisk in the olive oil, check the seasoning again, and add the arugula. Toss well and divide among 4 plates. Using a vegetable peeler, shave over the Parmesan cheese.

When I asked my friend Francesco Tripoli about his favorite bitter greens he mentioned *strigoli*, or bladder campion (*Silene vulgaris*). The young leaves of this plant are eaten in various parts of Europe, especially Italy, where they love bitter greens; in North America it is labeled a weed. I doubt you will find *strigoli* unless you harvest it yourself; however, you can substitute arugula, which can be foraged at the supermarket.

If you prefer more pungent tastes use wild arugula or the greens from turnips or radishes. You can also use leaves from any of the chicories, especially dandelion chicory.

ARUGULA WITH ORECCHIETTE | SERVES 2

Sea salt

7 ounces / 200 g
orecchiette

1 bunch arugula

3 tablespoons extra
virgin olive oil

3 anchovy fillets
packed in olive oil

2 cloves garlic, germs
removed, thinly sliced

1 small red serrano
chile, seeded and
finely chopped

Freshly ground
black pepper

Bring a large saucepan of salted water to a boil over high heat. Add the orecchiette, stir, and return to a boil. Adjust the heat so the water boils gently and cook until al dente. As the orecchiette is cooking, skim off the starchy water that rises to the top; you'll want ¼ cup / 60 ml.

Meanwhile, remove the roots and the thick stalks from the arugula. Rinse well and spin dry. Stack the leaves and slice them thinly; you should have about 6 cups / 5 ounces / 140 g.

Place a frying pan over low heat, then add the olive oil and anchovies. Cook, gently stirring, until the anchovies begin to break up. Add the garlic and chile and cook, stirring from time to time, until the garlic just begins to color. Remove from the heat.

Drain the orecchiette and add to the frying pan; return the pan to low heat. Stir in the sliced arugula and slowly add the pasta water so the arugula mixes evenly through the pasta. Season well with black pepper and salt; even with the anchovies you'll need it.

BRUSSELS SPROUTS

While I don't find cabbage bitter, its relative, brussels sprouts, were my childhood nemesis. I was not alone in my dislike of these mini cabbages; many people find them too bitter to eat.

It is easy to blame your parents for everything. I always blamed my aversion to this vegetable on my mother, who boiled them until they were soft enough to mash. I managed to avoid brussels sprouts until I married a man who loved them. Why would anyone go out of his way to eat brussels sprouts, I wondered? And while he may fall into a special category (he often eats them boiled for breakfast), marriage is about compromise, so I tackled them again. I found a recipe for hashed brussels sprouts in *The Union Square Café Cookbook* that changed my opinion of them: the brussels sprouts were shredded, quickly cooked, and then tossed with poppy seeds and lemon. I have never boiled a brussels sprout again; it was apparently the mushy texture that I didn't like, not their bitterness. Brussels sprouts are making a comeback on restaurant menus: in Chicago they came with my charcuterie platter, and in Zurich they accompanied game stew—they made an excellent match with both. And nowhere have I had them cooked whole with little crosses cut into their cores; these sprouts were pulled apart into individual leaves first. Like shredding them, it reduces the cooking time and changes the texture.

My friend Rony loves food and is a good cook. When I visited him in New York he made brussels sprouts for dinner. It was before my conversion and I was not that keen to try them, but being well brought up I did. They were delicious. Caramelizing the sprouts in the oil eases their bitterness, as does the addition of the starchy chickpeas. There are two keys to this recipe: cook your own chickpeas—they are superior to the canned ones—and cook the brussels sprouts in a very hot pan—as Rony said, "They should dance around in the pan."

RONY'S BRUSSELS SPROUTS AND CHICKPEAS

SERVES 4 TO 6

1 cup / 6¼ ounces / 180 g dried chickpeas, soaked overnight in water to cover

Sea salt and freshly ground black pepper

¼ cup / 60 ml extra virgin olive oil

1 shallot, finely chopped

¾ cup / 175 ml chicken stock, preferably homemade

17½ ounces / 500 g brussels sprouts, trimmed and halved

2 tablespoons dry sherry

Drain the chickpeas and place in a saucepan. Cover them with cold water by 2 inches / 5 cm and bring to a boil. Lower the heat, cover, and simmer until cooked. This can take from 30 minutes to over an hour depending on the age of the peas, so you need to keep an eye on them. Check them at 30 minutes. When they are cooked, remove from the heat, uncover, stir in 1 teaspoon of salt, and leave to cool for 30 minutes. Drain the cooked peas and spread them out on a baking sheet lined with a towel to dry.

Pour 2 tablespoons of the olive oil into a large heavy frying pan with a lid, and place over medium heat. When hot, add the shallot and cook until soft. Add the chickpeas, season with salt and pepper, and sauté until lightly browned. Add ¼ cup / 60 ml of the chicken stock and bring to a boil, stirring to deglaze the pan by scraping up any browned bits from the bottom. Tip the contents of the pan into a bowl.

Wipe out the pan and then add the remaining 2 tablespoons oil. Place over high heat, and when hot add the brussels sprouts. Try and get as many of the sprouts cut side down as you can; this will depend on the size of your pan. Cook the sprouts until dark brown on one side, then add the remaining chicken stock, season with salt and pepper, lower the heat, cover, and cook until the brussels sprouts are tender but still crisp.

Add the chickpeas, shallots, and any liquid and cook until warmed through. Check the seasoning and pour in the sherry. Serve hot or at room temperature.

I like all animal fats, but bacon or duck fat are my first choices here. Olive oil doesn't give the same flavor kick. I add chile in this recipe, though garlic, shallot, or poppy seeds all make interesting additions. What you do need is some acid—lemon, lime, or vinegar—and salt to tame the bitterness. And unless you are a supertaster you will change your opinion of brussels sprouts. Eat this dish once a month and you'll learn to love them. You might even be even persuaded to try them raw (opposite).

BRUSSELS SPROUTS REVISITED | SERVES 4

1 pound / 450 g
brussels sprouts

2 tablespoons fat

3 dried chiles or
½ teaspoon
chile powder

1 teaspoon sea salt

1 lime

Freshly ground
black pepper

Cut the stem ends off the brussels sprouts and, using a small knife, cut the leaves away from the core of the sprout. When you reach the center of the sprout where the leaves are tiny and compacted, stop and cut the sprout into quarters. Rinse the sprout leaves and pieces well, spin dry, and set aside.

In a large frying pan with a lid, heat the fat over medium-high heat. Add the chiles and cook, stirring, until you can smell the pepper, about 30 seconds. Add the brussels sprout leaves and centers and cook for 2 minutes, stirring, until the leaves are wilted and beginning to color.

Reduce the heat to low, add the salt, cover, and cook the brussels sprouts another 4 minutes, or until tender. Meanwhile, finely grate the zest from half the lime and squeeze the juice; you should have about 1½ tablespoons. When the leaves are tender, add the lime zest and juice and the pepper. Check the seasoning, and serve.

VARIATION You can also cook these brussels sprouts in the oven. Place the prepared brussels sprouts in a bowl, melt the fat, add it with all the other ingredients to the sprouts, and toss well. Place the leaves in a single layer on a baking tray and cook for about 7 minutes in a 400°F / 200°C oven. Some of the leaves will become quite crisp, creating another texture.

For me the secret to brussels sprouts is not to overcook them, but I didn't expect to like them raw; I am not a big fan of raw cabbage. However, with the pear's sweetness to soften the bitterness and the poppy seeds for crunch, they make an excellent early winter salad and a change from coleslaw.

BRUSSELS SPROUT SALAD / SERVES 4

1 pound / 450 g
brussels sprouts

1 barely ripe Bosc pear

2 tablespoons freshly
squeezed lemon juice

1 teaspoon very finely
grated fresh ginger

Sea salt and freshly
ground black pepper

2 tablespoons whipping
(35 percent fat) cream

¼ cup / 60 ml
extra virgin olive oil

2 tablespoons
poppy seeds

Trim the sprouts, then cut them in half lengthwise and rinse well. Thinly slice the sprouts and place in a large bowl. Peel and cut the pear in half lengthwise. Remove the core, then slice thinly crosswise and add to the shredded sprouts.

In a small bowl, whisk together the lemon juice and ginger and season well with the salt and pepper. Whisk in the cream and then the olive oil and check the seasoning. Stir in the poppy seeds and then pour over the sprouts and pear. Toss well and serve.

MYSTERIOUS BRUSSELS SPROUTS

Brussels sprouts have a mysterious and puzzling history. Some writers suggest they were eaten in classical times, but according to the English food writer Jane Grigson, they are first mentioned in the city of Brussels's market regulations in 1213. This would suggest they were being grown in the Low Countries at that time. However, not until two centuries later do they appear again, this time on the menus of Burgundian wedding feasts held at the court of Lille. At that time the powerful dukes of Burgundy controlled northern France and most of the Low Countries. After this appearance on the royal table, brussels sprouts vanish again; it seems they were never a popular vegetable, or perhaps they remained a very local specialty.

In the late eighteenth century they resurface, this time in gardening books rather than cookbooks. "Brussels sprouts are winter greens growing much like boorcole" is how they are described in Charles Marshall's *Plain and Easy Introduction to Gardening* (1796). This shows that it was the leafy green tops of the plant that were popular, not the small buds attached to the thick stem. Thomas Jefferson is often credited with bringing brussels sprouts to America. While he did plant them in his garden at Monticello in 1812, it is debatable whether this was their first appearance in the New World. They may well have arrived earlier with the French settlers to Louisiana, some of whom came from northern France.

However, it was their popularity as a garden plant that returned them to our tables, at least in England. By the mid-nineteenth century Elizabeth Acton, in her *Modern Cookery for Private Families* (1845), was explaining how to cook them Belgian style, boiled and smothered in butter. As a young woman, Elizabeth had spent time in France, where she had no doubt eaten them. A few years later in 1849, French chef Alexis Soyer included a recipe in his book *Modern Housewife*. In Victorian England, French chefs were very influential—not perhaps achieving the celebrity status of chefs today, but people took notice of their recipes. Brussels sprouts caught on in England, and if you ask any English person which vegetable to serve with the Christmas turkey you will get the same response: brussels sprouts—though unfortunately they are usually boiled. With their popularity cemented in England, brussels sprouts invaded the colonies—and my Australian childhood, much to my dismay.

But why are they called brussels sprouts and not cabbage sprouts or little cabbages? Before fast, reliable transportation took vegetables around the world, most were grown close to towns to guarantee supplies. As a result, vegetables often bore the names of these places, like "Argenteuil asparagus," "Hamburg parsley," and *"choux de Bruxelles"* or "brussels cabbage"; which goes halfway to explaining their name.

I used to make this dish with savoy cabbage, but now I prefer brussels sprouts as I think their bitterness balances the sweetness of the chestnuts better. The best chestnuts are those you roast yourself, although you can find them already cooked and vacuum-packed, which is a lot less work. If you can only find canned ones make sure they are not sweetened. This is the perfect dish to serve with roast goose, game, or turkey.

BRUSSELS SPROUTS, BACON, AND CHESTNUTS

SERVES 4

1 pound / 450 g brussels sprouts

4 ounces / 115 g pancetta or fatty bacon

2 tablespoons bacon fat or rendered pork fat

4 ounces / 115 g unsweetened cooked chestnuts

Sea salt and freshly ground black pepper

Trim the sprouts, then cut them in half lengthwise and rinse well. Thinly slice the sprouts and set aside. Cut the pancetta into matchstick-size pieces. In a frying pan with a lid, cook the pancetta slowly over low heat until it renders its fat and is very crisp. You should have enough fat to cover the bottom of your pan, if not add some extra fat. Chop the cooked chestnuts. Add the sliced brussels sprouts and chestnuts to the pan, stirring to coat with the fat. Season with the salt and pepper, and then cover the pan. Cook gently until the brussels sprouts are just tender and the chestnuts are heated through.

TURNIPS AND RUTABAGAS

Now, the turnip is a vegetable I love, while the rutabaga . . . I am still learning to like. Both are brassicas, but with very different temperaments. The turnip is sophisticated and subtle while the rutabaga is common and brash. No doubt my judgment is biased: I grew up with the rutabaga but I was introduced to the turnip in France. When I say "turnip," I mean the white and purple ones that appear in the spring and early summer. Their gentle bitterness makes them a natural match for sweet spring vegetables like peas, carrots, and new potatoes, and they are essential in a lamb navarin. They are also a perfect match for rich foods like duck and foie gras. Don't overcook turnips; they should retain some crunch. If you find them too bitter, peeling them will reduce it.

> "The turnip is the poor man's truffle, a product wrongly viewed as dull, which on the contrary brims with character if properly handled. Glazed turnips, turnips with salt or in a broth are all good. Their special taste makes them a basic ingredient of good cooking." —PIERRE GAGNAIRE

Turnips are often sold in bunches with their greens still attached. Keep the greens, rinse them, and toss them in with the cooked turnips, or add them to a salad, or cook them quickly in butter, or substitute them for arugula.

> "Once a turnip said, 'I taste very good with honey.' 'Go along you boaster,' replied the honey. 'I taste good without you.'" —RUSSIAN FOLK SAYING

You say "rutabaga"? I say "swede." It's strange to move to a country where they speak the same language, only to discover that you still sometimes need a translator. I grew up with "swede," not surprising since my grandmother came from Scotland. Mashed swede, or *neeps*, is the traditional accompaniment for haggis, and while I never ate haggis in Australia, I did eat a lot of mashed neeps. The swede, a relative of the turnip, arrived in Scotland from Sweden in 1781, and so was most sensibly called a Swedish turnip. But swedes are not Swedish. They probably originated in Bohemia before heading north to Scandinavia and on to Scotland. We think of them and cook them like other root vegetables, but they are not roots at all. The "root" part is simply an enlarged stem base, like celery root (celeriac) and the ridges on its surface are the marks left by leaves. Most vegetables get paler after cooking, but the swede intensifies in color, turning from yellow to orange, and that guaranteed it was noticed: according to the Encyclopaedia Britannica Dictionary of Arts, Sciences, and Miscellaneous Literature (1797), "The ruta baga, or Swedish turnip, is a plant from which great expectations have been formed." Alas, it didn't quite live up to its billing, but it has remained a staple in British (especially Scottish) kitchens, and its name was shortened to swede.

So where does the name *rutabaga* come from? It is an anglicized form of the Swedish name *rot bagge* meaning "baggy root," or "ram's root," depending on your source. Many writers claim that swedes are milder than turnips, while others say they are sweet. I disagree. In my taste universe they are much stronger flavored, and while I have tasted a little initial sweetness in some rutabagas, their pungency quickly overwhelms it and a bitter taste registers in my brain. Perhaps I need to eat a rutabaga a day to overcome this prejudice, but that isn't going to happen. So I am learning to like them by adding some sweetness, or lots and lots of butter, to keep that bitterness at bay. If, like me, you are not a rutabaga fan, I suggest you stick with the smaller roots, preferably unwaxed, as they are more likely to be milder. (Waxing may improve rutabaga's shelf like, but it also makes cutting into them a suicidal mission.) However, if you love rutabaga, try Cardoon Beef Tagine (page 187), replacing the cardoons with chunks of peeled rutabaga.

Some of my best recipes come from leftovers. It is good to be hungry with limited resources: it makes you think like a cook. Anyone can go to the store and buy ingredients to make a dish, but opening the refrigerator and creating a meal is more of a challenge. Once, my husband had been on a turnip binge while I'd been away, so there was half a rutabaga, which I passed over, but I grabbed three white and mauve turnips, a red pepper, and the remaining favas that I'd bought at the market. I wasn't really thinking "bitter" when I made this dish. I often cook this way. It is always edible, sometimes it's good, and often, like this time, it's worth making again. I threw the butter into a frying pan and then was distracted; suddenly a delicious, nutty, buttery aroma brought me racing back to the stove. It was the nutty browned butter flavor that made the dish. Good food is often a happy accident.

TURNIP AND FAVA BEAN STEW / SERVES 3 OR 4 AS A SIDE DISH

2 tablespoons / 1 ounce / 30 g unsalted butter

1 onion, halved and sliced

1 red bell pepper, seeded and diced

6 cloves garlic, germs removed

Sea salt and freshly ground black pepper

12 sprigs fresh thyme

3 medium white turnips

1 pound / 450 g fava beans in the pod

In a frying pan with a lid, over medium heat, cook the butter until it begins to turn brown and smells nutty. Remove the pan from the heat and add the onion. Stir to coat the onion in the butter and add the pepper and garlic. Season with salt and pepper and add 10 of the thyme sprigs. Reduce the heat to low, cover, and cook gently until the vegetables are soft.

Meanwhile, peel the turnips and cut into ½-inch / 1-cm chunks. Remove the fava beans from their pods.

When the onion is soft, add the turnip, and a tablespoon or two of water, just enough to keep the vegetables from sticking. Cover and continue to cook until the turnip is tender but still crisp, about 10 minutes.

Meanwhile, blanch the fava beans in boiling salted water for a couple of minutes until tender, then refresh in ice-cold water. Slip the beans from their outer skins. Pull the leaves from the 2 remaining thyme sprigs.

Remove the thyme sprigs from the pan, then add the favas and thyme leaves to the pan. Stir, check the seasoning, then remove from the heat. Leave to cool and serve at room temperature.

Young turnips are pleasantly bitter. You can make this dish using only turnips, but I like to add spring bulb onions, which come in bunches with green stems still attached. This helps offset the bitterness, as does the cinnamon stick. Cinnamon is slightly sweet, and as most of us associate cinnamon with dessert, it tricks our brain into thinking "sweet." It also has a warm and pungent taste that works well with savory dishes. Try to find real cinnamon (opposite); it is more refined than its harsher relative, cassia. Ideally, the turnips and onions should be the same size. I don't peel the turnips, as I like the extra bitterness from the skin and the way they look. This makes a good side dish or, for a starter, top the warm turnips with paper-thin slices of Spanish ham or smoked duck breast and let them soften.

BRAISED YOUNG TURNIPS / SERVES 4

8¾ to 10½ ounces / 250 to 300 g baby turnips, about 12

6 ounces / 170 g green bulb onions

1 tablespoon duck fat

Sea salt and freshly ground black pepper

¼ cup / 60 ml water or chicken stock, preferably homemade

A 4-inch / 10-cm piece of cinnamon (see opposite page)

Thinly sliced Serrano ham, optional

Trim the turnips, keeping the leaves if they are fresh. Rinse the turnips and leaves well. Thinly slice the leaves and set aside, and cut the turnips in half lengthwise. Trim the greens from the onions and keep for another use. Remove the onion roots and outer layer of skin if necessary. Rinse the onions, then cut in half lengthwise.

In a saucepan just large enough to hold the turnips and onions in a single layer, melt the fat over medium heat. Add the turnips and onions, then season with salt and pepper. Cook until lightly colored, about 5 minutes. Add the water and cinnamon stick, broken in half.

Cover and cook over low heat until the turnips are just tender, about 12 minutes. They should still have a little crunch to them. Remove the cinnamon stick, stir in the shredded leaves if using, and cook until just wilted. Serve as is, or topped with the thinly sliced ham.

VARIATION If you can't find baby turnips you can use larger ones, but peel them and cut them into large chunks. They will take longer to cook.

This simple recipe is surprising and delicious. It is an adaptation of a recipe from the French chef Guy Savoy. While I love turnips, I hadn't thought of eating them raw. The overnight bath in cream mellows their taste. The key is to slice the turnips very thinly, and using a mandoline makes this easier, although it is not impossible with a sharp knife. If they are small and very fresh, don't peel them. This mixture of raw turnips and cream is excellent with grilled, smoked, or cured meats or fish.

CREAMY TURNIPS WITH CHIKES / SERVES 4

7 ounces / 200 g
small turnips

¾ cup / 175 ml whipping
(35 percent fat) cream

3 tablespoons / ⅓ ounce /
10 g finely chopped chives

¼ teaspoon sea salt

Freshly ground
black pepper

Trim and rinse the turnips, peeling only if necessary. Cut them in half lengthwise, then slice into very thin half-moons and place in a bowl. Stir the cream and chives together, then pour over the turnips. Mix well so that all the turnip slices are covered in cream. Cover and refrigerate overnight.

Tip the turnips into a sieve set over a bowl to drain off the cream. Add the salt to the cream and whisk until the cream is softly whipped and just holds its shape. Fold the turnips and chives into the cream and season with black pepper and more salt if necessary.

CINNAMON

Cinnamon and cassia are the dried bark of Asian evergreens, which are members of the laurel family. This makes cinnamon and cassia distant cousins of both avocados and bay trees. Cinnamon is very aromatic, warming, and sweet, while cassia is harsh and strong. Unfortunately, most of the "cinnamon" sold in North America is cassia.

The bark is harvested during the rainy season, when it is more pliable. Only two or three branches are cut from each tree and the outer bark is removed. The valuable inner bark is bruised, then slit and carefully removed. Left to dry in the sun, it curls, forming the familiar quills or sticks.

The difference between the two cinnamons is easy to spot. Cassia is a single piece of rolled bark that is dark and difficult to break. A true cinnamon stick is made up of several layers of tan, paper-thin bark that breaks with almost no effort, crumbling into tiny, fine flakes.

I know what you're saying: Turnip ice cream? Really? Well, it's good to surprise your taste buds every so often, otherwise you become bored and don't pay attention to your food; much of the molecular style of cooking is about surprising the diner. Here, the bitterness of the turnip plays off the sweetness of the milk and cream. Serve this with baked apples or apple pie and see if your guests can guess the flavor. Mace is the lacy covering on whole nutmegs; I always add it to a béchamel sauce, and here it helps tame the turnip. You can buy mace in pieces called blades. If you can't find them, don't let that stop you from making this ice cream; you can substitute freshly ground nutmeg.

TURNIP ICE CREAM / MAKES ABOUT 2 CUPS / 500 ML

8¾ ounces / 250 g turnips, about 3 medium

1 cup / 250 ml whole milk

1 cup / 250 ml whipping (35 percent fat) cream

A blade of mace, or a good pinch of freshly ground nutmeg

3 egg yolks

⅓ cup plus 2 teaspoons / 2½ ounces / 75 g sugar

A pinch of fine sea salt

1 tablespoon vodka

Peel and coarsely grate the turnips, then place them in a medium saucepan and add the milk, cream, and mace. Bring to a boil over medium heat, remove from the heat, cover, and let stand for 15 minutes. Taste the mixture: it should taste of turnip; if not, let stand another 10 minutes. Strain the mixture into a large measuring cup, pressing down on the turnip to extract all the liquid.

Whisk the egg yolks with the sugar and salt in a large bowl until the mixture is light and thick and the sugar is dissolved. Whisk the strained milk and cream mixture into the egg yolks, then pour into a clean saucepan. Cook over medium heat, stirring, until the mixture thickens and coats the back of a spoon. Strain into a bowl and cool quickly by placing it in a larger bowl or sink filled with cold water and ice. Stir the mixture often. When it is cool, cover and refrigerate overnight. Also, place a container for the ice cream in the freezer to get cold.

The next day, remove the ice cream mixture from the refrigerator, stir in the vodka, and then churn in an ice cream machine following the manufacturer's instructions. Transfer to the cold container and freeze until ready to serve.

Anyone who knows me knows that rutabaga, or as I call it, swede, is not my favorite vegetable. Alas, my husband loves it: another vegetable he can eat for breakfast. If I'd known that before we were married . . . So over the years I have taught myself to like rutabaga (not for breakfast, mind you). Usually I calm its forceful bitterness with lots and lots of butter or by mixing it with sweet parsnips. The inspiration to add shallots to weaken rutabaga's force came from a recipe for mashed yellow turnips with crispy shallots in *The Union Square Café Cookbook*.

Instead of crisping shallots, I slowly caramelize them in butter while the rutabaga cooks, then I fold them into the smooth pureed rutabaga to add sweetness and texture. Unwaxed rutabagas cook in about the time it takes to caramelize the shallots, and I prefer their flavor. However, if your only choice is an older waxed one, you'll want to give it a head start, because if the caramelized shallots sit around they can solidify and stick to the pan. If this does happen, just reheat them in the pan over low heat with a splash of water before adding them to the puree.

RUTABAGA PUREE WITH CARAMELIZED SHALLOTS

SERVES 4

5 tablespoons / 2½ ounces/ 75 g unsalted butter

3 shallots, peeled and cut into rings

Sea salt

1 tablespoon sugar

2¼ pounds / 1 kg rutabaga, peeled and cut into 1-inch / 2.5-cm pieces

½ cup / 125 ml whole milk

Freshly ground black pepper

Melt 2 tablespoons / 1 ounce / 30 g of the butter in a small frying pan over low heat and add the shallots, a pinch of salt, and the sugar. Cook the shallots very gently, stirring from time to time, until they are caramelized, about 30 minutes.

Meanwhile, place the rutabaga pieces in a saucepan and cover with cold water. Add a good pinch of salt, cover, and bring to a boil. Lower the heat and simmer partially covered until very tender, about 30 minutes.

Drain the rutabaga well and place in a food processor. Heat the milk with the remaining butter until the milk is hot to the touch and the butter has melted. Puree the rutabaga, leaving the pusher out of the food processor's feed tube so that the steam can escape. Slowly add the hot milk and butter and continue to process until very smooth, scraping down the sides if necessary. Transfer the mixture to the saucepan and place over low heat. Stir in the shallots and any butter in the pan and season very well with salt and pepper. Reheat over low heat and serve hot.

VARIATION You can leave the shallots out completely and just have buttery pureed rutabaga.

HEALTHY BITTER

When I was a child, my mother told me to eat my vegetables and she always put fresh fruit in my school lunch. We all know that fruits and vegetables are good for you: they contain essential minerals and vitamins and are full of fiber. Research now shows that plants also have chemicals that have long-term positive effects on our health. I'm sure you look at leafy greens and dark chocolate differently today than you did ten years ago.

While science is providing the proof, the idea of food as medicine is as old as humankind. The ancient Greek physician Hippocrates said, "Let food be thy medicine and medicine be thy food," and since the beginning we have been looking for ways that what we ingest can treat infection, relieve pain, and cure illness. We turned to plants, and by trial and error we discovered which ones are medicinal, which ones stimulate our nervous system, and which ones alter our consciousness. Shen Nung was a legendary Chinese figure who supposedly lived during the late third century BCE. He is credited with developing the principles of Traditional Chinese Medicine (TCM) by testing out herbal remedies on himself. Unfortunately, so the story goes, he succumbed to a poisonous plant when he was unable to drink a remedial tea quickly enough. Whether Shen Nung was a real person or not, TCM has a long documented history of employing plants as medicine.

The Egyptians also had a vast knowledge of medicinal plants. Ancient papyri record numerous prescriptions based on plants. Many of these were made by steeping the plants in alcohol to extract their beneficial bitter compounds, and the resulting liquid was drunk. These medicinal drinks were the forerunners of today's bitters (see page 70). We often think we know more than our ancestors did, but they had a vast practical understanding of the curative power of plants. Tree bark is the basis of important medicines and today we still benefit from this knowledge. For millennia, willow bark was ingested to ease pain and relieve fever, and the active compound in it is still the major ingredient in the popular painkiller aspirin (although acetylsalicylic acid is now made in a laboratory rather than extracted from a tree). Quinine is another important medicine derived from tree bark. The cinchona tree provided an effective treatment for fever and malaria (see page 80) long before French chemists isolated its active compound in 1820. Both these compounds are very bitter.

To protect themselves against predators, plants produce chemical compounds, many of which are bitter tasting and even poisonous. This is why we have an innate negative reaction to bitter: the aversion protects us from being poisoned. Babies and young children can be poisoned by small amounts of toxins, so they are protected by a greater number of taste buds, making them react strongly to bitter tastes. Over time we have learned that many bitter plants can be safely consumed in small amounts or after special handling, and that many of them have positive effects on our health. Swiss physician Paracelsus, the founder of the science of toxicology, said: "All substances are poisons; there is none, which is not a poison. The right dose differentiates a poison from a remedy."

While bitterness signals the presence of healthy compounds, most of us prefer sweetness and we have selected and bred plants to reduce their bitterness. Lettuces were all once bitter weeds, and while their bitterness has disappeared over time, you'll get hints of their original bitterness if you eat the leaves from a plant that has gone to seed in your garden. Vegetables like cabbage, eggplant, and cucumber have also become less bitter through cultivation. Ever wonder why older cookery books suggest salting eggplants? It was a way to reduce the bitterness, but is no longer necessary. Grapefruit juice's bitterness comes from the flavonoid naringin. This powerful antioxidant fights cancer and lowers cholesterol, yet there is less of it in sweet red grapefruit. What does remain of this bitter-tasting chemical is deliberately filtered out of commercial juice.

> "Mediterranean people value 'bitterness' in weeds, as once did all European peoples . . . The Sculptor and I soon discovered the benefits conferred by weeds." —PATIENCE GRAY

Luckily some plants, like members of the chicory family, have retained their original bitterness and as a result have more healthy phytochemicals (see page 154) than sweet lettuces. Others are exploited for their bitterness. Hops are bred to give beer its distinctive bitter flavor (see page 55), and thanks to their antibacterial chemicals, they also preserve it. These same chemicals help us fight disease, and there are more antioxidants in a lager than in a glass of red wine or a cup of green tea. Like their relative cannabis, hops act as a sedative and muscle relaxant and contain a natural estrogen, which is now being used to treat cancer and help women through menopause. Bitter melon, or karela (see page 242), is a knobby type of cucumber appreciated by a few for its very bitter taste. Its fans believe that it cures fever, parasites, hypertension, and diabetes, and evidence is accumulating to prove them right: research shows that bitter melon lowers blood sugar levels and fights viruses. A study undertaken at the University of Colorado Cancer Center has shown that bitter melon juice destroys cancer cells. In sub-Saharan Africa, the local people eat the wild bitter leaf plant (*Vernonia amygdalina*) to cure themselves of intestinal parasites and treat malaria. The chemical compounds extracted from this plant back up its antiparasitic and antibacterial reputation. In Nigeria, its leaves are added to beer, performing the same functions as hops: preserving and adding bitterness to the brew. In Cameroon, they cook the bitter leaf, which resembles spinach, and balance its bitterness by mixing in ground peanuts to make a dish called *ndolé*. Bitter leaf is now cultivated in Africa, but it is less bitter and thus less beneficial than the wild variety.

So even as we gain evidence about the importance to our health of bitter compounds in our food, there are fewer of them available to us. If we want bitter in our diet we have to actively seek it out, and one place to find it is in wild plants. Wild plants rich in beneficial chemical compounds are not always our first choice for food. Efficient food transportation systems mean that we live in a world with no seasons and an overabundance of food, making foraging unnecessary. We might spend an afternoon in the woods looking for mushrooms, but dinner doesn't depend on our success. Yet throughout human history, and even in some places in modern times, foraging has been a necessity when crops failed, or as a source of stopgap food in early spring when winter supplies were exhausted. In Europe during World War II, food shortages forced people to forage for food. Even in the United Kingdom, food rationing led to an increased interest in harvesting plants from the woods, fields, and hedgerows to supplement a restricted diet. Some cultures have maintained their appreciation for bitter foraged foods. In *Honey from a Weed* (1986), Patience Gray recounts how during her travels around the Mediterranean in the 1960s she saw women and children gathering weeds in the early spring. You might imagine that people living in small villages at this time were simply happy to eat anything green and fresh after a limited winter diet. However, they harvested these bitter weeds not just to eat but also to use as medicine. In Italy, a young girl explained to Gray which weeds she could eat raw in salad, and which ones must be cooked before eating. The people there knew from long experience that cooking could reduce the toxins in the very bitter plants and make them more palatable.

" . . . food has become primarily an expression of each individual culture, needing to be learned anew from birth and passed on from generation to generation." —PAUL FREEDMAN

Collecting and eating wild plants in the spring is happening less, and much of this traditional knowledge is in danger of being lost. Professor Andrea Pieroni of the Slow Food University in Italy has studied descendants of Albanians living in southern Italy. He found that only the elderly women still gather wild bitter greens. Like the young girl Gray met, they differentiate among the plants in a very practical way, by taste rather than by botanical taxonomy. Plants are selected for food or medicine according to their degree of bitterness. Mildly bitter plants are eaten; moderately bitter ones are eaten and used as medicine; and the bitterest plants are only medicinal. Their way of classifying plants is backed up by pharmacological studies, but will it survive them? Does it matter? I believe it does. While we may think that we can grow these plants or replicate their beneficial compounds in a laboratory, neither of these methods delivers the same health benefits as plants harvested from the wild. We are continually learning about the signifciant role the compounds found in plants have for our health and well-being. The importance of safeguarding knowledge of wild plants was shown as recently as the 1990s, during the war in the Balkans. Bosnian botanist Sulejman Redžić was instrumental in helping many of the inhabitants of Sarajevo survive the longest siege in modern warfare, which lasted almost four years, from 1992 to 1996. He did so by explaining and demonstrating to his fellow citizens how to find, harvest, and cook wild greens and so provided them with a source of nourishing food.

Even if we possess the knowledge, most of us don't have the time or territory to forage. Perhaps we could recognize and harvest dandelions from our lawn, but we would have a hard time collecting enough to make a salad. Habitats where wild plants grow are fast disappearing, with large-scale agriculture destroying hedgerows and other field borders where wild plants flourish, while pesticides and pollution adversely affect any that do remain. Most of us live in cities and do our foraging at the supermarket, where wild plants are rare. All is not lost, however. There is a resurgence of interest in and appreciation for wild foods. "Wild," "gathered," and "foraged" are now positive descriptors on upscale restaurant menus, and restaurants employ foragers or send their chefs out to harvest wild foods. While this trend may seem new, it's not. French chefs Michel Bras and Marc Veyrat were using locally foraged foods more than twenty years ago, as was Chez Panisse in California, and there are many chefs whom no one has heard of cooking foraged food. Still, international acclaim sways the food world, and thanks in large part to restaurants in Scandinavia, wild food is now very fashionable. People line up to pay large amounts of money for food that is essentially free to anyone with knowledge and time. Interest in wild foods has spread beyond the restaurant world to the extent that there are now books, television programs, websites, and workshops all devoted to learning to gather and cook edible wild plants. As a result, foraged foods are showing up again in farmers' markets and even some supermarkets, especially in the spring.

I must admit to not being the first to order rutabaga when I see it on a restaurant menu. I was dining with my friend Lesley and she was doing a review, so I let her order all the food—and there was, as usual, a lot of it. Rutabaga and apple soup was one of her choices and I was surprised how much I liked it. The soup is sweet to begin with, thanks to the carrot and apple, then the peppery assertiveness of the rutabaga steps in, but doesn't overwhelm. The croutons are optional, but I think pureed soups are improved with a contrast in texture, and the croutons do just that.

RUTABAGA AND APPLE SOUP | MAKES 7 CUPS / 1.75 L

2 tablespoons / 1 ounce / 30 g unsalted butter

1 onion, halved and sliced

1 carrot, peeled and diced

1 stalk celery, sliced

Sea salt and freshly ground pepper

1 teaspoon curry powder

1⅓ pounds / 600 g peeled, diced rutabaga

1 sweet apple

1 clove garlic, germ removed

1 fresh bay leaf

4 cups / 1 l chicken stock, preferably homemade

2 slices sourdough bread, optional

In a large saucepan, melt the butter over medium-low heat. Add the onion, carrot, and celery and season with salt and pepper. Cook, stirring, until the vegetables soften a little, about 7 minutes. Add the curry powder and stir to mix, then add the rutabaga, apple, garlic, and bay leaf. Cook, stirring, for a minute or two until you can smell the curry powder.

Pour in the stock and bring to a boil. Lower the heat, cover, and simmer for 1 hour or until the rutabaga is very soft.

Meanwhile, cut the bread into cubes and place on a baking sheet in a 400°F / 200°C oven for about 7 minutes or until crisp.

Remove the soup from the heat, and let cool slightly. Discard the bay leaf and blend the soup in batches until smooth. Reheat the soup, thinning with water if necessary, and check the seasoning. Serve with the croutons.

A GLASS OF RAPINI?

Rapini, also called broccoli rabe, is a subspecies of *Brassica rapa,* and has more in common with a turnip than a brussels sprout. Rapini comes from the Italian word for turnip, and this vegetable is also called *cime di rapa,* or "turnip tops" in Italy. If you find broccoli bitter, you'll hate rapini, with its assertive pungency and bitterness. However, for bitter lovers, rapini's taste is perfect to wake up the taste buds and cleanse the palate.

Many people blanch rapini to tame its taste. It helps a bit but not much, and because rapini cooks quickly it will turn to mush if you don't pay attention. If you do decide to blanch it first, don't salt the cooking water and don't throw it away.

One of the best things about working on a book is that everyone sends you ideas and suggestions, and my agent stumbled across a recipe for *ciccoria* water in *Tomatoes, Basil and Olive Oil: An Italian-American Cookbook* by John Agresto. He grew up with rapini, or bitter broccoli as he calls it, and he remembers that when his grandmother cooked it, as well as dandelions or chicory, she never added salt to the water. Why? She kept a jug of *ciccoria* water in her refrigerator to drink.

> "At any given temperature, however, we are much more sensitive to bitter substances than we are to sweet, sour, or salty ones, by a factor of about 10,000." —HAROLD MCGEE

Rapini is full of vitamins and minerals and its bitterness signals lots of good phytochemicals, but I can't vouch for how good the cooking water is for you. I can tell you there are many other things I would rather drink. Although Agresto states you can drink it hot or cold, when hot it tastes like the worst herbal tea you've ever had. I recommend you put it in the refrigerator, like his grandmother did, and drink it very cold (remember, cold reduces the impression of bitterness). No doubt some people would say that it tastes better than Fernet-Branca, but at least the latter contains alcohol.

Rapini makes a delicious sauce for pasta. Adding the pancetta helps temper its taste and provides fat for the sauce, so it is important to have pancetta or bacon with a good ratio of fat to meat. Cook the rapini until it is meltingly soft, so it blends with the fat and pasta water to make a thick sauce.

RAPINI WITH PENNE | SERVES 2

1 bunch rapini, about 17½ ounces / 500 g

Coarse sea salt

7 ounces / 200 g penne

4 ounces / 125 g pancetta or bacon

2 cloves garlic, germs removed, sliced

Extra virgin olive oil

Freshly ground black pepper

Parmesan cheese

Trim the rapini stems at the base; I usually cut off about 1 inch / 2.5 cm or so. Drop the rapini into a sink of cold water and swoosh around, then drain in a colander. Chop the rapini stems, leaves, and florets coarsely.

Bring a large saucepan of salted water to a boil over high heat. Add the penne, stir, and return to a boil. Adjust the heat so the water boils gently and cook until the penne is al dente, 10 to 12 minutes. As the pasta cooks skim off about ¼ cup / 60 ml of the starchy cooking water and set aside.

While the water is coming to a boil, cut the pancetta into matchstick-size pieces. Place a large frying pan over very low heat and add the pancetta. Cook the pancetta gently so that it renders its fat. When the fat begins to render, add the garlic and stir; add a little olive oil if necessary—the fat should coat the bottom of the pan. Now add all the rapini and stir to coat with the oil, season with salt and pepper, cover, and cook gently until the rapini is very soft.

With a bit of luck you will have the rapini and penne cooked at the same time. You can start the rapini ahead of time to be sure.

Drain the penne and add to the pan with the rapini. Over low heat, toss together, adding some of the penne cooking water to make a sauce. Check the seasoning and serve with freshly grated Parmesan.

I love rapini; it has all the brassica bravado. I doubt whether rapini has ever gone unnoticed in a dish or on a plate. Serve it with a spicy sausage or duck confit and duck fat potatoes to wake up taste buds that are being lulled into a stupor with all that delicious duck fat. This is my favorite way to cook rapini, and this dish is also good at room temperature.

BRAISED RAPINI WITH GARLIC AND CHILE

SERVES 2 OR 3

1 bunch rapini, about
17½ ounces / 500 g

3 tablespoons extra
virgin olive oil

3 or 4 cloves garlic,
germs removed, sliced

1 serrano chile or a large
pinch of chile flakes

Sea salt and freshly
ground black pepper

Trim the rapini stems at the base; I usually cut off about 1 inch / 2.5 cm or so. Drop the rapini into a sink of cold water and swoosh it around. Pull out pieces, cut off the thicker stems, and toss the leaves and florets into a colander. Slice the stems into ½-inch / 1-cm pieces.

In a large saucepan with a lid, heat the oil over medium heat and add the garlic and the whole chile. Lower the heat and cook gently, stirring from time to time. As soon as the garlic begins to color, add the rapini stems and season with salt. Cook, stirring, until they render their liquid, about 3 minutes.

Add the rest of the rapini and the chile flakes if using. Stir until the rapini begins to wilt, then cover and cook over low heat until the rapini is soft, about 10 minutes. Check the seasoning and remove the whole chile before serving.

HORSERADISH

Horseradish (pictured on pages 94–95) is an interesting root: when you pick it up and sniff, it gives nothing away. Only when you grate it, releasing its volatile oils, do its bite, pungency, and bitterness become apparent. Just a small amount will grab your attention and cut the richness of whatever it's paired with. The power of horseradish dissipates when it sits or is heated, which is why it is always used either freshly grated or preserved in vinegar, which stabilizes its flavor.

The United States produces about 24 million pounds / 10.8 million kilos of horseradish root a year and only a small amount of it is used fresh. Most of it is turned into 6 million gallons / 22.7 million liters of prepared horseradish and the rest ends up in cocktail sauces, dips, and mustards. Sixty percent of the world's supply is grown around the town of Collinsville, Illinois, close to the Mississippi not far from St. Louis, Missouri. In the late nineteenth century German immigrants arrived in the area, bringing with them their love of horseradish. Long summers, cold winters, and a soil that is rich in potash make this region ideal for growing horseradish. There is a Horseradish Festival every May, with recipe contests, the obligatory horseradish eating competition, and what must be a very entertaining event—root tossing.

Horseradish is commonly used to represent one of the five bitter herbs, collectively called "*marrorium*," which are included in the Jewish Passover meal, or Seder. The eating of bitter herbs symbolizes the bitter, hard times Jews endured in Egypt. Strictly speaking, it shouldn't be there. The *maror* should be either the leaves or stalks of a vegetable, not the roots. So while wild bitter lettuces, endives, and chicories are all acceptable, horseradish is not. However, as the Jews moved north in Europe and bitter leaves were not available, horseradish was gradually substituted.

The name *horseradish* has nothing to do with horses. It refers to the taste of the root—"hoarse," meaning harsh and strong. It is not only a condiment; in Germany they make horseradish schnapps, while in England during the mid-seventeenth century they added it to ale, as this passage from Samuel Pepys reveals: "There met Mr. Pargiter, and he would needs have me drink a cup of horse-radish ale, which he and a friend of his, troubled with the stone, have been drinking of."

Pepys had his kidney stones removed, a dangerous option in 1657, so he would have understood the pain Mr. Pargiter's friend was enduring. I am not sure if drinking horseradish beer would have helped the kidney stones, but the root contains anti-inflammatory compounds that fight harmful bacteria. And as anyone who has grated fresh horseradish root knows, it will also clean out your sinuses.

I wish I could say that this recipe idea came to me in a moment of brilliance, but alas, no. At lunch at Moustache restaurant in Paris's fifth arrondissement, my poached shrimp were paired with avocado quenelles. Not until I tasted them did I have any idea that they were flavored with horseradish. The sweet shrimp and rich, fatty avocado were the perfect foil to the pungent, gently bitter horseradish.

I thought this recipe would be better with fresh horseradish, but it isn't. Prepared horseradish (I am referring to finely grated horseradish in vinegar, not creamed horseradish) is available in most supermarkets and if you like horseradish, you'll probably have a jar in the back of your refrigerator. How you serve these is up to you. Two quenelles with a couple of slices of Melba toast makes a great starter. They can accompany seafood, smoked fish, or cold meats, or you can even serve the mixture as a dip. Shaping the mixture into quenelles is optional, but it looks good and is simple to do.

HORSERADISH AND AVOCADO QUENELLES

MAKES ABOUT 7 OR 8 QUENELLES

1 ripe avocado, about 8¾ ounces / 250 g

2 tablespoons prepared extra-hot horseradish

½ teaspoon sea salt

Freshly squeezed lemon juice

Cut the avocado in half and remove the pit. Slip the flesh out of the skin into a bowl. Add the horseradish and salt and a squeeze of lemon juice, then using a fork mash together until well blended. Taste and adjust the seasoning, if necessary. If you are not serving the quenelles immediately, press a piece of plastic wrap directly onto the surface of the mixture and refrigerate.

To make a quenelle, take two equal-sized dessertspoons and dip one into the mixture; use the second spoon to form the avocado mixture into an egg shape. Using the second spoon, slide the quenelle onto a plate.

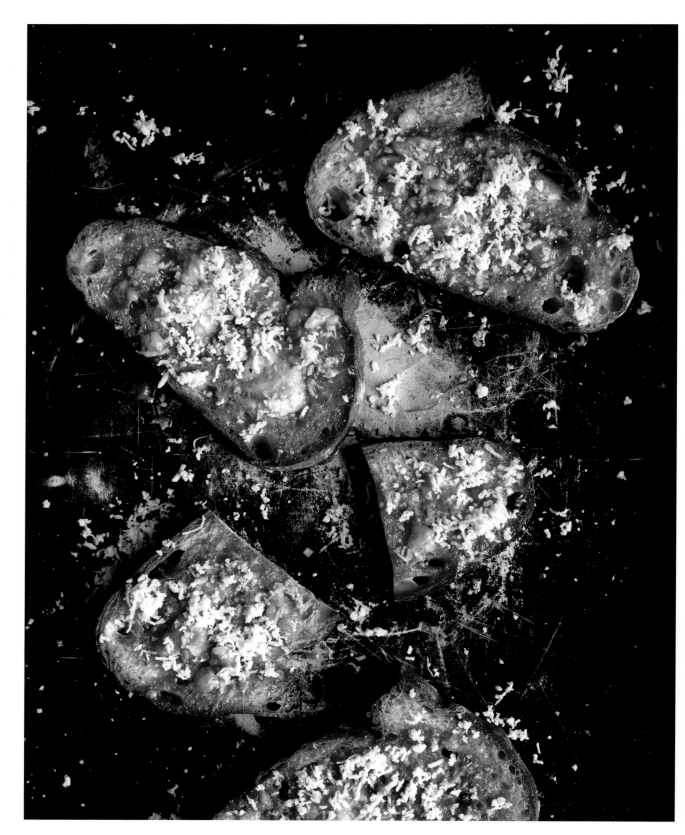

Horseradish cuts the fat of the bone marrow and makes it taste sweeter. It is important to use fresh horseradish for this recipe. Grate it finely just before serving so it retains all its pungency. Use a microplane grater to give the horseradish a light, fluffy texture. Make sure you buy marrow bones cut from the center of the leg bone, so the marrow is accessible from both ends of the bone and the marrow-to-bone ratio is highest. Four bones should yield about 7 ounces / 200 g of marrow; if you have a little more or less it's not a problem.

HORSERADISH AND BONE MARROW TOASTS

SERVES 4

4 marrow bones, about 4 inches / 10 cm in length

Coarse sea salt

4 slices country-style bread, preferably with fine grain

½ cup / 1 ounce / 30 g finely grated fresh horseradish

Fleur de sel or fine sea salt

Leave the marrow bones on the kitchen counter at room temperature for about 15 minutes; the marrow should just begin to soften slightly. Now run a small, flexible knife between the marrow and the bone at each end, to free the marrow from the bone as much as possible. Pick up the bone and, using your thumb, push the marrow from the narrow end toward the wide end out of the bone. Don't start at the wide end. The marrow will be soft and will tend to squish under the force of your thumb, but persist and eventually the marrow will emerge from the bone in one piece. Place the marrow pieces in a bowl of ice water, add some coarse salt, and refrigerate for a few hours to remove the blood. (You can leave it refrigerated overnight.)

Drain the marrow, place in a small bowl, and leave at room temperature for 20 minutes. Preheat the broiler to high.

Toast the bread on one side. Spread the marrow evenly over the untoasted sides of the bread and place on a rimmed baking sheet; some of the marrow will melt and liquefy. Broil until just melted and warm. Remove from the heat and sprinkle with the grated horseradish and fleur de sel. Serve as is, or with a bitter green salad.

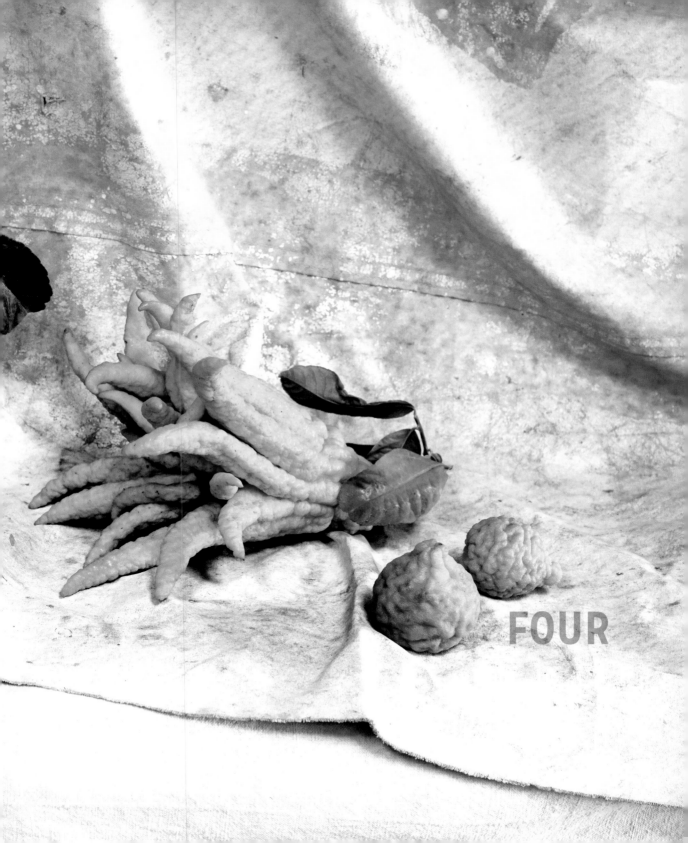

FOUR

SUBTLY BITTER

Fruit doesn't typically make you think of bitter; quite the opposite, in fact. Ripe strawberries, fragrant melon, juicy peaches—all of them sweet. However, there are fruits that harbor bitterness; the most obvious are members of the citrus family, such as grapefruit and Seville oranges. Recipes constantly warn you to cut away the bitter pith when using citrus zest, and while there is some bitterness in the flavorful volatile oils in the skin, most is concentrated in the pith. The peel and pith of citrus fruits are common ingredients in bitters and bitter alcohols, and they are full of antioxidants. Take full advantage of their phytochemicals: next time you add citrus zest to a recipe, leave on a little of the pith. It will add a hint of bitterness to sugar syrup, milk, or savory stew.

> "I used to love dishes that were rich on rich—but the older I get, the more I look forward to that bitterness, the cleansing bite that makes you want to go back for your next forkful of a dish." —SHARON HAGE

Other fruits, like red currants and apricots, have tannins that develop when you cook them, giving these fruits a slight bitterness. Walnuts get most of their bitterness from their skins, while green olives give high-quality extra virgin olive oil its hint of bitterness. The bitterness of fruits can be exploited to make more complex dishes. When it comes to sweet dishes, bitter fruits can make them a little less cloying and much more seductive and satisfying. Sweetness can kill your appetite; a touch of bitter will keep you wanting to have another mouthful.

GRAPEFRUIT

The grapefruit is a relatively new addition to our fruit bowl, and it's the only citrus fruit that doesn't originate in Southeast Asia. Citrus trees hybridize easily and grapefruit are the result of an accidental cross between an orange and the largest of all citrus fruit, the yellow, thick-skinned pomelo. Grapefruit were discovered growing on the island of Barbados. The Reverend Griffith Hughes called them "the forbidden fruit" in his *The Natural History of Barbados* (1750). Perhaps he thought Barbados was the Garden of Eden? Oranges had arrived in the Caribbean Islands much earlier—with Christopher Columbus—but just when and how the pomelo made its way there from Southeast Asia is uncertain. An often quoted story suggests that a certain Captain Shaddock carried it with him on a voyage from Malaysia to Barbados in the mid-seventeenth century. There is no way to verify this tale, but it does explain, perhaps a little too neatly, why in English, a pomelo is also called a shaddock.

In 1820 the French botanist Chevalier de Tussac described the grapefruit he saw growing in the botanical gardens of Jamaica as " . . . a variety of shaddock whose fruits, which are not bigger than a fair orange, are disposed in clusters." Because he was writing in French, he used the word *grappe* for "cluster," and his description was probably responsible for the English name grapefruit. It is not, as some have speculated, because the grapefruit bears any similarity to a grape. The French introduced grapefruit to Florida in 1823, but as they were harder to peel and more bitter than oranges, the fruit didn't become popular until the twentieth century. The first hybrid pink grapefruit appeared in 1907, and then red grapefruit was developed in Texas in 1929.

"With a rich main course there is no need for an elaborate starter. Follow our advice and serve grilled grapefruit." —CORDON BLEU COOKERY SERIES

What gives grapefruit its characteristic bitter flavor is the chemical naringin, of which there is a higher percentage in white grapefruit than in pink or red. More than half of the world's grapefruit is turned into juice, and during its production the naringin is filtered out in a process called debittering. Not only does this make grapefruit juice less complex in flavor, but it also removes a powerful antioxidant. It is worth searching out white grapefruit and squeezing your own juice—it is a lot better for you. I know that white grapefruit are still grown in Florida, because I can buy them at my market in Paris, complete with a Florida sticker!

This recipe has a long history. I first made it while at university when I was taking a course to learn French by cooking. It is much easier to learn a language if you are interested in what everybody is talking about, plus having a good food vocabulary in any language is always useful. I made this tart for my husband early in our marriage, and then like many things I forgot about it. He requested it several times, but I could never find the recipe—it was lost for a decade or more. Then several years ago I found it tucked inside another cookery book. I immediately made several copies, so I wouldn't lose it again. It is one of those typically vague French recipes, a list of ingredients in no particular order with no real instructions. Since I rediscovered it I've been playing with it or, as I think of it, improving it.

GRAPEFRUIT TART / SERVES 8

½ recipe Sweet Butter Pastry (page 141)

3 eggs

Fine sea salt

2 small grapefruit

6 tablespoons / 3 ounces / 90 g unsalted butter

½ cup / 3½ ounces / 100 g superfine (caster) sugar

¾ cup / 5¼ ounces / 150 g granulated sugar

¾ cup / 175 ml water

Roll out the pastry on a floured surface and line a 9-inch / 23-cm tart pan. Prick the base of the tart with a fork, right through to the metal, then refrigerate for at least 30 minutes.

Place a heavy baking sheet or pizza stone in the oven and preheat it to 375°F / 190°C.

Separate 1 of the eggs, and add the yolk to the other 2 eggs. Whisk the egg white with a pinch of salt.

Line the tart with parchment paper and fill it with dried beans. Place it on the hot baking sheet and bake until the pastry is set, about 15 minutes. Remove the paper and beans and continue to bake for another 5 minutes or until the base is lightly colored. Remove the tart shell from the oven on the baking sheet and lower the oven temperature to 325°F / 160°C.

Meanwhile, finely grate the zest from 1 grapefruit and squeeze the juice. Pour the juice into a measuring cup, you should have ⅔ to ¾ cup / 150 to 175 ml. Pour the juice into a small saucepan, add the zest, and bring to a boil over medium heat. Boil until reduced to ½ cup / 125 ml, about 4 minutes. Let cool, then strain through a fine-mesh sieve, pushing on the zest to extract all the juice. Place the butter in a small saucepan and melt over low heat; set aside to cool.

CONTINUED

GRAPEFRUIT TART
CONTINUED

In a bowl, whisk the eggs and yolk, then whisk in the super-fine sugar. Continue to whisk until the sugar is well blended, then whisk in the juice, melted butter, and a pinch of salt.

Brush the base of the tart shell with the beaten egg white, making sure it goes into all the holes. Return it to the oven, on a baking sheet, for 4 minutes.

Pour the filling into the tart shell, and bake until barely set, 15 to 18 minutes; the filling should still be wobbly, but not runny, in the center. Transfer the tart to a wire rack and allow to cool completely.

Cut the remaining grapefruit in half from top to bottom. Cut each half into thin half-moon slices, about ⅛ inch / 3 mm. You need about 20 slices. Line a baking sheet with parchment paper and place a large wire rack on top.

Put the granulated sugar in a saucepan and add the water. Place over low heat and stir until the sugar dissolves, then bring to a boil and boil for 1 minute. Add only enough grape-fruit slices to make a single layer of fruit in the syrup. Cover, and simmer gently until the pith is translucent, 5 to 6 minutes. Using a slotted spoon, remove the slices, drain, and transfer them to the rack on the baking sheet. Add the remaining slices in batches and continue simmering, covered, until they are all cooked. You'll need 16 slices for the tart, so if 1 or 2 fall apart don't worry, you can eat them.

Mentally divide the tart into 8 portions. On each portion, place 2 slices of cooked grapefruit, overlapping them so the rind edge is to the outside and they make a stylized fish shape. You can, of course, cover the tart in cooked grapefruit slices, and while this looks very pretty, it makes the tart very difficult to cut. I prefer practicality to looks in this recipe.

Rich and buttery, this is my favorite pastry, and I use it for all sorts of sweet tarts. It is important to use superfine sugar, also known as fruit or caster sugar, which dissolves more easily into the crust. The high butter content of this pastry can make it a little harder to roll than others; remove it from the refrigerator about 15 minutes before you roll it. If the pastry becomes too sticky, place it between two sheets of parchment paper to roll it out. Not only will this stop it from sticking, but it will also help you ease the pastry into the tart pan. This pastry freezes well.

SWEET BUTTER PASTRY

MAKES ENOUGH FOR TWO
9-INCH / 23-CM TARTS

2 cups / 8¾ ounces / 250 g flour

A pinch of fine sea salt

⅔ cup / 5 ounces / 150 g cold unsalted butter, diced

1 egg

⅓ cup / 2 ounces / 65 g superfine (caster) sugar

Combine the flour and salt in a food processor and pulse to mix. Add the butter and pulse until the mixture resembles very coarse bread crumbs. Transfer the mixture to a large bowl.

In another bowl, whisk together the egg and sugar. Pour the egg mixture over the flour and butter mixture and then mix with a fork. Squeeze a bit of the mixture between your fingers. If it holds together, transfer the dough to a lightly floured surface; if not, add a couple of teaspoons of ice water and test again.

Gently knead the dough into a ball, then divide the pastry in half, and flatten into 2 disks. Wrap each disk in plastic wrap and refrigerate for at least 30 minutes before using.

TALKING TASTE

Trying to describe exactly how a food tastes is difficult. We use comparisons to describe the flavor with more or less success. We choose words that are onomatopoeic, mimicking the sound the food makes when we cook or eat it, like "sizzling," "crisp," and "crackling." However, describing a food like this is only useful if we share a common experience of it. It becomes even more challenging if the food is unfamiliar, or its taste is thought of negatively. The French explorer Jean de Léry described the newly discovered pineapple as having the taste of raspberries. It makes you question the Frenchman's taste buds, or wonder just what raspberries tasted like in late sixteenth-century France. Perhaps it is easier in some languages than others?

Food writer A. A. Gill argues that the fault lies with the English language: "English, which is so gloriously verbose about so much of life's gay tapestry, is summarily tongue-tied when it comes to describing food and eating."

"Language is the agent of cognition, the currency of thinking, the tool-box of communication and the custodian of culture. To be useful, it must map onto the world with some precision." —GREGORY KIMBLE

But is it? Brillat-Savarin, the French gastronome and writer, complained that French did not always have the term he needed, so he was happy to borrow the words from other languages, or simply make them up. Does any language have a vocabulary rich enough to adequately describe all tastes and flavors? Language reflects its culture, and each culture has its own unique appreciation of food. The Japanese, for example, are very serious about texture. A comparative study of words used to describe food textures found that they have more than four hundred words to describe the texture of their food. The Chinese have around one hundred and forty-four while English speakers seem impoverished with a mere seventy-seven terms. Do we not care about texture, or is it just too much pudding and mushy peas? The French, whose cuisine is renowned for its sauces, have more than nineteen words just to describe the viscosity of a sauce. Food is an integral part of a culture, and so it strongly influences its language. Can we translate these words? Can the language of one culture adequately describe the food of another? As food historian Rachel Laudan asks, "Can we be bilingual and bicuisinal?" All we can do for certain is try.

We can expand and improve our own food vocabulary by talking about food. Language is how we communicate and, as Brillat-Savarin pointed out, without language and discussion you have cooking but not gastronomy. My experience of French table talk led to my lifelong love of the country and its food. The talk wasn't pretentious abstract "foodie" nonsense or one-upmanship, it was simply the pure pleasure of sharing past meals with others. I love the way my friends can recall meals from decades ago and conjure up the tastes and flavors of what they have eaten. I didn't realize that all this talk served another purpose. By continually evoking past food experiences—their flavors and tastes, good, bad and indifferent—then sharing them with others, they are creating a collective memory and a vocabulary of food that is constantly growing. Talking about food not only increases our food word power but also places what we are eating into the everyday as well as a social, historical context.

> "*La seule issue pourtant est de parler, de parler sans cesse pour parvenir à une meilleur analyse.*" —JEAN-ANTHELME BRILLAT-SAVARIN

Once we have an expanded vocabulary of food we must take care in how we use it. Everything from a recipe headnote to the name of a dish will influence whether or not we try the dish. Then if we do make it, that title will influence how we think it tastes, as Heston Blumenthal's experience shows. Customers at his Fat Duck restaurant found the Frozen Crab Bisque less sweet than the Crab-Flavored Ice Cream although it was exactly the same recipe. Language is a very powerful tool.

I've been mulling this over as I try to describe bitterness. Bitter, while a positive taste in many cultures, is not well loved among Anglo-Saxons. It is hard to evoke a positive taste image for bitter. *Astringent, pungent, bittersweet, bitter as gall* (bile) or *wormwood, acrid, caustic, tart, astringent, harsh*, and *sharp* are some of the words you find in a thesaurus when you look up *bitter*. Not a very appetizing list. *Bittersweet* is the most encouraging, thanks to its connection to chocolate. As we learn to appreciate bitter tastes, we will have to describe them, and so we should give serious creative thought to creating a positive vocabulary to describe the range of bitter tastes. Bitter greens is now a positive description on a menu; perhaps soon to follow are a hint of bitter caramel, bitter like darkly roasted coffee, a touch of burnt toast, soft tannins, welcome astringency, intriguingly bitter, mouth-puckeringly delicious, quenchingly bitter . . .

There is a lot of work to do.

I've made lemon and grapefruit curd before, but never this way, and I have two friends to thank, both of them pastry chefs: Lesley Chesterman, who suggested I try this method, and Dorie Greenspan, for putting the recipe in the book she wrote with the French superstar pastry chef Pierre Hermé. This recipe is worth the effort—it make a sublime silky cream, as Dorie calls it.

I have changed the recipe to showcase grapefruit's bitterness. You will need a kitchen thermometer for this recipe; I like to use a probe thermometer—it is easier to put into the bowl and has an alarm. I serve quenelles of this curd for dessert.

GRAPEFRUIT CURD | MAKES 2 CUPS / 500 ML

⅔ cup / 5¼ ounces / 150 g unsalted butter

1 large grapefruit, about 17½ ounces / 500 g

½ cup / 3½ ounces / 100 g sugar

2 eggs

Cut the butter into 1 by ½-inch / 2.5 by 1-cm pieces and leave at room temperature to soften.

Using a microplane grater, finely grate the zest from the grapefruit and then squeeze ⅓ cup / 75 ml of juice from the grapefruit.

Place the zest and sugar in a food processor and process to blend. The sugar will become moist and pale yellow. With the motor running, add the eggs, blend, then add the juice and process again.

Pour the mixture into a saucepan and cook over low heat, stirring, until it just thickens and coats the back of a spoon. It should be about 176°F / 80°C. Strain the mixture through a fine-mesh sieve into a large measuring cup, pressing hard on the zest to extract all the flavor.

Transfer the mixture to a blender and check its temperature; it should have dropped to 122°F / 50°C or less.

With the blender on high speed, add the butter, one piece at a time (about every 5 seconds; watch out—the first couple will splash), until all the butter is added. Give the blender a quick rest if it is overheating, then blend the mixture on high for 2 minutes.

Transfer the grapefruit curd to a container and stir from time to time until the mixture cools. Cover and refrigerate; the curd will keep for several days refrigerated, or you can freeze it.

To make a quenelle, dip two equal-size dessertspoons into warm water. Scoop the grapefruit curd onto one spoon and with the second one form the curd into an egg shape. Using the second spoon, slide the quenelle onto the plate.

VARIATIONS

Make individual tart shells using the Sweet Butter Pastry (page 141) and bake them completely. Fill them with the curd and top with a cooked grapefruit slice (page 139).

Use the curd to top a pavlova and balance its sweetness, or make a composite grapefruit dessert (see Variation on page 146).

Like the Beer Jelly (page 56), this is savory; it is an excellent match with fish. I first had it with a thin slice of raw fish at Spring restaurant in Paris. I don't serve much raw fish at home, but I love sardines (yes, out of the can), and this jelly is excellent with them, or any fatty or smoked fish. Try it on top of freshly shucked oysters, too. This jelly also makes a good palate cleanser—remember that bitter stimulates the appetite—so serve a small portion between courses of a rich meal.

GRAPEFRUIT JELLY / MAKES 1 CUP / 250 ML JELLY

1 cup / 250 ml freshly squeezed grapefruit juice, about 2 grapefruit

½ package / 1½ teaspoons / 4 g powdered gelatin

A pinch of fine sea salt

A squeeze of lemon juice

Pour ¼ cup / 60 ml of the grapefruit juice into a small saucepan and sprinkle over the gelatin. Let stand for 5 minutes.

Add the salt to the gelatin mixture and place the pan over low heat. Stir to dissolve the gelatin, then remove from the heat. Stir in the remaining grapefruit juice and the lemon juice.

Pour into 3 small ramekins and refrigerate until set, then using a damp, warm spoon to place a small spoonful or two on the plate with the fish. Or, if you want to serve it as a palate cleanser between courses, set the jelly in 8 small egg cups.

VARIATION Serve a trio of grapefruit: a spoonful of the jelly with a quenelle of the Grapefruit Curd (page 144) and fresh grapefruit segments, a perfect sweet-and-bitter finish to a meal that will also aid digestion.

SEVILLE ORANGES

Bitter oranges are so much more complex in flavor than sweet ones. My favorite is the Seville orange, a throwback to days when oranges were prized for their bitterness, not their looks or sweetness. Grown mainly in Spain, which explains their moniker, they are seasonal, arriving on the market in mid-January and staying less than a month. Not very attractive, these oranges have lumpy, ridged skin, a thick layer of pith, lots of seeds and very tart juice. Seville oranges are now grown in California, and while the fruit maintains its bitterness it has had a makeover—so much so I didn't recognize them, their skin is less wrinkled—how very Californian.

While Seville oranges are the *ne plus ultra* for making marmalade (page 151) they are not the only bitter orange. The Bergamot, a hybrid of the Seville orange and the sweet Palestine lime, grows mainly in Calabria, in southern Italy. It is not eaten as a fruit, but its sour juice is used in place of vinegar. It is most renowned for its fragrant, bitter peel, which is candied, or distilled into the oil that flavors Earl Grey tea. The peel of both these oranges is also the base of many orange flavored liqueurs, bitters and bitter alcohols and is excellent for flavoring for both savory and sweet dishes. In Belgium they add bitter orange peel to wheat beer, and in Scandinavia it is an ingredient in Christmas baking and mulled wine. Bergamot peel is minced and mixed with the juice to make a bitter-sour puree that is paired with everything from fish to dessert. The bitter orange flowers are distilled producing oil for perfumes and orange flower water a popular flavoring for desserts in the Middle East, France and Portugal. In North Africa it is added to tagines and salads, while in Lebanon they mix it with boiling water to make white coffee.

As the season for Seville oranges is short, you must act quickly when you see them. Remove the peel in strips and dry it in a low oven; store in an airtight container. Drying concentrates the orange's bitterness. The dried strips can be infused in milk or cream and added to stews for a bitter orange flavor; it is particularly good with beef. If you cut the peel into thin strips before drying it, you can then pound them into a powder. Sprinkle it over everything from a grilled veal chop to a bowl of strawberries just before serving to add a wonderful, surprising note of bitterness. The Chinese use it medicinally to reduce fevers and cure coughs; they believe that the older the dried peel is, the more effective it is as medicine, and they often keep it for many years. Make sure you freeze some whole Seville oranges; despite being a fruit of the sun, they survive a sojourn in the freezer very well. If you do all this—peeling, drying, and freezing—you will be able to enjoy their bitterness all year long.

One of the first "foreign" desserts I ever made was the Italian zabaglione—egg yolks and sugar whisked with wine, usually Marsala from Sicily. It was light, frothy, and very, very sweet. This recipe is a lot less sweet and, as a result, much more interesting to eat. It is good by itself or over strawberries. Strawberries and Seville oranges are not in season at the same time, but if you've squirreled away a few oranges in your freezer you'll be able to enjoy the combination. Remember, you have to soak the rind a day in advance.

SEVILLE ORANGE SABAYON / SERVES 4

2 Seville oranges, about 5¼ ounces / 150 g each

3 tablespoons brandy

4 egg yolks

¼ cup / 50 g superfine (caster) sugar

Rinse the oranges well and pat dry. Using a vegetable peeler, remove the zest of 1 orange, taking a little of the white pith, too. Cut the zest into pieces and place them in a small bowl. Pour over the brandy, cover, and leave at room temperature for 1 day, stirring from time to time.

Squeeze the juice from the peeled orange; you should have about 2 tablespoons. Strain the juice into a measuring cup, cover, and refrigerate.

Next morning, strain the brandy into the measuring cup with the orange juice. Take a couple of pieces of the marinated zest and remove the pith, then cut the pieces into thin strips or a fine julienne; set aside. Dry the remaining rind (see page 147).

Place the yolks in a large heatproof bowl. Finely grate the zest from the remaining orange and add it to the yolks. Squeeze the juice from the orange into the measuring cup to make ½ cup / 125 ml of brandy-orange mixture. You can freeze any leftover juice.

Add the sugar to the yolks and orange zest. Then, using an electric beater, whisk until the sugar is dissolved. Add the brandy-orange mixture and whisk to mix. Place the bowl over a saucepan of barely simmering water and continue to whisk until the mixture is pale, fluffy, and thick enough so it just holds its shape. Spoon into serving glasses and top with the julienned orange rind.

I like the gently bitter, sour taste of this vinaigrette. This dressing is perfect on sweet vegetables: try it on a grated carrot salad, roasted beets, or roasted root vegetables to make a winter salad. It also works well on Boston lettuce or avocado, or in a chicken salad.

SEVILLE ORANGE VINAIGRETTE

MAKES ABOUT ½ CUP / 125 ML

1 Seville orange

2 teaspoons
Dijon mustard

Sea salt and freshly
ground black pepper

⅓ cup / 75 ml
extra virgin olive oil

Finely grate the zest from the orange into a bowl. Cut a thick slice off the top and bottom of the orange to reveal the flesh. Stand the fruit upright on a cutting board and, cutting from the top down to the bottom, remove the skin and pith. Holding the fruit over a bowl, use a small knife to cut along either side of each segment to the center to free it from the orange, catching the juice in the bowl. Once you've removed all the segments, set them aside and remove the seeds. Squeeze the juice from the membranes into the bowl. Finely chop the orange segments.

Add 2 tablespoons of the juice to the mustard in a measuring cup, add the grated zest, and season well with salt and pepper. Whisk well, then slowly whisk in the olive oil. Stir in the chopped orange segments.

This is the only jam I make. Seville oranges arrive in Toronto around Robbie Burns's day, so I make marmalade as a tribute to my Scottish heritage. It is the perfect way to spend a cold winter's day, and the resulting jars look like potted sunshine, giving me hope that spring will come eventually. Originally, marmalade was made from one of my favorite fruits, the quince. Oranges became increasingly available in Europe at the end of the Middle Ages, and by 1587 marmalades using them were made in England, often with the addition of pippins (a type of apple) to ensure the marmalade set. Gervase Markham published a recipe for "Excellent Orange Marmalade" in *The English Huswife* (1631). Numerous other orange marmalade recipes appeared using Seville oranges, as the thick layer of bitter pith on these oranges ensured that the jam set. In 1797, thanks to a Dundee grocer's wife named Janet Keiller, marmalade changed from a thick paste to the "chip," or Dundee-style marmalade. This is the jam we know today: shredded pieces of Seville orange peel suspended in a jelly. It is ideal for spreading on toast (well-made toast, that is; see page 221). For me, marmalade made with any other fruit just isn't marmalade. As it is Scottish, and I make it on Robbie Burns's birthday, the addition of whiskey is essential.

SEVILLE ORANGE WHISKEY MARMALADE

MAKES ABOUT TWELVE
1-CUP / 250-ML JARS

3 pounds / 1.5 kg
Seville oranges, 10 to 12

6 cups / 1.5 l water

2 lemons

11¼ cups / 5 pounds /
2.25 kg sugar

¼ cup / 60 ml
Scotch whiskey

Scrub the oranges well under running water, and then place them in a large, deep stockpot. Add 4 cups / 1 l of the water and bring to a boil over medium heat. Reduce the heat, cover, and simmer gently until the oranges are very soft, about 1 hour. Using a slotted spoon, rotate the oranges from time to time so they cook evenly. Leave the cooked oranges in the pot to cool. Once they are cool enough to handle, remove them using a slotted spoon; set the cooking water aside.

Cut the cooked oranges in half, then, using a spoon, scoop out the flesh, seeds, and pith into a saucepan. Add the remaining 2 cups / 500 ml water to the pan and bring to a boil; lower the heat and simmer, uncovered, for 10 minutes. Strain this mixture through a fine-mesh sieve into the pot with the cooking water from the oranges. Discard the pith, flesh, and seeds.

CONTINUED

While the pith and water mixture is cooking, cut the orange halves in half again and then finely chop or shred. I prefer shreds, but you can cut them into chunks or dice; it won't change the flavor.

Add the shreds to the pot containing the orange cooking liquid and strained water from the pith mixture. Now zest the lemons and squeeze their juice. Add the lemon zest and juice and the sugar to the pot.

Place the pot over medium-low heat and stir to dissolve the sugar. Once the sugar has dissolved, increase the heat and bring to a boil. At this stage, the marmalade must be watched carefully, as it boils up quickly. Clip a sugar thermometer to the pot and cook over high heat for 20 minutes, or until the jam reaches 220°F / 104°C.

Transfer the pot to a trivet and leave for 20 minutes. Stir to distribute the orange shreds, and add the whiskey. Ladle the jam into warm, dry, sterilized jars (see below), filling to within ½ inch / 1 cm of the top. Stir the jam in each jar to distribute the orange shreds, then wipe the edges of the jars clean. Cover and process in a boiling water bath for 15 minutes.

PROCESSING

The canning jars and lids should be clean and sterilized. Place the jars in a low oven to keep warm. Place the lids and rings in a saucepan, cover with water, and bring to a boil. Remove from the heat and leave in the pan until ready to use.

Put a rack in the bottom of a canning pot or large saucepan, fill with water, and bring to a simmer. Place the filled jam jars on the rack in the pan, making sure they are covered by at least 1 inch / 2.5 cm of water. Bring the water to a boil and boil for 15 minutes. Transfer the jars to a towel to cool. You will hear the jars make a popping sound, indicating that they are sealed; check to see that all the lids are concave.

Seville oranges are often used in Mexican cooking, especially in the Yucatán. However, only the juice of the *naranja agria* finds its way into the kitchen. I've never been to Mexico, so I began my search for a more savory way to use Seville oranges with two noted authorities, Rick Bayless and Diana Kennedy. The juice is an ingredient in a red seasoning paste made with achiote (annatto) paste. I decided to make my own so that I could add the aromatic bitter zest of the orange to complement the rich, sweet pork meat.

SEVILLE ORANGE PORK SHOULDER | SERVES 6 TO 8

1 tablespoon achiote seeds

1 teaspoon coriander seeds

1 teaspoon black peppercorns

1 teaspoon dried oregano (Greek)

A 1-inch / 2.5-cm piece of cinnamon (see page 117)

½ teaspoon cumin seeds

4 cloves

2 small dried chiles

1½ teaspoons coarse sea salt

5 cloves garlic, germs removed, coarsely chopped

2 Seville oranges

4½ pounds / 2 kg well-marbled, fat-coated bone-in pork shoulder, skin removed

2 cups / 500 ml water

2 banana leaves

1 teaspoon cornstarch

Place the achiote and coriander seeds, peppercorns, oregano, cinnamon, cumin seeds, cloves, chiles, and salt in a spice grinder. Grind finely, add the garlic and grind again; tip into a bowl.

Finely grate the zest of 1 orange and add to the spice mixture. Squeeze the juice from the orange and stir into the puree to make a paste. Cut a crosshatch pattern into the fat on the shoulder. Spread the paste all over the pork, then cover, and refrigerate for 48 hours, turning 4 times.

Preheat the oven to 325°F / 160°C.

Place a rack in a large ovenproof casserole or Dutch oven and add the water. Place the banana leaves overlapping on the counter, shiny side up. Put the shoulder on top, fat side up, and fold over the leaves. Place the shoulder in the pot, cover, and cook for 2 to 2½ hours or until the pork registers 155°F / 68°C.

Remove the pork and increase the temperature to 400°F / 200°C. Unwrap the pork and return it to the oven. Cook until the fat is dark golden brown, 15 to 20 minutes.

Transfer the pork to a serving dish and cover loosely with aluminum foil. Pour the cooking juices into a large measuring cup. Let stand 10 minutes, then pour off the fat.

Finely grate the zest from the remaining orange and place in a small saucepan; add the cooking juices. Squeeze 1 tablespoon of juice from the orange and mix in the cornstarch. Whisk into the cooking juices and bring to a boil.

Carve the shoulder into thick slices and serve with the sauce.

PHYTOCHEMICALS

Every plant contains hundreds of different phytochemicals, or biologically active chemicals that occur naturally in them. Scientists have identified thousands of these compounds, with more being discovered all the time, and it is easy to get confused among the antioxidants, phytonutrients, and flavonoids. We've all been encouraged to eat plants for the vitamins and fiber they contain; now we are learning that these phytochemicals are equally important, especially for our long-term health. Some are antioxidant, protecting our tissues from damage and disease; some are anti-inflammatory or analgesic, easing our pain; some are antipyretic, or fever reducers; and some are multifunctional, delivering more than one of these benefits. A number of these compounds are responsible for the bitterness in vegetables and fruits and other edible plant parts, and are placed into groups according to their chemical composition, including phenols and polyphenols (like tannins), flavonoids, glucosinolates, terpenes, and alkaloids.

Perhaps you think you can enjoy the benefits of plants by swallowing a pill: pharmaceutical companies certainly hope so. They have worked hard to isolate many of the beneficial chemicals in plants and create "healthy" supplements. But while research backs the importance of phytochemicals for our overall health, it also shows that each plant has a unique combination that is more effective when eaten in its natural state than taken via a pill. Nature still does it better than us.

The same chemicals that protect plants from wear and tear can protect us, too. Processes within our bodies make unstable molecules called free radicals, which can damage our cells and organs; other molecules called antioxidants fight these free radicals, binding them so they can't damage our tissues. Our bodies make antioxidants, but we can obtain them from plants, too. The significant role antioxidants play in maintaining good health is backed by a large and growing body of research. Their effect is cumulative: they inhibit the growth of cancer cells and tumors, prevent damage to our arteries; slow the development of heart disease; and help us fight numerous other illnesses. No single antioxidant is the answer, and each plant has a different combination of them, so the best way to benefit from phytochemicals in this way is to eat many different plants—and not avoid the bitter-tasting ones, which often have the most of these beneficial chemicals. Yet while bitterness signals the presence of phytonutrients, it also indicates the presence of toxins, so it is prudent not to eat extremely bitter foods.

There are thousands of different *phenolic* compounds, and they each have distinctive aromas and flavors; they abound in foods like cardoons, chicories, dandelion, olives, cocoa beans, and tea. *Tannins* are a group of phenols found in tea, red wine, and some fruits like walnuts and citrus; they are rich in antioxidants. They are very soluble in water, making their taste tenacious and persistent; it registers via the trigeminal nerve as dry, puckery, and astringent on your tongue and inside of your mouth. Tannins get their name from their long history of being used to tan animal skins. *Flavonoids* are polyphenolic compounds found in all plants, and they can act as antioxidants. They impart bitterness to grapefruit, tea, hops, and citrus peel.

Glucosinolates are organic sulfur compounds commonly found in the brassicas. They can be very bitter, with hot, pungent flavors and an unpleasant sulfur smell. Some research shows that they help detoxify our bodies, eliminating unwanted chemicals, and also fight cancer cells. However, some glucosinolates can hinder proper function of the thyroid gland if your diet is low in iodine. *Terpenes* are responsible for many of the aromas in fruits and vegetables, and they have anti-inflammatory properties. You'll find them in citrus fruits and hops.

Alkaloids are bitter tasting compounds that plants produce to protect themselves from being eaten by mammals. It is important to understand that the majority of alkaloids, like most phytonutrients, are poisonous in high doses, but they are also stimulating and can be beneficial in small amounts. The most well known are caffeine, morphine, and quinine. Alkaloids have varying effects on the human nervous system and can alter our metabolism, which is why we are drawn to them despite their bitterness. They can act as analgesics, anesthetics, vascular constrictors, antispasmodics, tranquilizers, and even cause hallucinations.

OLIVE OIL

As many of you know, I love animal fats and use them all the time for cooking. I even make salad dressing with animal fat, but that doesn't mean I avoid olive oil. I love the taste of fine extra virgin olive oil, and like good-quality animal fat, it is full of compounds that are beneficial to my health. Olive oil has one advantage over animal fat: it has some bitterness. Take a spoonful of olive oil into your mouth and swirl it around: you may get a hint of bitter, but mostly you'll feel the oil, tasting its weight and voluptuous qualities. Now swallow, and you'll probably cough. The peppery bitterness in oil is picked up by the receptors in the back of your throat that are specifically designed to signal bitterness. They detect the phenolic compound oleocanthal present in high-quality extra virgin olive oil, which is made with unripe green olives. It is believed that oleocanthal is a powerful antioxidant that plays a role in protecting us against numerous diseases.

> "This inherent bitterness (of olive oil) can be very useful to the cook. Its subtlety adds a tantalizing hint of sophistication to foods . . . "
> —SYBIL KAPOOR

It shouldn't be a surprise that olive oil has bitterness—have you ever tasted a raw olive? You may think of olive oil as fat, and it is, but it is also a simple way to add a touch of bitterness to a dish. Drizzle it into a rich soup or stew just before serving. Remember this bitterness when making salad dressing or serving sweet ripe tomatoes.

I drizzle my best olive oil over tomatoes, dip crusty bread in it, and swirl it into soup. I also like to make a simple dressing of very good oil, lemon juice, a little Dijon mustard, and salt and pepper, which I use on green salad or warm new potatoes.

One evening, I was about to make the dressing again, but I was feeling a little lazy, so instead I took out my best olive oil—the one that makes me cough—and kept adding it to my hot cooked potatoes until they no longer appeared thirsty and the oil was beginning to pool in the bottom of the bowl. A little salt and pepper, and we ate them at room temperature. It was a perfect dish: ridiculously simple, but so good, the sweet new potatoes with the mildly bitter olive oil. Make as much as you want!

NEW POTATOES WITH OLIVE OIL / SERVES AS MANY AS YOU WANT

Baby new potatoes

Sea salt

1 fresh bay leaf

Best-quality extra virgin olive oil

Freshly ground black pepper

Place the potatoes in a saucepan in a single layer. Cover with cold water and add salt and a bay leaf, or two if you are cooking a lot. Bring the water to a boil, lower the heat, cover, and simmer the potatoes until they are cooked.

Drain the cooked potatoes, and as soon as you can handle them, cut them in half. Place them in a wide, shallow bowl and drizzle with olive oil while gently tossing with a rubber spatula. Season the potatoes with salt and pepper and serve warm or at room temperature.

My friend Fran Gage is a wonderful baker and an olive oil expert. I wanted to make a pound cake with a little bitterness, and I thought of olive oil and Seville oranges. As I've always made pound cake with butter, I turned to Fran for advice. She kindly shared a recipe with me; instead of the candied oranges she used, I decided to try it with Seville oranges. This is a pound cake that even a butter lover will enjoy, and the olive oil and oranges have antioxidants that are not only good for you but also help keep the cake fresh.

OLIVE OIL AND ORANGE POUND CAKE

SERVES 8

Extra virgin olive oil, for the pan

1⅔ cups / 7 ounces / 200 g all-purpose flour

1 teaspoon baking powder

¼ teaspoon fine sea salt

6 tablespoons / 90 ml extra virgin olive oil

1 cup / 7 ounces / 200 g sugar

2 Seville oranges

2 large eggs, at room temperature

½ teaspoon pure vanilla extract

¼ cup / 60 ml full-fat yogurt, at room temperature

Preheat the oven to 350°F / 180°C.

Oil an 8½ by 4½-inch / 21 by 11-cm loaf pan and line the base with parchment paper. Sift the flour, baking powder, and salt together into a bowl. Set aside.

In the bowl of a stand mixer with the paddle attachment, beat the olive oil and sugar on medium speed, scraping down the sides of the bowl from time to time, until well mixed and slightly fluffy.

Finely grate the zest from the oranges into a small bowl. Cut a thick slice off the top and bottom of the orange to reveal the flesh. Stand the fruit upright on a cutting board and, cutting from the top down to the bottom, remove the pith. Holding the fruit over a bowl, use a small knife to cut along either side of each segment to the center to free it from the orange, catching the juice in the bowl.

Squeeze any remaining juice from the orange and set aside. Remove the pips from the segments, then finely chop them and add to the zest.

Break the eggs into a small bowl, add 1 tablespoon of the juice, and whisk them lightly with a fork. With the mixer running, add the egg mixture a little at a time to the sugar and olive oil. Wait until each addition is well mixed before adding more. Stir the vanilla into the yogurt with the remaining juice; you should have ⅓ cup / 75 ml.

Beginning and ending with the flour mixture, add to the egg mixture in three parts, alternating with the yogurt, mixing until just incorporated. Stir the orange zest and the segments into the batter until mixed.

Pour the batter into the prepared pan and smooth the top. Bake the cake for 20 minutes, then, using a sharp knife, quickly make a cut down the center of the cake so it cracks evenly. Continue baking the cake until browned and a skewer inserted into the center of the cake comes out clean, about 25 minutes. If the top of the cake is getting too dark before the cake is cooked, cover it with a piece of foil. Transfer the cake in the pan to a wire rack to cool. Remove it from the pan and serve. The cake can be stored in an airtight container for up to 4 days.

HEARING TASTE

We don't often consider that our hearing influences our perception of what we eat. There are several ways that sound affects how food tastes. First, there is the background noise. In France, restaurants rarely play music; the only noise comes from the other diners. In North America, restaurants often play music, and in restaurants with bare walls and hard surfaces the result is a noisy environment where it is impossible to talk to your dinner companions. At home, some of us eat with loud music or the television blaring. Why is this bad? Well, even if we don't want to have a conversation, our food has less taste when the environment is very noisy. Noise distracts us and reduces the attention we pay to what we are eating. The constant engine noise is one of the reasons (there are many others) why the food on airplanes always seems so bland.

Loud noise alters our behavior, too. Studies reveal that couples in a bar ordered more drinks when the music was cranked up than when it was quietly playing in the background. The noise limits conversation, making us drink more. Even the tempo of the background music is important. As you might guess, slower music encourages us to linger, while fast-paced music makes people eat quickly. This, of course, can be exactly what some establishments want.

> "Even before we put food into our mouths, our brains have made a judgment about it, which affects our overall experience." —CHARLES SPENCE AND VANESSA HARRAR

There are the sounds we hear before we eat: the preparation of the food, the chopping of ingredients, the rattle of dishes, the hissing crackle of French fries hitting hot oil, the bacon sizzling in the pan, or, if we listen really hard, the popping of bubbles in a sparkling drink. With all these sounds we anticipate taste and they subtly influence how we will perceive the flavor of the food and drink by setting up expectations.

Food makes noise inside our head when we eat. Most of the time we overlook the sounds we make chewing our food, because we are so used to them. However, the snap of a green bean or the crunch of a potato chip captures our attention with the sound it makes inside our head and we concentrate on the food and taste it better. It's their sound that keeps us eating them; we take longer to tire of eating a food that is crisp and crunchy. According to chef Mario Batali, the term *crisp* (or his word, *crispy*) is a favorite on menus because it sells more food than any other adjective. We all like crisp foods no matter what our cultural background. Scientists ran experiments where they played crackling sounds to people eating potato chips. The participants in the trial reported that the chips they ate when they could hear the crackling sounds were crispier and fresher than the chips they ate in silence. They were, of course, exactly the same chips. Next time you bite into something crisp, pay attention to the sound it makes in your head. If there was silence, would it taste so good? I don't think so.

Heston Blumenthal has taken the role of sound in taste another step further at his Fat Duck restaurant. On his tasting menu is a dish called Sound of the Sea, which arrives with an iPod placed in a scallop shell. You eat the dish while listening to the sound of crashing waves, which intensifies the taste of the dish.

Other studies have explored the link between the pitch of a sound and taste, finding that sweet and sour tastes are matched with high-pitched tones, while bitterness is more often linked to low-pitched sounds. So Poncelet (see page 42) may have been on the right track when he compared taste to musical notes, although he put bitter in the mid-range rather than at the lower end of the scale. Scientists have even demonstrated that the type of instrument playing the background music can alter peoples' perception of taste. Toffee eaten while brass instruments played low-pitched, solemn music was judged more bitter than the same toffee eaten to bright, higher-pitched piano music.

So the sound outside and inside our head plays a role in how we discern the flavor of our food. The right sounds can improve the experience, while the wrong sounds can destroy it. So what about the next time you serve something bitter? Put on some higher pitched piano music, but not too loud of course, and add a crisp, crunchy topping to the dish.

I find that apricots become more tannic with cooking, which gives them a slight bitterness. In this tart, the dark, bittersweet caramel both enhances this bitterness and magnifies the flavor of the apricots. The tart tastes intensely of apricot, and the touch of tannic bitterness shows that dessert doesn't have to be very sweet to be very satisfying. Have the apricots ready to add to the caramel as it finishes, as adding them will stop the caramel from cooking too far. And you will need to begin the pastry at least 45 minutes before starting the tart filling. The amount of caramel sauce with the tart will depend on the juiciness of the apricots.

APRICOT TARTE TATIN / SERVES 6 TO 8

1 cup / 4½ ounces / 125 g flour

A pinch of fine sea salt

7 tablespoons / 3½ ounces / 100 g cold unsalted butter, diced

2 tablespoons ice water

¾ cup / 5¼ ounces / 150 g sugar

8 to 12 firm, small apricots, halved and pits removed

Place the flour and salt in a food processor and pulse to mix. Add ⅓ cup / 2½ ounces / 75 g of the butter and pulse until the mixture resembles fine bread crumbs. Turn the mixture into a bowl.

Pour the water over the flour mixture and mix with a fork. Squeeze a bit of the mixture between your fingers. If it holds together, transfer the dough to a lightly floured surface; if not, add another couple of teaspoons of ice water and test again. Gently knead the dough into a ball. Flatten into a disk and wrap in plastic wrap. Refrigerate for at least 30 minutes before using.

Place the pastry on a floured surface and roll into a 10-inch / 25-cm circle; place on a baking sheet and refrigerate until ready to use.

Preheat the oven to 425°F / 220°C.

Sprinkle the sugar evenly into a heavy ovenproof 9-inch / 23-cm frying pan, then place over medium heat. Cook, shaking the pan from time to time, until the sugar melts. As the sugar melts, gently swirl the pan to mix the sugar granules with the liquid sugar; you can give the mixture a gentle stir with a wooden spoon to blend in any uncooked sugar. Once all the sugar has turned into liquid caramel, continue to cook, swirling gently to make sure it cooks evenly, until it is a rich, dark caramel color. You will smell the caramel and see it smoking quite a bit.

Remove the pan from the heat and then quickly and carefully place as many of the apricots as you can, cut side down, in the pan, in concentric circles. Remember, the caramel is very hot. Cut the remaining butter into small pieces and scatter over the apricots.

Once the caramel has stopped bubbling, place the pastry on top of the apricots, tucking in the edges. The warmth of the pan will soften the pastry. Place the pan on a baking sheet and bake for 10 minutes. Lower the oven temperature to 350°F / 180°C and continue to bake for another 10 minutes, or until the pastry is puffed and lightly browned. Some caramel will bubble up over the pastry.

Remove the tart from the oven, remembering the handle is very hot, and let it sit for at least 10 minutes before turning out. Loosen the edges of the pastry with a knife, then place a large pan lined with a piece of parchment paper over the tart (I use a pizza pan with a lip). Quickly flip the tart and pan over in one bold move. If any apricots stick to the pan, you can place them back on top of the tart, as the caramel is still quite liquid. Scrape any caramel in the pan over the tart and let cool. The parchment paper will allow you to reposition the tart or move it to another plate.

I have a prolific red currant bush in my tiny city garden, so I am always looking for ways to use them. Now they are more available in markets, so you no longer have to grow your own. There is no need to pick off the leaves or stems for this recipe; the food mill will remove them. Plus, those leaves will add to the flavor. Red currants have tannins that develop when they are cooked, and adding the mildly bitter Campari highlights these and gives this ice a more complex flavor.

RED CURRANT ICE | MAKES ABOUT 2 CUPS / 500 ML

1 pound / 450 g
red currants

½ cup / 3½ ounces /
100 g sugar

A pinch of fine sea salt

2 tablespoons Campari

Rinse the red currants and place in a frying pan with a lid. Add the sugar and place over low heat. Cover and cook gently, stirring from time to time, until the currants are very soft, about 20 minutes.

Remove from the heat and pass the currants and liquid through the fine disk of a food mill; you should end up with about 2 cups / 500 ml. Add the salt, stir, and refrigerate overnight; the mixture will thicken. Also, place a container for the ice in the freezer to get cold.

The next day, remove the ice mixture from the refrigerator, stir in the Campari, and then churn the mixture in an ice cream maker according to the manufacturer's instructions. Transfer it to the cold container and freeze until ready to serve.

WALNUTS

I listened to an interview that Mitchell Davis, host of *Taste Matters* on Heritage Radio, did with Andrew Zimmern, the man famous for eating bizarre foods. When asked what food he didn't like, Zimmern replied, "walnuts." Quite a statement coming from a man who eats bugs and fried bats like they were everyday foods. Perhaps Zimmern has never eaten a good walnut?

Good-quality walnuts have a pleasant bitterness and an astringent quality that can be exploited in both savory and sweet dishes. Walnuts are rich in omega-3 fatty acids, making them very good for us. However, omega-3 fatty acids oxidize and turn rancid easily, and this is often the reason why we don't like walnuts: we've eaten rancid nuts. Also, the skin on shelled walnuts is bitter, and that is another reason we avoid them. However, the skin of the walnut is responsible for most of the nut's taste, and it is rich in phenols; its tannins also protect the nut from turning rancid, so leave it on. Poorly stored nuts are very susceptible to oxidization; keep walnuts in the shell in a cool dry place and shelled walnuts in the freezer.

Toasting the nuts lightly before using them enhances their taste. Walnut oil is another way to add bitterness, but it is even at higher risk of spoiling than the nut itself. Once opened, it should be kept out of the light, refrigerated, and used up quickly.

There are a dozen varieties of walnuts, and the black walnut, a native of the East Coast of America, is especially interesting. It has a wonderful floral aroma and a slightly fermented flavor that is great for baking.

This rich, moist, dense, not-too-sweet cake is perfect with an espresso. If you have a Seville orange, use it, but a regular orange is fine, too. If you can locate black walnuts, try using them; they'll add a wonderful fragrance to the cake. As the cake bakes, it will rise and then fall; that is normal. This cake improves with keeping and is really better a day or two later, if you can wait. Adding the cocoa is another way to play up the bitterness of the nuts.

WALNUT CAKE / SERVES 8 TO 12

5½ ounces / 160 g walnut halves

2 slices white bread

⅔ cup / 5¼ ounces / 150 g unsalted butter, diced

⅔ cup / 4½ ounces / 130 g sugar

4 eggs, separated

¾ teaspoon ground cardamom

A pinch of fine sea salt

1 Seville or regular orange

A pinch of cream of tartar

Cocoa powder

Preheat the oven to 350°F / 180°C. Butter a 9-inch / 23-cm springform cake pan and line the bottom with a round of parchment paper.

Spread the walnuts and bread slices on a baking sheet and place in the oven for 10 minutes or until the bread is dry and the nuts are lightly toasted. Let cool slightly. Lower the oven temperature to 325°F / 160°C.

Put the butter in the bowl of a stand mixer with the paddle attachment. Set 3 tablespoons of the sugar aside and add the remaining sugar to the butter. Cream the butter and sugar until they are light and fluffy. Meanwhile, place the walnuts and toasted bread in a food processor and pulse until finely ground.

Add the egg yolks, one at a time, to the creamed butter and sugar, beating well after each addition. Stir in the ground walnut and bread mixture, then add the cardamom and salt. Finely grate the zest from the orange and add to the mixture; set the orange aside for another use.

In a clean bowl, whisk the egg whites until frothy; add the cream of tartar, and continue to whisk until white. Add the reserved 3 tablespoons of sugar, 1 tablespoon at a time, whisking until the whites are glossy and resemble whipped cream. Add a large spoonful of the egg whites to the walnut batter and stir to lighten. Tip the batter onto the egg whites and fold lightly until mixed.

Pour the batter into the prepared pan and smooth the top. Bake for about 50 minutes or until dark golden and a skewer inserted into the middle of the cake comes out dry.

Let the cake cool for 5 minutes, then run a knife around the edge of the cake and unmold onto a cooling rack. Let cool completely, then dust with cocoa powder.

This is a great late-summer sauce when you have basil to use up. Basil, a sweet herb, is often matched with rich pine nuts, but balancing it with bitter walnuts makes an interesting change. Simple to make, the sauce can be kept in the refrigerator, covered, for up to 2 weeks.

WALNUT SAUCE FOR PASTA | MAKES ABOUT 1 CUP / 250 ML

1 cup / 3½ ounces / 100 g freshly shelled walnut halves

2 cups / 1 ounce / 30 g packed basil leaves

1 clove garlic, germ removed, chopped

¼ cup / 2 ounces / 60 g ricotta cheese

1 teaspoon sea salt

Freshly ground black pepper

3 tablespoons walnut oil

2 tablespoons extra virgin olive oil

2 teaspoons champagne or other mild vinegar

Pasta, for serving

Preheat the oven to 350°F / 180°C. Place the walnuts on a baking sheet and toast in the oven for 10 minutes, or until fragrant and lightly colored. Let cool.

Place the basil and garlic in a food processor and process until chopped; add the nuts, cheese, salt, and black pepper. Process again until pureed. With the motor running, gradually add the oils and vinegar. Check the seasoning. Transfer the mixture to a bowl and cover with plastic wrap, pressing the plastic onto the surface of the sauce. This is the way to store whatever sauce you don't use right away: covered airtight with plastic wrap and refrigerated.

For 3½ ounces / 100 g of pasta (my preference is linguine), you will need about 2 tablespoons of sauce which will serve one as a main course. When you cook the pasta, keep 2 tablespoons of pasta water per serving. Drain the cooked pasta, return it to the hot pan, and add half the water and the sauce; stir, and then add enough of the remaining pasta water to make a creamy sauce. Check the seasoning to see if you need more salt, and serve.

Well, I couldn't talk about walnuts without considering this classic salad. Oscar Tschirky was the maître d'hôtel at New York's Waldorf Hotel from 1893 until 1943. Originally from Switzerland, Tschirky was not a cook, but he did create a simple salad of celery, apples, and mayonnaise, which he called Waldorf salad. This salad was featured in an episode of the television show *Fawlty Towers*, when Basil Fawlty has to explain to an American guest that he cannot make him the salad because he has just run out of waldorfs! While this is an American classic, there are no two recipes the same; most, unlike Tschirky's original, add walnuts (apparently the salad's creator detested walnuts). Walnuts are an inspired addition to the salad, adding bitterness and pairing brilliantly with the celery (see page 202). This is my version with walnuts, but without the mayonnaise: I am not very fond of mayonnaise, so I've replaced it with a vinaigrette—or mayonnaise without the egg yolk.

WALDORF SALAD REVISITED | SERVES 6

7 ounces / 200 g leafy celery stalks, 3 to 4

2 sweet apples

3½ ounces / 100 g shelled and toasted walnut halves

2 tablespoons chopped parsley

2 tablespoons white wine vinegar

1 tablespoon grainy mustard

Sea salt and freshly ground black pepper

¼ cup / 60 ml walnut oil

⅓ cup / 75 ml extra virgin olive oil

Rinse the celery, and then slice the stalks in half lengthwise. Thinly slice the stalks and leaves, then place them in a bowl. Cut the apples into 8 wedges, removing the cores. Slice the apples crosswise into thin slices and add to the celery. Coarsely chop the walnuts, and add to the celery mixture along with the parsley.

Whisk together the vinegar and mustard, then season with salt and pepper. Slowly whisk in the two oils. Pour the dressing over the salad mixture and toss well; check the seasoning again, and serve.

ALMONDS

Almonds are one of the oldest nuts known to humans. They appear in the Old Testament, "the rod of Aaron for the house of Levi was budded, and brought forth buds, and bloomed blossoms, and yielded almonds," and they have been cultivated since the Bronze Age.

There are two types of almonds: sweet and bitter. Both have more calcium than other nuts and are good sources of vitamin B and E and other essential minerals. While the nuts look similar, bitter almonds are slightly smaller in size and have an intense almond flavor. Sweet almonds, the readily available nut we use in cooking and to snack on, are mild tasting. The distinctive taste and aroma of bitter almonds comes from the compound benzaldehyde, which is also found in cassia (see page 117). In the past, bitter almonds were taken in small doses medicinally, and according to Frederick Accum in his book, *A Treatise on Adulterations of Food, and Culinary Poisons (1820)*, they were added to table wine to give it a "nutty" taste.

Their bitterness signals poison and bitter almonds contain prussic acid (cyanide), as do the kernels of apricots, plums and peaches—all members of the genus *Prunus*. While the nut can be toxic when eaten raw, you would have to crush and eat a large number for them to have fatal consequences. Luckily, the nut's bitterness would prevent you from consuming very many. Heat destroys their toxicity and reduces their bitterness, so they are blanched and roasted before being pressed to make almond oil, which is used in high quality confectionery. Small quantities of bitter almonds flavor marzipan, almond liqueurs, ratafia, orgeat syrup and almond cookies like amaretti. The leftover almond mash is steeped in water then distilled to make a concentrated almond extract or essence. Bitter almonds are available in Europe, but they are illegal in the United States.

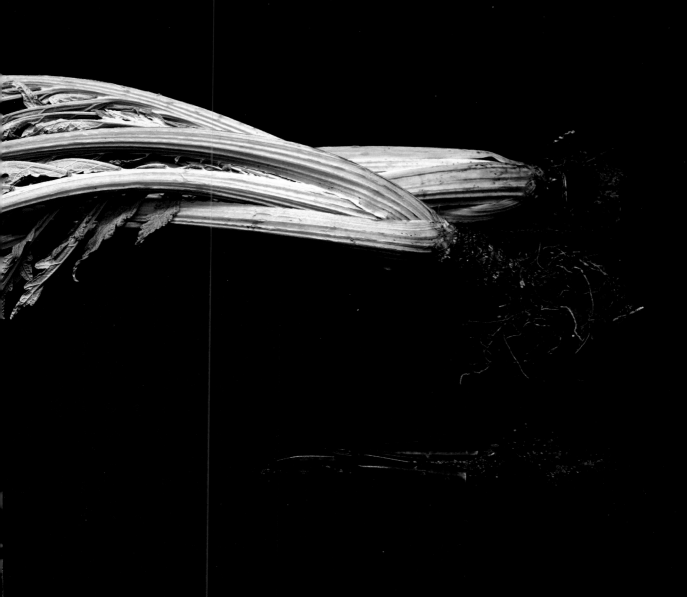

FIVE

SURPRISINGLY BITTER

While brassicas and chicories dominate the bitter vegetable world, there are other vegetables with varying degrees of bitterness. They are subtly bitter so we often don't consider them bitter, but bitter is still an important part of their flavor spectrum, and makes them distinctive. Two of them are among my favorites: white asparagus and cardoons, neither of which is particularly well known in North America. Green asparagus dominate the North American continent so much so that they are available all year round. Grassy and vegetal, they lack the subtle complexity of their rarer, seasonal white cousins—they have no hint of bitterness. White asparagus do, and that is what makes them so interesting to cook and eat.

> "The cardo was sometimes eaten with pepper and salt—with pepper, because it will not generate wind and cleans the liver." —FREDERICK HACKWOOD

Cardoons are a vegetable that most of us only see in still life paintings, but their beauty and their bitterness make them worth seeking out. Much beloved by Italians, these members of the artichoke family complement rich sauces and meats. Then there is celery, ubiquitous and underappreciated. Celery is added to stews and salads, but rarely celebrated as a vegetable in its own right. While centuries of breeding have resulted in a plant not nearly as bitter as its forebears, its stalks are still deliciously astringent—and just try chewing some celery leaves that way you'll taste its bitter heritage.

You may not agree with my choices in this chapter, however it is worth remembering bitterness does not have to assail your taste buds and is usually at its best when muted and surprising.

CARDOONS

While to some they are just noxious weeds, others consider thistles food. As a child I bravely collected thistles for my canary; he ate the seeds from the flower head. Never once did I consider eating them myself; surely only the desperately hungry would tackle such a plant.

Thistles grow wild from the Mediterranean to Siberia and from Japan to Australia, their vibrant purple flowers attracting our attention and their prickly leaves and stinging stems keeping us away. However, the flower heads, stems, and even roots of thistles have a long history as nutritious foods and useful medicines. Like other bitter plants, thistles support the liver, gallbladder, spleen, and kidneys, and aid digestion. They contain good amounts of folic acid and minerals, notably copper, manganese, magnesium, and iron, and are a source of phytonutrients. And some thistles, when relieved of their thorns, are very tasty.

Wild thistles are still collected in many places, but most of the thistles that enter our kitchen are bred to make them easier to handle and eat: the artichoke and the cardoon. The most familiar of these is the artichoke, which is a thistle's unopened flower head. It requires insider knowledge to tackle either raw or cooked; the first time I was presented with one in a restaurant, I had no idea how to eat it. Despite this, it has become popular. What interests me more is its bitter relative, the cardoon. Despite being easier to eat, cardoons have bitterness that deters many from trying them, and finding cardoons requires work.

Cardoons (pictured on pages 172–173) are an invasive plant; they self-seed easily and are considered a weed in North America and Australia. Depending on where you live, you may be able to try wild cardoons. Rosa Mitchell of Rosa's Kitchen in Melbourne, Australia, harvests wild cardoons in the Victorian countryside, a skill she learned from her Italian parents. Smaller and thinner than cultivated ones, they are closer in size to celery and their stalks are tinged with purple. I'm told they are more aromatic and bitter than cultivated cardoons, which is no surprise. Wild cardoons occasionally appear in markets in Europe.

Cardoons are an autumn vegetable, although in North America they also appear for a short time in early spring. In Piedmont, Italy, where they love cardoons, they take great care growing them. The most prized are the *gobbi* cardoons, which have a bowed shape. *Gobbi* is the Italian word for "hunchback," and these plants are bent over and covered with soil as they grow. This blanches the plant; protecting it from the light makes the stalks paler in color and more tender. Outside of Italy you'll generally find straight, silver-green *lunghi* cardoons.

Cardoons look like pumped-up celery with stalks, up to 5 inches / 13 cm wide and 19 inches / 48 cm long. Their large outside leaves, which often have sharp spikes, are already removed, and they are sold in heads, like celery. The head should be firm, not floppy, and the stalks are paler than celery, with deep ridges. The stalks are often split and tinged with brown, as cardoons oxidize easily; don't let any browning on the cut ends put you off. The inner stalks are delicate silver-green with feathery leaves, and are cloaked on the inside with a velvety down. Cardoons are commercially grown in California, and you'll often find them in markets in areas with a large Italian or North African population, as both these families of cuisines love cooking with cardoons.

> "Eeyore led the way to the most thistly-looking patch of thistles that ever there was, and waved a hoof at it. 'A little patch I was keeping for my birthday,' he said; 'but after all, what are birthdays? Here to-day and gone tomorrow. Help yourself, Tigger.'" —A. A. MILNE

It is hard to predict just how bitter the cardoons you buy will be, as it depends on several factors: the soil, climate, and time of year. Cardoons are generally harvested in the autumn, as lower temperatures reduce their bitterness; as the temperature increases, they become more bitter. Many a cookbook will tell you that they are too bitter to eat raw. I don't think so, but we all have different bitter thresholds. The inner stalks are milder and have a better texture; they are the ones I tackle raw. Try a slice of peeled stem, if you find it too bitter, begin your exploration of cardoons by cooking them, which mellows their bitterness.

Once you begin to appreciate their bitterness, cardoons have an earthy meatiness and mild artichoke-and-mushroom flavor that will seduce you. Cardoons are rich in phenolic compounds, which are responsible for their bitter, astringent taste and the reason why they discolor when cut. These compounds make cardoons a rich source of antioxidants and anti-inflammatories. There is no denying that cardoons require preparation before cooking, but unlike artichokes, everything is edible, so you don't need instructions explaining how to eat them.

Most bunches I buy weigh around 2¼ pounds / 1 kg, which is enough for four people as a vegetable. All these recipes are forgiving, so if you have a bigger or smaller bunch, don't worry. It's a good idea to buy two bunches when you find cardoons; that way, you can use the stringy outside stalks for soup and the paler inside ones for a gratin or salad. Before attacking the cardoons, fill a large bowl with cold water, add the juice of a lemon, and throw in the squeezed halves.

Cut the stalks from the base with a sharp knife and then remove all the leaves. The leaves are very bitter. In the center of the bunch are a couple of very thin stalks with lots of leaves; these are worth the time preparing if you are going to eat the cardoons raw. Rinse the stalks well and with a small sharp knife, remove the strings from the stalks, as you would with celery. You can use a vegetable peeler, but there are a lot of strings and you spend all your time cleaning the peeler, so a small knife is easier. Cut the stalks into about 2-inch / 5-cm pieces. Some cooks remove the velvety coating on the inside of the stalks, but this is not necessary unless you are going to eat them raw. If you are, simply rub it off. As you cut the stalks into pieces you will discover strings you missed; pull them off and drop the pieces into the bowl of water and lemon juice.

The old-fashioned way to cook cardoons is *à blanc*, where you make a paste of flour and water then whisk it into a pot of boiling water, to prevent the cardoons from discoloring. A much simpler way is to squeeze a good amount of lemon juice into your pot, and it doesn't hurt their flavor. I simply add the lemon halves to the cooking water, since my cardoons have been soaking in acidulated water. No matter what you do, your cooked cardoons will always be a dull green color.

Bring a large pot of water to a boil over high heat. Drain the cardoon pieces, keeping the squeezed lemon halves, and add them all with a large handful of salt to the pot. Lower the heat and simmer the cardoons until they are just tender—this should be 20 to 25 minutes; however, check them from time to time. Don't cook them for 3 hours as some older cookery books tell you.

Drain them well, then place on a towel to absorb any excess water. You might find a few strings you missed on the cooked pieces; just pull them off. Cooked cardoons can be kept refrigerated for several days.

IDEAS FOR CARDOONS

Raw

Thinly slice inside stems in a salad

Serve cardoon crudités with a spicy dip, or Bagna Cauda (page 190)

Cooked

Toss with a garlic vinaigrette

Mix with a little olive oil, place in a baking dish, top with a little cream and grated cheese, then bake in a hot oven

Coat the slices with flour, egg, and bread crumbs and fry in olive oil and butter

I was at the University of Gastronomic Sciences in Pollenzo, Italy, to give a lecture. Pollenzo is a tiny village where the only signs of life are around the university complex, so most of the students live in the nearby town of Bra. That's where the offices of the Slow Food Foundation are also located—luckily, right next door to an official Slow Food restaurant, Osteria del Boccondivino. I shared a meal there with two of the students and as it was autumn I chose a gratin of cardoons. Now these were not just any cardoons; they were the *gobbi* cardoons that are championed by Slow Food.

CARDOON GRATIN | SERVES 4

1¾ cups / 425 ml whole milk

6 black peppercorns

1 fresh bay leaf

1 blade of mace or a good pinch of nutmeg

3 tablespoons / 1½ ounces / 45 g unsalted butter, plus extra for greasing

2¼ pounds / 1 kg cardoons, prepared and cooked (see page 178)

2 tablespoons / 15 g flour

1½ cups / 1¾ ounces / 50 g freshly grated Parmesan cheese

½ teaspoon sea salt

¼ teaspoon chile powder

Freshly ground black pepper

¼ cup / 25 g fresh bread crumbs

Pour the milk into a medium saucepan and add the peppercorns, bay leaf, and mace. Place the pan over medium-low heat and bring to a simmer. Remove the pan from the heat, cover, and let stand for 20 minutes. Strain the milk through a fine-mesh sieve into a large measuring cup.

Preheat the oven to 400°F / 200°C and butter a large gratin dish. Place the cardoon pieces in the dish, spreading them out so they are no more than three pieces deep.

In a saucepan, melt the butter over medium heat; add the flour, and stir with a wooden spoon until smooth. Continue to cook, stirring, until the mixture turns a light golden color, about 3 minutes. Slowly whisk in the milk and whisk continuously until the sauce is very smooth. Bring the sauce to a simmer and, whisking from time to time, simmer until the sauce thickens, about 5 minutes.

Set 3 tablespoons of the cheese aside and whisk the remaining cheese with the salt and chile powder into the sauce. Season with black pepper and more salt if necessary.

Pour the sauce over the cardoons in the gratin dish as evenly as you can. Mix the reserved 3 tablespoons cheese with the bread crumbs and sprinkle over the top. Bake in the oven for about 30 minutes, or until golden brown and bubbling.

WHICH CAME FIRST:
THE CARDOON OR THE ARTICHOKE?

Both artichokes and cardoons are natives of the Mediterranean region and members of the Asteraceae (daisy) family. There is a lot of debate and speculation over the history of the domestication of these two plants. Many people believe that artichokes were eaten in the classical world. Pliny the Elder is often quoted to back these claims up, and while he did write about a spiky vegetable, it may have been an artichoke but could just as easily have been a wild cardoon or another member of the thistle family. The best guess by scholars is that artichoke cultivation began in the first century CE, but that it took time to be successful.

The first concrete evidence of artichokes being commercially available is at the beginning of the fifteenth century, when records show that artichokes were shipped from Sicily to Florence. Then, over 150 years later, they appear in several Renaissance paintings: Vincenzo Campi's *Fruit Seller* (1580) has a pile of them in the left-hand corner, while Giuseppe Arcimboldo added one to the lapel of his portrait of a man's head composed entirely of vegetables and fruits, depicting summer (1563). Cardoons don't make their appearance in art until the early seventeenth century, when they show up in Italian and Spanish still-life painting. The rebellious Italian painter Caravaggio painted them, but it is the exquisite renditions by the Spanish artist Juan Sánchez Cotán that make you lust after this vegetable even if you don't know what it is. My favorite image is the simplest: silver-gray *gobbi* cardoons painted with four carrots. The vegetables sit in a niche or window that is lit from the left. The carrots emerge from the black background and overhang the edge of the frame, but it is the cardoons that capture your attention. They lean their crooked forms against the right-hand side of the window, bathed in light; you see every detail of their wide, ridged stems trimmed with feathery leaves. Obviously, Sánchez Cotán loved cardoons, too.

While paintings give us clues as to when and where certain vegetables arrived in our kitchens, it's science that has the precise answers. Genetic markers illuminate the origins of every living thing, if less poetically than a Spanish painter might. DNA analysis reveals that the wild cardoons growing around the Mediterranean now are the ancestors of both the artichokes and the cardoons we eat today. Artichoke cultivation began at the start of the first millennium, just as the historians guessed, probably on the island of Sicily. However, it was not until one thousand years later, in Spain and France, that Europeans turned their attention to growing cardoons. Cultivated for less time, cardoons have kept the bitterness of their wild antecedents.

Cardoons were first cultivated in England in 1656, and the English word *cardoon* comes to us from Latin via the French, who introduced the English to many foods. *Cardus* is Latin for "thistle;" it is also the source for the English verb *card* and the noun *chard*. When you card wool you clean and remove the fibers, while "chard" is usually paired with "Swiss" to describe a vegetable, a relative of the sugar beet with a stalk that resembles that of a cardoon.

One year, desperate to eat cardoons, I planted two plants in my small garden. They colonized it, growing over 6 feet (3 meters) tall. Luckily, they are pretty plants, with their silvery green foliage, and they added a touch of exoticism to my city plot. Indeed, many gardeners plant cardoons simply for their decorative value. The French love to use them in autumn flower borders, and they often show up in Paris's Luxembourg Gardens. That year, my Italian neighbors harvested most of them in the middle of the night, leaving only a couple of spiky buds that burst into brilliant purple flowers. Now I pick up cardoons at the market, but every time I see them in a Paris park I am very tempted to return late at night with a knife and a bag.

This is a good way to use fibrous outer cardoon stalks. The advantage of devising recipes for a cookbook is that you make them over and over again, so you discover things about a recipe that you never would if you only made it once. This soup improves with time. I liked it when I first made it, but a day later, it was even better, so if you can, make this soup a day or two in advance. It will keep for a week refrigerated, and you can freeze it, too. You should weigh your dried mushrooms, or check the weight on the package.

Despite its drab color, the soup is delicious and a spoonful of crème fraîche will dress it up.

CARDOON SOUP / SERVES 6 TO 8

½ ounce / 15 g dried porcini mushrooms

2 cups / 500 ml boiling water

2 tablespoons olive oil

1 onion, chopped

2¼ pounds / 1 kg cardoons

2 cloves garlic, germs removed, chopped

1 pound / 450 g potatoes, peeled and diced

1 large branch fresh thyme

2½ teaspoons sea salt

Freshly ground black pepper

Crème fraîche (optional)

Place the porcini in a bowl and pour over the boiling water; let stand for 30 minutes.

In a stockpot, heat the olive oil over medium-low heat. Add the onion and cook, stirring, until the onion is softened, about 7 minutes. Rinse the cardoons, trim, and remove all the leaves and thick strings. Slice into 1-inch / 2.5-cm pieces and set aside.

Remove the mushrooms from the soaking water, squeezing out the excess liquid. Carefully strain the soaking water through a fine-mesh sieve, discard any debris, and keep the mushrooms and the liquid separate. Chop the mushrooms and add them with the garlic to the onions. Cook, stirring, until the mixture begins to stick to the bottom of the pan. Add the sliced cardoons, potatoes, and thyme. Season with salt and pepper, and add enough water to barely cover the vegetables, about 6 cups / 1.5 l.

Bring to a boil over medium heat, then lower the heat, cover, and simmer until the cardoons are soft, about 1 hour. Let cool, remove the thyme, and then blend in batches, passing the pureed soup through a coarse sieve into a large bowl. You should have about 8 cups / 2 l of soup and you'll be left with about 1½ cups / 375 ml of cardoon debris.

Check the seasoning, adding more salt and pepper as necessary. Refrigerate the soup overnight. To serve, gently reheat the soup and ladle into bowls. If you like, swirl in a spoonful of crème fraîche.

Potatoes and cardoons work well together. In this dish, the cardoons take the lead role, but you can always reverse the quantities if it is your first time trying cardoons. The salad is good warm and at room temperature, but don't serve it straight from the refrigerator. A few shavings of fresh truffle before serving it warm would be a wonderful addition—one can always dream. Any waxy potato is good for this recipe; I chose red ones to add a little color to the cooked cardoons. Add the dressing to the cardoons and potatoes while they are still warm, so they drink it up. This anchovy dressing has more lemon than the dressing for chicories (page 19), because the juice and zest really brighten the cardoons' flavor.

WARM CARDOON AND POTATO SALAD

SERVES 6

2¼ pounds / 1 kg cardoons, prepared and cooked (see page 178)

1⅓ pounds / 600 g small red-skinned potatoes, cooked and sliced

½ cup / 125 ml extra virgin olive oil

4 cloves garlic, germs removed, thinly sliced

1 can (1¾ ounces / 50 g) anchovies in olive oil, diced

Zest and juice of ½ lemon

Sea salt and freshly ground black pepper

3 tablespoons chopped Italian parsley

Cut the cardoon pieces in half and place in a salad bowl with the potatoes. In a frying pan over medium-low heat, heat the olive oil. Add the garlic and anchovies and cook gently until the garlic is just golden and the anchovies melt into the oil, then add the lemon zest and juice. Season with salt (being a little more judicious if your anchovies were very salty) and pepper.

Pour the dressing over the cardoons and potatoes, toss gently until everything is well coated, and then check the seasoning. Sprinkle with the parsley. Serve warm or at room temperature.

VARIATIONS

You can vary the amount of potatoes, or leave them out altogether.

Forget the potatoes and cut the cardoons into batons. Add them with more olive oil to the dressing in the pan and cook until warm. Toss in cooked pasta, and finish with a good grating of Parmesan cheese.

Cardoons are a popular vegetable in North African cooking, often added to stews. In this Moroccan-style tagine, they yield their flavor to the sauce making it the best part of this dish, so you need something to soak it up. It could be bread or potatoes, but steamed couscous is ideal and a better cultural match. Many cooks think that instant couscous, where you pour boiling water over the couscous and wait a few minutes, is fine. Well, it isn't. Like cardoons, couscous needs more respect, so please follow the recipe on page 189; it's worth the effort. Prepare the couscous ahead of time, then steam it for the final time after you've added the olives and preserved lemon to the tagine.

CARDOON BEEF TAGINE / SERVES 6

2½ pounds / 1.2 kg stewing beef, with a good amount of fat

Sea salt and freshly ground black pepper

2 tablespoons olive oil

1 tablespoon beef drippings, or more olive oil

2 onions, halved and sliced

1 teaspoon paprika

1 teaspoon ground ginger

1 teaspoon ground cumin

½ teaspoon turmeric

3 large cloves garlic, germs removed, sliced

1 cup / 250 ml water

2¼ pounds / 1 kg cardoons

1 lemon

½ cup / 100 g kalamata olives

1 preserved lemon

1 cup / ½ ounce / 15 g cilantro (coriander) leaves, chopped

Preheat the oven to 300°F / 150°C.

Cut the meat into large pieces, about 2 inches / 5 cm. Pat the meat dry and season well with salt and pepper.

In a heavy flameproof casserole or Dutch oven, heat 1 table-spoon of the oil and all the fat over medium-high heat. When it is hot, brown the beef in batches, transferring the pieces to a plate as they brown.

Lower the heat and add the onions. Stir well, using the moisture from the onions to deglaze the pan. Add the remaining table-spoon of olive oil only if necessary. Add the paprika, ginger, cumin, and turmeric with a good amount of black pepper, about 20 turns of the pepper grinder. Continue to cook, stirring, until the onions soften slightly and you can smell the spices.

Add the garlic and water, stirring to deglaze the pan again. Return the beef with any juices to the pan and bring to a boil. Cover the surface of the meat with a piece of wet parchment paper, place the lid on the pot, transfer to the oven, and cook for 1½ hours.

While the beef is cooking, prepare the cardoons (see page 179) and cut them into ½ by 3-inch / 1 by 7.5-cm pieces; place in a bowl. Cover with water and squeeze in the juice of the lemon, then toss in the squeezed halves.

CONTINUED

Remove the pan from the oven. Drain the cardoon pieces and stir them into the beef mixture with 1 teaspoon of salt. There will be a lot of cardoons, and the cooking liquid will not cover them; it doesn't matter. Cover again with the parchment paper and the lid, then return to the oven and cook for another 30 minutes. Stir again to mix the cardoons into the cooking liquid. Cover with the parchment and the lid again and cook another 30 minutes, or until the cardoons and beef are tender.

Rinse the olives, then remove the pits by hitting the olives with the flat side of a chef's knife. Cut the preserved lemon into quarters, remove the pulp, and discard. Cut the preserved lemon into matchstick-size pieces.

Stir the olives and lemon into the beef mixture and cover just with the lid this time; return to the oven for 20 minutes. Sprinkle with the chopped cilantro and serve with couscous.

VARIATIONS

Cardoons are not always available, so try this dish with celery instead. The flavor is different but still good, and it will improve your opinion of cooked celery. You will, however, still have to spend time removing the strings from the celery stalks.

My husband said I have to point out that you could also make this same recipe using rutabaga. Cut it into good-size chunks so the pieces stay whole.

This method is taken from Paula Wolfert's instructions in *Couscous and Other Good Food from Morocco*. You will need a colander that fits snugly into your saucepan and a piece of cheesecloth.

COUSCOUS / SERVES 6

2⅔ cups / 14 ounces /
400 g couscous

Flour

1 teaspoon sea salt

½ cup / 125 ml
cold water

Place the couscous in a sieve under running water and stir the grains with your fingers so that all the grains are wet. Then spread the couscous onto a baking sheet and leave it for 10 minutes to dry. Wet your hands, then run your fingers through the grains to break up any lumps.

Fill a large saucepan halfway with water, then place a colander on top. Rinse a piece of cheesecloth under cold water and squeeze out any excess water. Spread out the cloth and lightly dust it with flour. Line the colander with the cheesecloth, flour side in, and then add the couscous. Bring the water in the pot to a boil, then lower the heat so it boils gently. Steam the couscous, uncovered, for 20 minutes, stirring it gently with a fork from time to time so that it steams evenly.

Tip the steamed couscous onto the baking sheet again and spread it out using a fork. Add the salt to the cold water and stir to dissolve. Gradually pour it over the couscous, stirring the grains with your fingers so they are evenly moistened. Leave the couscous to dry for 10 minutes. Now cover with a damp cloth and set aside until you are ready to cook it for the final time.

Return the couscous to the cheesecloth-lined colander and steam, covered, for 20 minutes, then turn the couscous into a serving dish. Couscous is usually tossed with butter before serving, but if you are making it to serve with the Cardoon Beef Tagine (page 187), there will be enough fat in the tagine sauce to enrich it.

This warm garlic and anchovy sauce is a traditional accompaniment for raw cardoons in Piedmont. The name comes from the Italian *bagno cauldo,* meaning "hot bath." Try it with prepared raw cardoons (see page 179). Or, if you find your cardoons too bitter to eat raw, you can serve it with cooked ones instead. If you can't get cardoons, serve the bagna cauda with a selection of vegetables, making sure you include some bitter ones, like Belgian endive, radicchio, and baby turnips, which I like to lightly blanch in boiling water first. Serve the sauce warm in small hot ramekins, or place a pot over a low flame at the table, as you would for a fondue. The sauce should be warm, but if it gets too hot it will break. If this happens, tip it into the blender with a tablespoon of hot water and blend it to bring it back together. Or just give it a good stir before you dip; while the broken sauce doesn't look as good, the flavor is the same. You can also use the sauce as a hot dressing on bitter greens.

BAGNA CAUDA | MAKES ABOUT 1⅓ CUPS / 325 ML

½ cup / 125 ml
extra virgin olive oil

⅓ cup / 2½ ounces /
75 g unsalted butter

6 large cloves garlic,
germs removed,
finely chopped

1 can (1¾ ounces / 50 g)
anchovies in olive oil

⅓ cup / 75 ml whipping
(35 percent fat) cream

1 tablespoon freshly
squeezed lemon juice

Sea salt and freshly
ground black pepper

Place the oil and butter in a saucepan over low heat. When the butter begins to bubble, add the garlic and cook very gently so the garlic softens but doesn't color, about 5 minutes. Add the anchovies with their oil and continue to cook gently for another 5 minutes, or until the anchovies melt into the sauce.

Slowly whisk in the cream and continue to cook, whisking, until the sauce comes together. Add the lemon juice and season with salt and pepper; serve warm.

VARIATION If you run out of vegetables before you run out of sauce, put the sauce back over low heat and add a beaten egg, whisking until it thickens. This idea, from Antonio Carluccio, gives you a soft, rich, and very flavorful scrambled egg that makes the perfect topping for a piece of toast—well toasted, of course (see page 221).

CARDOON CHEESE

Cardoons are grown primarily for their fleshy stems, but the roots and flowers are also edible. The brilliant purple flower heads look like a cross between a thistle and an artichoke flower; they are used in cheese making. Cheese is pressed curdled milk that is usually coagulated using rennet from a calf's stomach. Other substances, like figs, papayas, and even black snails, will curdle milk, and since Roman times cheese has been made using the dried purple stamens from wild cardoon flowers.

While the cardoon enzymes curdle all milk, when added to cow's milk they produce numerous bitter amino acids, resulting in cheese with a very bitter, unpleasant taste. Cardoon rennet, however, works very well with sheep's and goat's milk. This way of making cheese is particularly popular in the Iberian Peninsula, and Portugal and Spain are the main producers of cardoon cheese. Many of them are certified by the European Union with a DOP (Denominazione di Origine Protetta) label to protect their quality. Among the better known Portuguese cardoon cheeses are Azeitao, Castelo Branco, Serpa, Serra da Estrela, and Nisa, which was nominated as one of the world's 100 best cheeses by *Wine Spectator* magazine. Spanish cardoon cheeses include Queso de la Serena, Torta de los Pedroches, and Torta del Casar.

Cardoon cheese is also made in Italy. Producers, inspired by the writings of the Roman agriculturalist Columella, are making Caciofiore, a type of Pecorino Romano using cardoons. In France, in Poitou and the Vendée, you find fresh creamy goat's milk cheeses *à la chardonette*, made using flowers of wild thistles and cardoons. Even in Somerset, England, a goat's milk cheese, appropriately called cardo, is made with cardoon flowers. Often, cardoon cheeses are very creamy; the texture of Torta del Casar, from Extremadura, rivals a perfectly ripe French Vacherin. Cardoon cheeses all have a residual bitterness that contrasts with and complements the richness of the cheese.

This is a great salad to have after a rich, fatty main course, like cassoulet or duck. The bitter leaves stimulate your gastric juices and help you digest the meal. You could also begin with this to give you an appetite. The proportions of leaves don't matter, but the mixture does—it gives the salad different textures and makes it more interesting to eat. And do add the celery leaves; they have a pleasantly bitter taste.

CARDOON AND BITTER LEAF SALAD WITH HARALDS'S VINAIGRETTE | SERVES 6

12 cups mixed salad leaves, including Belgian endive, radicchio, curly endive, and celery

3 inside cardoon stalks, prepared (see page 179)

Haralds's Vinaigrette

1 tablespoon raspberry syrup

1 tablespoon Dijon mustard

1 tablespoon balsamic vinegar

1 teaspoon wine vinegar

Coarse sea salt and freshly ground black pepper

¾ cup / 175 ml extra virgin olive oil

½ clove garlic, germ removed, crushed

Rinse the leaves and dry, then cut or tear them into small pieces and place them in a large salad bowl. Drain the cardoon pieces and cut into thin slices, cutting the pieces in half if necessary.

In a glass measuring cup, whisk together the raspberry syrup, Dijon mustard, and vinegars. Season with salt and pepper and slowly whisk in the olive oil. Add the garlic clove and whisk again.

Toss with enough dressing to coat the leaves but not drown them, and serve.

VARIATION Try this salad with the Anchovy Dressing (page 19).

I make this with sliced cardoons and various mixtures of bitter leaves, depending on what is in season and in my refrigerator. I like curly endive and escarole, and I often add the coarse, bitter outside leaves from a head of romaine lettuce. Radicchio, dandelion, and even brussels sprout leaves all work, too. This is delicious hot, warm, or at room temperature. You can replace the cardoon stalks with celery, but don't forget to remove the strings. It may seem like a large volume, but the leaves cook down to nothing.

CARDOON WITH BRAISED BITTER GREENS

SERVES 4

12 packed cups /
14 ounces / 400 g
bitter green leaves,
rinsed

3 tablespoons olive oil

1 shallot, diced

4 inside cardoon stalks,
prepared (see page 178)
and thinly sliced

2 cloves garlic,
germs removed, sliced

1 small serrano chile,
seeds removed and
sliced, optional

Sea salt and freshly
ground black pepper

1 lemon

Slice the leaves into ½-inch / 1-cm strips and place in a large bowl. In a large frying pan with a lid, heat the olive oil over medium heat. Add the shallot and cook, stirring, until softened, about 3 minutes. Add the cardoons, garlic, and chile if using, and cook until the garlic just begins to color.

Add the sliced leaves to the pan and reduce the heat to low. Cover with the lid, forcing it down if necessary. Don't worry if the lid doesn't fit properly, it will as the leaves wilt. Cook for 5 minutes; the leaves should have softened a little. Season with salt and pepper, then stir to coat the leaves with the oil and the shallot and garlic mixture. Cover again and cook for 5 minutes until all the leaves are wilted and softened. Uncover and continue to cook until all the liquid has evaporated. Check the seasoning, then add a good squeeze of lemon juice and serve.

FEELING TASTE

Touching food with our fingers gives us lots of information about its texture and temperature, yet we can feel taste without using our hands. Put a walnut half in your mouth. You can tell the temperature of the nut and its texture—firm, but not so hard that you cannot bite it in half. You'll taste both its fatty richness and bitterness with your taste buds, and then its astringency and tannins kick in. We can *feel* its taste. We know if we are eating something hot or cold, soft or hard, rough or smooth, dry or moist, thick and creamy, or watery and light. Often whether we like a food or not depends as much on its texture as its taste. Slippery, soft, mushy textures are not as popular as crunchy, crisp ones. Texture plays a role in our perception of taste. Although we are more aware of texture with solid foods, even liquids have texture: consider the difference between a glass of water—light and clean and a glass of full cream milk—heavy and rich.

All this information comes to us via the nerves in our fingers, lips, teeth, and tongue, called the somatosensory system. One of its largest and most important components is the trigeminal nerve. It senses the temperature, texture, astringency and tannins of our food. It also detects chemical (rather than temperature) sensations of hot and cold. The cool freshness of a mint is not physically cold, but it creates a sense of coolness in our mouth. The opposite occurs when a room-temperature glass of cognac gives us the same sense of warmth as a hot drink. Scientifically speaking, the taste of bitter is triggered by our taste buds, while astringent, tannic, and pungent sensations are relayed through the trigeminal nerve. Sensitive enough to discern the bubbles in Champagne, this nerve registers the pungency of horseradish and the tannins in tea signalling bitterness and increasing our impression of it. While most chefs are not supertasters (see page 24), they do have above average trigeminal nerve responses, making them more sensitive to what they eat.

There are also receptors at the back of our throat that perceive bitterness. Swallow a spoonful of high-quality extra virgin olive oil, you will feel the bitter pepperiness of the oil in the back of your throat rather than taste it on your tongue, and it will probably make you cough.

There are also nerves inside our bodies that "feel taste" too; a process called *interoception*. In our digestive system they tell us whether we are hungry or full, or have eaten spicy or rich food. They relay both the pain and the pleasure of what we ate. A bitter alcohol will stimulate our gastric nerves, sparking our appetite; it will also help us digest rich food. We don't simply taste bitter with our tongues: we feel it with our bodies, too.

WHITE ASPARAGUS

Like *gobbi* cardoons, white asparagus are a very European vegetable. They too are blanched and have a bitter edge that isn't present in green asparagus. In my taste world, green asparagus are grassy and vegetal, while white are more intense and complex thanks to that touch of bitterness. I rarely eat green asparagus, preferring the taste of white ones: I am, I admit, an asparagus snob. White asparagus are misunderstood on this side of the Atlantic. They need care and some skill to cook, and you can't treat them like green ones. Most importantly, you need fat ones, which are almost impossible to find. Sometimes fat imported European ones turn up in Montréal, but in my part of Canada the white asparagus are too thin and not worth buying; in Europe they can be 1½ inches / 4 cm in diameter. Fat white asparagus are expensive and you need them, because removing the stringy outer layer of white asparagus is essential. It's best done with a small knife—a vegetable peeler is rarely sharp enough. So unless you begin with thick asparagus, you'll be left with nothing to eat.

Begin by trimming the asparagus, cutting off the bases so that they are roughly uniform in length. Take a small, sharp knife and, beginning just below the tip, remove the outside layer. What you remove should be about the thickness of an apple peel. As you peel you will become aware of what is stringy and what is not. My husband says you can feel with the knife how much you have to remove. I make him peel so many in the season he goes into an asparagus Zen state.

Chefs like to tie asparagus into neat bundles, which makes sense if you are cooking large amounts. The other common suggestion is to cook them standing up, to protect the tips. But how many people own a special steamer for asparagus? I don't. Besides, the tips of white asparagus are more robust than green ones, so don't bother looking for one. If I am cooking a few fat stems I will use a frying pan; for larger numbers I prefer a roasting pan. Put the asparagus in the pan, making sure they fit in a single layer, and cover them with cold water. Remove the asparagus and add about 1 teaspoon or so of sea salt, depending on how many you are cooking, and a good pinch of sugar to the pan.

Place the pan over high heat and bring the water to a boil. Add the asparagus, so the tips are all facing the same direction, then lower the heat so that the water simmers. Move the pan so that most of the heat is concentrated away from the tips; if you have a stove with an oval burner, it is ideal, but you can also do this with a frying pan on a regular burner if you're careful. No matter what you read, you need to cook white asparagus longer than green, at least 15 and maybe 25 minutes, depending on their freshness. The older they are, the longer they'll take to cook.

Test by piercing the base of the asparagus with a cake tester or a fine skewer. You want them cooked, NOT crunchy, but you don't want them overcooked, soft, and mushy, so pay attention. The advantage of not tying up your asparagus is that you can remove them as they cook. There are often one or two that cook more quickly than the others. Drain them well, then place on a towel to help absorb the water. Put the asparagus in a dish and keep them in a warm oven, if you plan to serve them hot, while you make the sauce. You can cook asparagus ahead of time and reheat them in a single layer on a baking sheet in the oven.

Warm white asparagus are perfect with a thick coating of melted butter, but you can use the butter to make hollandaise sauce, or my favorite variation, Maltaise sauce, with blood orange juice (opposite). Or, if you are serving the asparagus cold, add some orange juice to mayonnaise to thin it out to a sauce consistency, or try them with Seville Orange Vinaigrette (page 149). You can turn white asparagus into a meal by adding sliced ham, a soft-boiled egg, or both. The Germans often add boiled new potatoes, or serve them with scallops (page 198).

If we all demand big fat white asparagus, perhaps some growers will cover up their asparagus and produce them for us. But be prepared to pay for them.

WHY WHITE ASPARAGUS ARE SO EXPENSIVE

White asparagus are good for you: they're full of folic acid and vitamins A, B, and C, and they also act as a diuretic. They are grown buried under hills of soil covered with black plastic to trap the sun's warmth and prevent any sunlight from reaching the plants. Most of the harvest is done by hand, as the spears from the same plant mature at different times. The plastic is rolled back and pickers prowl the hills looking for any sign of the asparagus. A crack in the soil can signal an asparagus ready for picking. Some pickers even claim they can feel the asparagus through the earth. Once located, each ripe asparagus must be cajoled from the ground. The picker removes some soil, then plunges a specially designed knife deep into the earth, cutting the spear at its base to remove it without damaging it or any other spears nearby. It is a skilled job, but also hard, backbreaking work. Even experienced workers can accidently damage a neighboring spear, or miss a ripe spear that will break through the soil the next day, turning its tip violet and halving its value. About 70 percent of the asparagus grown in Europe are white, and harvesting them accounts for 35 to 50 percent of their cost.

With labor costs rising and skilled workers harder to find, the European Commission has invested in technology to create a fully automated harvester; the machine is already in the testing phase. It uses a sophisticated image recognition software that can locate the position of each spear, tell whether it is ready for picking, and then cut it gently and more precisely than a human worker can. It is the way of the future; however, the machine does have some teething problems, one being that in trials it only cuts eight stalks a minute, while an experienced worker can harvest up to fourteen. The machine is expected to cost around 40,000 euros, but if it can speed up the picking it may also lower the price of a bunch of white asparagus.

The season for white asparagus and blood oranges just overlaps at the beginning of spring, making this a perfect combination. If you can't find blood oranges you can use a regular orange, but the flavor won't be quite the same. This sauce is an orange butter sauce made exactly the same way you would make a white butter sauce (beurre blanc), but using orange juice instead of wine. The cream is added to make the sauce more stable. Two important things to remember when making this sauce: use a heavy pan that transfers the heat slowly and evenly, and watch carefully as you whisk in the butter. If your sauce overheats, you can let it cool down slightly, add a splash of water, and whisk it back together.

WHITE ASPARAGUS WITH BLOOD ORANGE SAUCE

SERVES 4

12 large fat white asparagus

1 blood orange

1 tablespoon whipping (35 percent fat) cream

Sea salt and freshly ground black pepper

½ cup / 4 ounces / 115 g cold unsalted butter

Cook the asparagus following the instructions on page 195. While the asparagus are cooking, finely grate the zest from the orange and then squeeze the juice. Place both the zest and the juice in a small saucepan and bring to a boil over medium-high heat. Reduce the heat and boil gently until the mixture is reduced to about 2 tablespoons. Stir in the cream and season with salt and pepper.

Drain the cooked asparagus and keep warm in a low oven.

Cut the butter into 6 pieces. Place the pan with the juice and cream mixture over very low heat and slowly whisk in the butter, thoroughly incorporating each piece before adding another. While you're whisking, keep the sauce warm, but not hot, so that the mixture emulsifies and the butter doesn't melt into the sauce. When all the butter is incorporated, taste, adjust the seasoning, and serve over the cooked asparagus.

Remember that butter sauce is a warm sauce, not a hot one, and it should be served as soon as it is made. You can hold it for a few minutes by placing the sauce in a pan of barely warm water, around 120°F / 48°C.

CONTINUED

WHITE ASPARAGUS WITH BLOOD ORANGE SAUCE
CONTINUED

VARIATION

You can turn this dish into a main course by adding scallops. They are sweet, and a perfect match with the asparagus and orange sauce. You'll need 12 large sea scallops for 4 people.

Pat dry the scallops and season well with salt and pepper. Once the asparagus are cooked, heat a couple of tablespoons of clarified butter in a frying pan over medium-high heat. When the butter is hot, add the scallops and cook for 2 minutes, then turn and cook for another minute, or until just opaque in the center. Transfer them to the oven with the asparagus to keep warm. Make the blood orange sauce.

Place 3 scallops and 3 cooked asparagus spears on each of 4 plates and spoon over the blood orange sauce.

PAN-ROASTED WHITE ASPARAGUS

Cooking asparagus this way was a discovery for me. I ate "pan-roasted" asparagus for the first time at Spring restaurant in Paris. They were served in a shellfish broth, which was delicious, but all asparagus really needs is a lot of butter.

This method requires attention, so I only cook a smaller number of asparagus at a time this way. You must trim and peel your asparagus first (see page 195). Then melt a good amount of butter with a drizzle of olive oil in a heavy pan that will fit all the asparagus in a single layer. When the butter begins to foam, add the asparagus and cook over medium heat, turning them in the pan until they are nicely colored, about 12 minutes.

Now test your asparagus with a cake tester or skewer to see whether they are cooked. They will probably need a little more cooking, so reduce the heat to low and cover the pan. After another 5 minutes or so, they should be perfect.

Add more butter and, as it begins to melt, serve the asparagus with butter and pan juices or, if you have it, some shellfish broth.

SEEING TASTE

There is a large Korean community close to my home in Toronto. One morning while walking by a Korean bakery I saw the cooks frying doughnuts and spied a pile of sugar-dusted ones on the counter. I have a weakness for warm jam-filled doughnuts, so I went in. I could see large red stains on the sides of the doughnuts that I assumed was raspberry jam, and I bought one. Well, as soon as I took it out of the bag I realized it wasn't hot; no matter, the fat and sugar coated my fingers. Then I bit into it—total disappointment. The dough was sweet, but the raspberry jam wasn't. It wasn't even jam, it was red bean paste. You've probably had a similar experience with a crunchy-looking cracker that was soft and mushy, or a juicy ripe peach that was dry and floury. We can't trust our eyes.

We live in a very visual society, and the look of a food is more important today than it was even a generation ago. Older cookbooks had few pictures; today they are filled with tempting photographs to inspire the reader and convey how the dish will taste. All cookbook authors learn that it is hard to describe a recipe's taste with only words. Visual clues give us information about food, setting up expectations of its taste even before we smell or put it in our mouth. While sight is an important indicator as to how something will taste it is not a reliable one. Often our visual assumptions are incorrect, as they are based on previous experience. We can be proved right, pleasantly surprised, or, like me with that doughnut, disappointed.

> "Our sense of sight confounds what we think we savor. In test after test, researchers have proved that we default to our visual system even when our taste and smell systems work just fine." —BARB STUCKEY

When we taste, our nose and tongue work together to determine the food's flavor in our brain. However, our eyes can prejudice and confuse our brain, making sight just as important as our sense of taste and smell. We eat with our eyes, or as food scientist Tony Acree noted, sight is such a powerful sense that we can "see" flavors. One of the shortcuts our brain uses to create flavor expectations is color: I associated red with sweet when I bought that doughnut. Sight can even trump the information coming from the taste and smell of what we are eating. Experimental psychologist Charles Spence explains that half our brain responds to visual information, while only a small part translates the other senses, taste, smell, sound, and touch. He has carried out several experiments to show the importance of sight. In the United Kingdom, he switched the packaging of flavored crisps (potato chips), placing salt and vinegar ones into the cheese and onion package and vice versa. Many of the people in the experiment believed they were eating cheese and onion crisps even though they were really salt and vinegar flavored. Why? The color of the package. The color cues made their brain ignore all the other sensory information they were receiving from the crisps. Now before you dismiss people who eat packaged crisps as having inferior palates, you should know that the same results have been shown with wine. A group of experienced wine tasters was asked to try several white wines and then describe them. They all used adjectives common for white wine like grassy, honey, flinty, and lychee. Then the same wines were tinted with a tasteless red dye and presented to the tasters again. Now they described them as having berry, chocolate, and tobacco flavors, words usually reserved for red wine. The color of the wine had triggered an expectation of how it would taste. Even the experts were fooled: they tasted the color of the wine rather than the wine itself.

Molecular chefs love to play with the visuals of food to surprise us and make a dish more memorable. Heston Blumenthal's orange and beetroot jelly is an interesting example. The jelly has two layers, one orange and the other dark red. Not until diners taste the jelly with their eyes closed do they realize that the orange-colored jelly is made with orange beets and the purple jelly with blood oranges. Practitioners of molecular cooking like Ferran Adrià, Heston Blumenthal, and Grant Achatz fool with our senses and perceptions, showing us we cannot trust our eyes.

Odd colors, or lack of color, attract our attention. Blue is not a color we associate with food, yet it dyes everything from jelly beans to energy drinks. Studies show that our color preference is based on our experience of foods, our culture, and of course, fashion. However, despite being à la mode, blue remains a tricky color in the world of food. In one experiment steak was dyed blue and presented to volunteers to eat in a darkened room so they couldn't see its color. When the lights were turned on, most of the subjects were repulsed at the thought of having eaten a blue steak, a few so much so that they vomited. The popularity of blue foods may be more about bravado than real appeal.

Dark colors often signal bitter. We know dark brown tea is strong and bitter, brown alcohols are usually bitter, and those dark, burnt edges of a pie or toast are less sweet. We can use color to reduce the impression of bitterness. A 1974 study of how color influences flavor expectations tested the reaction to clear bitter liquids and to bitter liquids dyed red. Participants judged the red-colored liquids as less bitter than the colorless ones. However, adding yellow or green had no similar effect. Red is the color most closely associated with sweet, as ripe, sweet fruits are often red. Does this explain why Campari is more popular than Fernet-Branca, and why bitter radicchio trumps rapini? Do people think they taste less bitter?

CELERY

Celery was once a very bitter plant. A member of the parsley family, celery is also an old plant in a culinary sense, appearing in the writings of Confucius and in Homer's *Odyssey*. Wild celery, also called smallage, had thin, hollow stalks and lots of leaves. It was used medicinally and to flavor dishes, rather than eaten as a vegetable. In the late fifteenth and early sixteenth centuries, growers in Italy began reducing its bitterness by blanching its stems (see page 11), then with breeding developing the thick-stalked celery we know today. They were trying to broaden its appeal, but I am not sure they were very successful. How many people do you know who really love celery?

> "... of all the vegetables I have grown, cooked with, or talked about, celery is the most unpopular." —NIGEL SLATER

We still use celery mainly as a flavoring, not as a vegetable. It's mixed with carrots and onions as a base for stocks, stews, soups, and many sauces and turns up on platters of raw vegetables. Rarely, however, does celery shine by itself, and it deserves to. Thanks to plant breeders, celery has lost a lot of its bitterness, but it still maintains an astringent, bitter quality, especially in its leaves, which are delicious in salads. Cooked celery is a revelation.

Despite being less bitter than it was, celery is still good for you. It contains phthalides, which are responsible for its distinctive flavor and aroma and also help lower your blood pressure.

In French markets you can buy celery by the stalk rather than the head, which is more practical when you are making the classic mirepoix, a mix of carrots, onions, and celery for a braise, or adding a stalk or two to stock. When you buy a head of celery usually half of it is left to languish in the back of the refrigerator. The best part of celery is often what we don't eat: the leaves. Celery leaves are pleasantly bitter and are softer than the stems; they, and the inner leafy celery stems, are what you need for this salad, so look for heads with lots of leaves.

This salad is strongly flavored, so don't serve it as a separate course, but as a condiment with rich fatty meats or spicy, sweet dishes liked barbecued ribs.

CELERY AND OLIVE SALAD | MAKES ABOUT 1½ CUPS / 375 ML

7 ounces / 200 g
celery hearts and leaves

3½ ounces / 100 g
green olives

1 lemon

2 tablespoons
extra virgin olive oil

1 tablespoon
fresh oregano leaves,
chopped

Freshly ground
black pepper

Rinse and trim the celery stalks. Cut off the leaves and slice thinly, then dice the stalks. Make 3 or 4 cuts lengthwise down each olive and then cut off the flesh and discard the pits. Chop the olives. Mix the celery leaves, stalks, and olives in a bowl.

Finely grate 1 teaspoon of zest from the lemon, then squeeze 1½ teaspoons of juice. Add the lemon zest and juice with the oil to the celery and olives. Season the salad with the oregano and freshly ground black pepper. Cover and leave to marinate for several hours or overnight in the refrigerator before serving. Check the seasoning; the olives should provide enough salt.

Here the celery leaves star, and I hope this recipe will stop you tossing them into the compost. Their pleasant bitterness matches with the peppery, pungent arugula. Use small, baby arugula if you can, and while it sounds like a lot of celery leaves, two leafy heads should provide enough. You can always make up the difference with more arugula leaves. This salad is very good with roasted marrow bones, or try it with Horseradish and Bone Marrow Toasts (page 131). And don't worry about how you'll use up those stalks: Tarragon Roasted Celery (opposite) is the answer.

CELERY AND ARUGULA LEAF SALAD

SERVES 4

4 cups / 2½ ounces / 75 g celery leaves, from 2 bunches

4 cups / 2½ ounces / 75 g baby arugula leaves, stems removed

2 tablespoons finely diced shallot

1 tablespoon capers, preferably salt-packed, rinsed and chopped

1 lemon

1 teaspoon Dijon mustard

Coarse sea salt and freshly ground black pepper

⅓ cup / 75 ml extra virgin olive oil

Rinse and spin dry the celery and arugula leaves. Place them in a bowl with the shallot and capers.

Finely grate the zest of half the lemon and squeeze 1 tablespoon of juice. In a small bowl, mix the zest and juice, add the mustard, and season well with salt and pepper. Whisk together, then slowly whisk in the olive oil. Pour over the leaves and toss; check the seasoning and serve.

I hate to throw food away, and one day when I was roasting some root vegetables, I sliced up a couple of celery stalks that had been in the refrigerator a little too long, and threw them in with the other vegetables. The bittersweet roasted celery was a revelation, so good that I thought it deserved its own recipe. Sure, you can add it to your roast vegetables, but go out and buy a whole head, and use the leaves and hearts in Celery and Olive Salad (page 203) and the outer stalks here. You can serve this as a vegetable side dish or as a snack, with drinks. It may seem like a lot of celery, but remember, celery is mainly water and it shrinks quite dramatically. Roasting it changes it from boring, watery, and crunchy to earthy, caramelized, and gently bitter, while the tarragon adds a licorice flavor. Celery never tasted so good. I guarantee it will change your opinion of this vegetable.

TARRAGON ROASTED CELERY

SERVES 4 AS A VEGETABLE, 2 AS A SNACK

17½ ounces / 500 g outside celery stalks, about 5 stalks

2 tablespoons extra virgin olive oil

Sea salt and freshly ground black pepper

Several large sprigs of tarragon

Preheat the oven to 425°F / 220°C.

Rinse and trim the celery stalks. Cut each stalk into 3 or 4 pieces crosswise, then cut each piece into 4 or 6 sticks.

Place them in a bowl and add the olive oil, salt, and pepper, then toss. Put them in a single layer in a roasting pan, top with the tarragon, and cook for 20 minutes. Stir and cook for another 20 minutes. Stir again and cook for a final 10 to 20 minutes, until soft, well colored, and slightly caramelized on the edges. Check the seasoning and serve.

BITTER IN RECIPES

In cooking school during a class on catering, we were advised to always start our dinner menus with an appetizer that was slightly sweet; a fruit cocktail was suggested (well, it *was* the 1970s). Being sweet, it would suppress the guests' appetites: they would be satisfied with smaller portions for the rest of the meal and we would be rewarded with bigger profits. I never got a chance to put the lesson into action, but I was at a reception recently and the spinach salad was full of fruit and candied nuts: it seems this practice is still in play.

Bitter, as we know, has the opposite effect: it stokes the appetite. Bitterness enhances a dish, subtly adding complexity and depth, often without any marked bitter taste. Understanding the role of bitter in balancing a recipe, a plate of food, or an entire meal is an essential skill for a cook.

To explore bitter's effect, consider one of the simplest (if, alas, infrequently made) recipes: a dressing for salad. It begins with salt and pepper, an acid (lemon juice or vinegar), and oil. Now add mustard to the mix, or use a high-quality extra virgin olive oil with bitter notes, and you have elevated the simple formula into something more interesting. Use this dressing on sweet Boston lettuce; then make a salad with Boston lettuce and a little bitter frisée. Next, try a salad entirely of bitter greens and rework the dressing: less mustard or a milder olive oil, or replace it with bacon fat and an extra kick of salt to mellow the bitterness of the leaves. And on you can go. It's that easy to work bitter into your cooking.

I prefer to begin a meal with something slightly bitter to stimulate the appetite. You can also do this by enjoying a bitter aperitif before dinner, a very European habit (see page 70). Or bitter could be in your first course: stir some escarole into a vegetable soup, add some Beer Jelly (page 56) to the smoked salmon, or begin with a plate of Bitter Greens Ravioli (page 47).

Later in the meal, introducing a little bitterness is a good way to temper rich and fatty foods. Pairing these with a bitter vegetable like rapini will make them seem lighter and less rich. In return, the fat will take the edge off the bitter ingredient, making it taste less bitter. This is why sautéed bitter greens make a good match with a fatty meat like pork belly. Bitter not only balances rich foods, but it also makes them more digestible by keeping those gastric juices working. Bitterness has a cleansing effect on the palate, encouraging us to take another mouthful of the dish. It intensifies other tastes and adds complexity and depth, all this without making the dish taste bitter.

In a multicourse dinner try something bitter between the courses: a salad of bitter leaves, a bitter ice or jelly. This gives your palate a break and your stomach a chance to digest. You'll eat the rest of your meal with much more enthusiasm. Bitter is also a way to add an element of surprise to a meal, capturing your guests' attention and making them concentrate on what they are eating. They'll remember a dish more if it surprised them (pleasantly, of course).

Bitter works well at the end of the meal. A rich dessert with a hint of bitterness is less cloying and much more satisfying than a sugary sweet one. Slightly bitter caramel is more intense and multilayered, and chocolates coated in bitter cocoa powder (see page 212) are more interesting than those dipped in icing sugar. Or you could simply finish your meal with a bitter digestive alcohol.

". . . ignoring bitter is as ill-considered as a painter eschewing a primary color."
—WAYNE CURTIS

We are naturally very sensitive to bitter and can detect even the smallest amounts of bitterness in a food. Our sensitivity is affected by the temperature of the food: cold food will taste less bitter, while bitterness is at its most intense around 64°F / 18°C. So use bitter with discretion; nobody wants to eat a meal composed entirely of bitter tasting foods. Once or twice in a dinner is enough, and no more than one bitter food on the plate. Matching meat cooked in a bitter alcohol with a bitter vegetable is too much for even the most fervent bitter lover.

If you find something too bitter, you may be tempted to add sugar. This works in your coffee, but when it comes to vegetables, salt is a better choice. Salt enhances sweetness; in Asia they sprinkle it on fresh fruits to make them sweeter. It works by suppressing bitterness; a cucumber is a good example. Take a slice of fresh cucumber and taste it: it is mildly bitter and slightly astringent. Now sprinkle it with a little salt and taste it again: all bitterness has disappeared and the cucumber tastes sweet. So strong, salty tastes make good companions to bitter vegetables. Acids like lemon juice and vinegar can mellow bitterness, while fat and bitterness make the perfect couple, each complementing and balancing the other in a dish. Bitterness enhances other tastes: I have paired sautéed bitter greens with sweet potato, making the potato taste very sweet. Peaches poached in tea taste more intensely peachy than those poached in a simple syrup (see page 67). And of course you can use bitterness to reduce sweetness, by cooking sugar until it is dark caramel (see page 224) or adding dark chocolate or cocoa to a sauce (see page 212).

Pungent, astringent, puckering, and tannic are all part of my bitter spectrum. Tea is bitter and tannic, while arugula and horseradish are bitter and pungent. In the kitchen you can make use of all these different components of bitterness. The goal is not to make a dish bitter, but to use bitter to balance all elements and improve the dish as a whole.

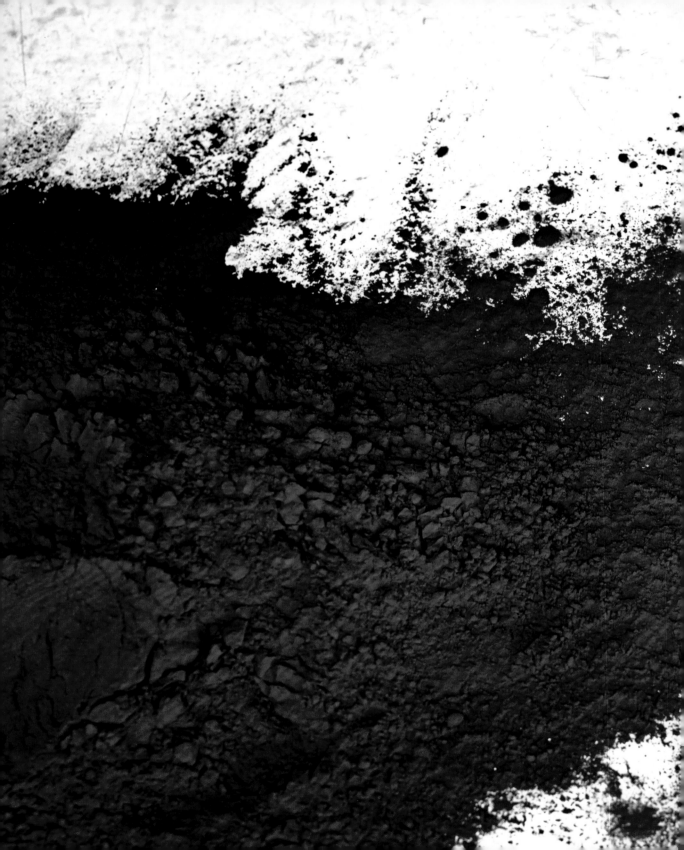

SIX

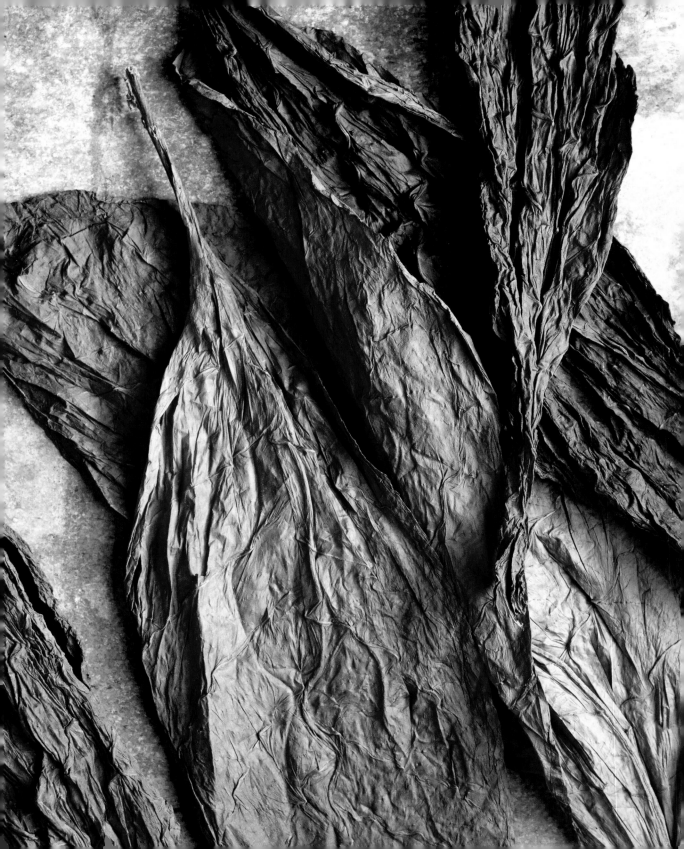

DARK, FORBIDDEN, AND VERY BITTER

his chapter gathers bitter notes from all over the culinary map, and some off its edges. First, I consider a favorite food—chocolate, which wasn't always sweet. I also include toast: yes, good toast has a caramelized bitterness, as does caramel itself. Caramel, if you didn't know, is more complex and interesting tasting if you give it a bitter edge. So much for "dark"; what is "very bitter" in this chapter? Well, try fenugreek and bitter melon, two exceedingly bitter ingredients that are very popular in Indian cuisine. And just to throw some truly forbidden territory into the mix, there are a couple of recipes with bitter tobacco. Here there may be dragons—or at least, a few surprises.

COCOA GRAVY

You probably limit your use of cocoa to baking, a coating for truffles, or mixing with hot milk. It is more versatile than that.

Cocoa powder is what is left after most of the cocoa butter has been extracted from the beans. The paste is dried and ground to make cocoa powder that ranges from 8 to 26 percent fat. Its flavor is intense, concentrated chocolate and it is very bitter and astringent. Van Houten, a Dutch chemist, developed a method to improve this powder's ability to blend with water by treating it with alkaline salts, a process that came to be called "Dutching." Dutched cocoa powder is darker in color and less astringent than untreated, or natural, cocoa powder. Not only can cocoa flavor a dish, it can thicken a sauce.

To make cocoa gravy, you need a Dutch-process cocoa powder. I mix a small amount, a teaspoon or two, with the same amount of water to make a paste, and then whisk it into the sauce as I would cornstarch. It will thicken the sauce slightly and add a touch of bitterness. It is particularly good with game.

CHOCOLATE AND COCOA

We often forget that chocolate is a bitter food; although most of the chocolate consumed today is sweetened, cocoa beans are naturally bitter and astringent. Not until the beans are fermented, roasted, and ground do they become palatable. Rich in fats, cocoa beans contain two bitter alkaloids, caffeine and theobromine, which stimulate our nervous system. The civilizations of Central America did not eat chocolate; they drank it. The Maya flavored it with chile and vanilla and consumed it hot, while the Aztecs drank it infused with flowers, sweetened with honey, and cold. Both cultures reserved chocolate drinking for important royal and religious occasions.

When chocolate arrived in Europe in the mid-sixteenth century, it was expensive and considered a medicinal beverage. Doctors prescribed it to settle the stomach and aid digestion. Flavored with cinnamon, anise, black pepper, citrus peel, and even ambergris, and sweetened with sugar, chocolate still tasted bitter, making it an ideal beverage to mask a poison. It is believed that in 1774 Pope Clement XIV was poisoned with a cup of chocolate. By the late seventeenth century, chocolate found its way into the kitchen, and was added to both savory and sweet dishes. It became so popular in Italy that the poet Francisco Arisi complained it was being put into everything from polenta to nougat. He even feared it might be used with quail.

There are about 30 mg of caffeine in 1 ounce / 30 g of unsweetened chocolate and 20 mg in 1 tablespoon of cocoa, while a cup of coffee has about 100 mg. Many people claim they are addicted to chocolate, and while it does contain chemical compounds similar to those in marijuana and the chemical responsible for the euphoric feeling you get when you fall in love, the amounts are far too small to have any real effect. Better to eat chocolate for its astringent phenolic compounds, which are full of antioxidants—and its taste, of course! The greater the amount of cocoa solids in the chocolate, the more intensely bitter and astringent it will be, and the more antioxidants it will have. Adding milk and sugar inhibits our bodies from absorbing the antioxidants, so dark chocolate is better for you.

Learning to appreciate higher percentage bitter chocolate is not easy if you have only eaten sweet candy bars. But retraining your palate will give you an excuse to eat chocolate every day. The trick is to bite into the chocolate, revealing its texture, then let the pieces melt on your tongue; you will taste its richness and fruity flavors, and then its bitterness and astringency.

Too often we think of chocolate only as dessert, but it is excellent in savory dishes, adding richness and bitterness.

This recipe is adapted from the great French chef Joël Robuchon in his book *Les Dimanches de Joël Robuchon*. The book is a collection of articles that Robuchon wrote for the French newspaper *Le Journal de Dimanche*. You can, of course, make this tart with a higher percentage chocolate, but I like 70 percent; it gives a good blend of bitter and sweet. Yet another layer of bitterness is added with the cocoa powder. This rich, bittersweet dessert makes a very satisfying end to a meal; you'll only need a small slice.

CHOCOLATE TART | SERVES 8

½ recipe Sweet Butter Pastry (page 141)

7 ounces / 200 g chocolate (70 percent)

⅔ cup / 150 ml whipping (35 percent fat) cream

¼ cup / 60 ml whole milk

1 egg, beaten

1 tablespoon cognac or whiskey

A pinch of fine sea salt

Cocoa powder

Roll out the pastry on a floured surface and line an 8-inch / 20-cm tart pan. Prick the base of the tart with a fork and refrigerate for at least 30 minutes. Place a baking sheet in the oven and preheat to 400°F / 200°C.

Line the tart shell with parchment paper and fill it with dried beans. Place the tart shell on the baking sheet, and bake for 12 minutes. The pastry should be just set. Remove the parchment paper and beans and return the tart shell on the baking sheet to the oven. Bake for another 5 minutes, or until it is lightly colored. Set aside to cool and lower the oven temperature to 300°F / 150°C.

Finely chop the chocolate. Pour the cream and milk into a small saucepan and place over medium heat. Bring the cream mixture to a boil, then remove from the heat and add the chopped chocolate and stir until smooth. Let cool slightly. Whisk the egg, cognac, and salt together, then slowly whisk into the chocolate.

Pour the chocolate mixture into the baked tart shell and shake the pan gently so that the chocolate fills the tart and is level. Return to the oven on the baking sheet, checking that your oven temperature has dropped to 300°F / 150°C. Bake for 15 to 18 minutes, or until the filling is barely set; it should wobble slightly in the center. Use your nose: when you can smell the chocolate, check the tart; it's probably cooked.

Transfer the tart from the baking sheet to a rack and let cool to room temperature. The filling will firm up as it cools.

Place a spoonful of cocoa powder in a fine-mesh sieve and dust over the top of the tart. Serve at room temperature.

I remember the first time I went to La Maison du Chocolat in Paris. It was for a tasting of hot chocolates (there were five different flavors at that time; they only have three now). My first surprise was that the hot chocolates weren't really hot, but rather lukewarm, and not one of them was sweet. Each cup of chocolate had its own special taste, ranging from rich and earthy, fresh and fruity, toasty and nutty to intense and long lasting. To recapture that moment I decided to make my own. Hot chocolate is simple: all you need is good-quality dark chocolate and whole milk. Better chocolate companies make grand crus of chocolate from a single or special blend of cocoa beans and hot chocolate is a good way to try them—that's what I use to make my hot chocolate. The addition of the water stops the milk from scorching when you heat it. Try this recipe with different chocolates to see which ones you prefer. Remember, the milk adds a little sweetness to the chocolate.

HOT CHOCOLATE / SERVES 1

3 tablespoons water

½ cup / 125 ml whole milk

1½ ounces / 45 g chocolate (70 percent), chopped

Pour the water into a small saucepan, then add the milk and chocolate. Place the pan over medium-low heat and stir with a whisk until the chocolate is melted and the milk is very hot and beginning to simmer. Lower the heat so the milk barely simmers and cook gently for 5 minutes, stirring with a wooden spoon from time to time. The mixture will thicken. Remove the pan from the heat and let stand 3 minutes. Stir again and then pour into a cup.

I tested the hot chocolate recipe on a hot, steamy July day, and while it didn't slow my consumption, it did leave me longing for a cold drink. So why not iced chocolate? This is not really a thirst-quenching drink, but if you drink it mid-afternoon it will keep you going until it's time for a bitter aperitif or a beer. It takes on the bitter sweetness from the ice cream—and caramel and chocolate is a great combination.

ICED CHOCOLATE CARAMEL DRINK / SERVES 1

1 recipe Hot Chocolate (see above), cooled

1 scoop Caramel Ice Cream (page 225)

3 ice cubes

Place the ingredients in a blender and blend until the ice is crushed; serve in a glass.

This recipe shows how you can use chocolate to enrich a sauce. Often cold butter is whisked into pan juices to create a sauce; here, the chocolate thickens and adds a touch of bitterness, as does the black pepper. This works well with the lamb, but you can use it with other pan-fried meats, such as a rack of venison. You don't need very much chocolate—just enough to slightly thicken the pan juices. I rarely suggest wine matches, but an Australian Shiraz is very good with this.

LAMB WITH DARK CHOCOLATE PEPPER SAUCE

SERVES 2

One 8-rib lamb rack, about 1½ pounds / 700 g, frenched

Sea salt and freshly ground black pepper

2 tablespoons olive oil

1 cup / 250 ml lamb stock, preferably homemade

½ ounce / 15 g chocolate (70 percent), chopped

Remove the lamb rack from the refrigerator 30 minutes before cooking and allow it to come to room temperature. Preheat the oven to 450°F / 230°C.

Pat the lamb rack dry and season with salt and pepper. In an ovenproof frying pan just large enough to hold the rack, heat the oil over high heat and brown the lamb on the fat side and the base. Then place the pan in the oven and roast for 15 to 20 minutes or until the internal temperature registers 135°F / 57°C on an instant-read thermometer. Remove the pan from the oven. Transfer the lamb to a plate and let the rack rest, loosely covered with aluminum foil.

Meanwhile, remembering that the handle will be very hot, discard the fat from the pan, add the stock, and bring to a boil, deglazing the pan by scraping up the browned bits from the bottom. Continue to cook for 8 minutes, or until reduced to about ⅓ cup / 75 ml. Meanwhile, coarsely grind 1 teaspoon of black pepper; add it to the sauce with the chocolate, stirring until melted. Check the seasoning.

Slice the lamb into individual or double chops and serve with the sauce.

In Paris's tenth arrondissement there is a neighborhood wine bar/bistro named Albion. Despite being run by a New Zealander and having an English chef, it is very French. I love pigeon and always order it when I see it on a menu. At Albion it came with a ganache sauce that made me just a little nervous. Ganache is a mixture of chocolate and cream, usually sweet, used to fill and ice chocolate cakes, or to make the centers of chocolates. Despite my initial hestitation I ordered the dish and was rewarded with a perfectly cooked game bird coated in a rich, dark, intense sauce that was not at all sweet. It was an excellent combination.

ROASTED SQUAB WITH GANACHE / SERVES 4

2 squab, about 12 ounces / 350 g each

Sea salt and freshly ground black pepper

2 tablespoons chicken or duck fat

½ cup / 125 ml chicken stock, preferably homemade

½ cup / 125 ml whipping (35 percent fat) cream

1 ounce / 30 g chocolate (70 percent), chopped

Preheat the oven to 450°F / 230°C. Remove the wishbones from the squabs, then pat dry and season inside and out with salt and pepper. Truss, or just tie the legs and the tail together, then fold the neck flap under, securing it by tucking the wings under the bird.

Heat the fat in a large ovenproof frying pan over medium-high heat. Brown the birds on all sides. Turn the birds on their backs and place the pan in the oven and roast for 20 minutes or until the internal temperature in the thigh registers 155°F / 68°C on an instant-read thermometer.

Remove the pan from the oven, transfer the cooked birds to a warm platter, breast side down, cover loosely with aluminum foil, and let them rest.

Meanwhile, remembering that the handle will be very hot, discard the fat from the pan, add the stock and cream, and bring to a boil, deglazing the pan by scraping up the browned bits from the bottom. Continue to cook the sauce until reduced to about ⅓ cup / 75 ml.

Remove the string from the squabs and cut in half, removing the backbone. Cut each squab half into 2 pieces between the breast and thigh. Place 2 squab pieces on each of 4 warmed plates. Add the squab juices to the pan and reduce the heat to low. Whisk in the chocolate and season the sauce with salt and pepper. Spoon the sauce over the squab and serve.

TOAST: THE POWER OF CARBON

Toast is not just for breakfast or an afternoon cup of tea; toast can also flavor soup (see pages 58 and 222). If you throw your bread in a toaster and turn a dial to regulate how you cook it, you obviously don't consider making toast a skill. However, it most definitely is, albeit a neglected one. Getting a good piece of toasted bread is not easy. How many times at breakfast or brunch in a restaurant have you ordered toast only to be presented with a barely warmed slice of bread—or a cold, dried-out one?

> "It is impossible not to love someone who makes toast for you. People's failings, even major ones . . . fall into insignificance as your teeth break through the rough, toasted crust and sink into the doughy cushion underneath." —NIGEL SLATER

I love a good slice of toast, and that's why I don't have a toaster; I make my toast under the grill, or broiler, as they call it in North America. A secret to good toast is to pre-heat the broiler; that way, you can color the outside of the bread very well, and still have a soft texture in the center of the toast. The thicker the slice, the more texture you'll have. The other important thing is to toast it well. It seems that everyone is afraid of burning toast, but a little carbonization adds to the flavor because it adds bitterness. Now, the amount of bitterness is important: you want some, but not too much. That smell of bread toasting is wonderful: that hint of the caramel as the sugars begin to burn is deliciously comforting. Perhaps it is my madeleine.

So in these recipes for toast, please don't use a toaster: show your bread more respect and cook it under a preheated broiler.

My perfect breakfast is a cup of café au lait and a slice of toast with homemade jam. Now you might not think you need a recipe for toast and jam, but I believe you probably do. The choice of bread is up to you; my preference is a country-style sourdough, but one that is not too acidic, and it shouldn't be fresh. Day-old bread is drier and toasts better; fresh bread with butter and jam is a different experience.

Make your toast just before eating it so the butter melts and soaks into it. Cold toast is awful, so if you want two slices you'll have to wait until you've finished the first one. While I like unsalted butter, lightly salted butter is very good with a not-too-sweet apricot jam.

TOAST AND JAM | SERVES AS MANY AS YOU WANT

Day-old bread

Good-quality butter, at room temperature

Seville Orange Whiskey Marmalade (page 151)

Preheat the broiler to high. Slice the bread about ½ inch / 1 cm thick. Place it on a baking sheet, a slice at a time, unless you are making toast for more than one person. Toast the bread, watching carefully, and moving it with a pair of tongs so that it colors evenly. Toast until you see specks of black, then turn the bread and toast the other side. Butter the toast generously, then spoon on the marmalade.

I remember the first time I tasted this soup at L'Astrance. It was before this Paris restaurant had three Michelin stars and you could still get a reservation without booking months in advance. I had a tasting menu, and when the soup arrived I had no idea what the flavor was. There was a taste of bacon, but what was the main ingredient, mushrooms? No; it was toasted sourdough bread. Many dishes are based on leftover bread; this is one you buy the bread to make. This recipe is a version of L'Astrance owner and chef Pascal Barbot's, adapted to my taste; you can find the original in his cookbook. The French aren't afraid of darkly caramelizing baked goods (look at the edges of fruit tarts and the underneath of palmiers and croissants); they know that caramelizing, even a little burning, adds taste. Best of all, it balances sweet, or, as in this soup, the bacon, milk, and butter. So don't be afraid, toast that bread until it is burnt on the edges and very dark in the middle.

TOAST SOUP / SERVES 4

1¾ ounces / 50 g bacon

2 cups / 500 ml veal or chicken stock, preferably homemade

5¼ ounces / 150 g sourdough bread, about 3 slices

1 cup / 250 ml hot milk

1 tablespoon Dijon mustard

1 tablespoon vinegar from a jar of cornichons

Sea salt and freshly ground black pepper

1½ ounces / 45 g butter, cut into 6 pieces

Cut the bacon into small pieces and place in a saucepan. Cook over medium-low heat until the fat renders and the bacon is cooked. You want the bacon cooked, but not crisp. In another saucepan, bring the stock to a boil and then pour it over the cooked bacon. Remove the pan with bacon from the heat, cover, and let stand for 20 minutes.

While the stock is infusing, toast the bread slices very well, allowing them to burn a little on the edges. Add the toast to the stock, breaking it into pieces if necessary, cover, and leave for 10 minutes. During this time the bread will soak up the stock.

Add the hot milk, mustard, and vinegar to the saucepan, then season with salt and pepper. Transfer the soup to a blender and blend until smoothly pureed. Return the soup to the saucepan and heat gently, stirring to scrape up any browned bits on the bottom of the pan.

When the soup is warm, whisk in the butter, check the seasoning, and serve.

THE TONGUE MAP

In 1942 a Harvard historian of psychology, Edwin Boring, was interpreting data from German researcher David P. Hänig and the tongue map was born. In this simplified map, the tip of the tongue was designated as the area sensing sweet foods and the outside front edges of the tongue picked up salty tastes, while further back the edges told us if what we were eating was sour. In the middle of our tongue we tasted nothing at all, and bitter tastes didn't register until they reached the back of our tongue. This map explained how the tongue, our primary tasting organ, recognized the basic tastes—of which, of course, there were only four. The diagram looked good, and the tongue map became the accepted doctrine that many of us learned at school. Some of us may still believe it, but it doesn't hold up to the simplest test.

Place some salt in the palm of your hand; now stick just the tip of your tongue into it. Salty, right? Sprinkle some salt onto the back of your tongue: salty again. Rinse your mouth out with water and try the same on the sides, front and back; even in the wasteland in the middle of your tongue you taste salt everywhere, right? Try it with lemon juice (sour everywhere) or powdered cinchona bark (bitter, bitter, bitter no matter where you put it). Unfortunately, the tongue map is still quoted by many people, including manufacturers of wine-tasting glasses, even though it's wrong and doesn't include umami and fat.

> "The organ of taste is not the tongue, but the brain, a culturally (and therefore historically) determined organ through which are transmitted and learned the criteria for evaluations." —MASSIMO MONTANARI

In his book *Zur Psychophysik des Geschmackssinnes* (1901), Hänig was trying to measure which areas of the tongue were more sensitive to one or another of the "basic" tastes. In 1974 the tongue map was exposed as false when Virginia Collins reassessed Hänig's work. She demonstrated that he was talking about small variations in sensitivity to the basic tastes in different areas of the tongue, not defining areas of basic taste. Different sensitivities exist over our tongues, but they are not significant, as we can detect all tastes on any part of our tongue. We also discern different tastes in other areas of our mouth and at the back of our throat, where more taste buds are located.

CARAMEL

Caramel immediately conjures up sweet thoughts, and while I am not denying caramel is sweet, the best caramel also has a touch of bitterness. To make caramel you cook sugar until it melts into a liquid and then turns a reddish brown color. The simple act of heating the sugar changes it from dry sweet granules to a multiflavored liquid. The chemistry of cooking sugar is very complicated: as you heat the sugar, hundreds of different compounds are created, many of them aromatic and bitter. Caramelizing sugar produces wonderful toasty, buttery aromas. It is important to cook the caramel until it is well colored. A dark caramel reduces the sweetness and intensifies the flavor, but be careful not to burn it. Caramel goes from perfect to burnt very quickly and is very hot and sticky. As the liquid sugar turns darker, the syrup becomes more acidic and bitter, as beneficial antioxidants are formed. There is a point at which the sugar will burn and the caramel will turn bitter and acrid, so you want to stop before you reach it. If you burn the caramel, tip it out and start again. When I worked in kitchens we cooked sugar until it was very dark, then thinned it down with water and kept it in a bottle. It was called blackjack and we added it to sauces to give them color. A similar product is used to color drinks, alcohol, and industrial food products. Caramelized sugar not only adds color and flavor, but the antioxidants created in making it also help preserve the food.

The word *caramel* was first recorded in English in 1725. It came from the French, who had adapted the Spanish word *caramelo.* Before that, its origins can't be verified, although it is probably originally from the Latin word *calmellus,* meaning little reed or cane, a reference to sugar cane.

This rich, intensely flavored ice cream is a treat for caramel lovers. The sugar should begin to liquefy at the 4-minute mark. Then it should be ready at about the 7-minute mark. Cooking caramel to the right color takes practice, so use your nose and eyes; they will give you lots of information. If you find the ice cream too sweet, you will know to cook it a little longer next time. A scoop of this ice cream should make you want a glass of water.

CARAMEL ICE CREAM | MAKES 2 CUPS / 500 ML

1 cup / 250 ml
whole milk

1 cup / 250 ml whipping
(35 percent fat) cream

¾ cup / 5¼ ounces /
150 g sugar

5 egg yolks

A pinch of fine sea salt

In a medium saucepan, bring the milk and cream just to a boil and then remove from the heat. Set 1 tablespoon of the sugar aside.

In a heavy-bottomed saucepan, add the remaining sugar, then shake the pan so that the sugar forms an even layer. Place the pan over medium heat and cook, shaking the pan from time to time, until the sugar melts. As the sugar melts, gently swirl the pan to mix the sugar granules with the liquid sugar; you can give the mixture a gentle stir with a wooden spoon to blend in any uncooked sugar. Once all the sugar is liquid, continue to cook, swirling gently to make sure it cooks evenly, until it is a rich, dark caramel color. You will smell the caramel and see it smoking quite a bit. Remove from the heat and immediately start pouring in the milk and cream mixture; pour it slowly and carefully because the caramel will bubble and spit. Stir until the caramel is dissolved in the cream mixture, placing it back over very low heat if necessary.

Whisk the egg yolks with the reserved 1 tablespoon sugar and the salt in a large bowl until light and thick and the sugar is dissolved. Whisk the caramel cream mixture into the egg yolks, then pour into a clean saucepan. Cook over medium heat, stirring, until the mixture thickens and coats the back of a spoon. Strain it into a bowl and cool quickly by placing it in a larger bowl or sink filled with cold water and ice. Stir the mixture often. When it is cool, cover and refrigerate overnight. Also, place a container for the ice cream in the freezer to get cold. The next day, remove the ice cream mixture from the refrigerator, stir again, then churn in an ice cream machine following the manufacturer's instructions. Transfer it to the cold container and freeze until ready to serve. This ice cream stays very soft in the machine, but it will firm up in the freezer.

This is one of the first recipes I ever made for dinner guests. I was following the Cordon Bleu cookery course in the magazines that arrived at our newsagent every month. These caramelized oranges graced the cover of the very first issue. They were part of a dinner party menu that included *potage madrilène*, a rich tomato soup with sherry, and *poulet Veronique*, or chicken with grapes. Those French names were really exotic in the 1970s. I've kept all the magazines and carried them with me around the world. While the photography is now very dated, they are a good reference. I still make the oranges in caramel sauce, although often I replace them with tangerines. And now I cook the caramel longer than the ladies of the Cordon Bleu school recommended. A simple and delicious dessert, it is much more interesting when the caramel has a bitter edge. This is a good recipe to try if you are scared of burning the caramel. You can taste the sauce to assess its bitterness before pouring it on the oranges.

CARAMELIZED ORANGES | SERVES 6

6 oranges or tangerines

1 cup / 7 ounces / 200 g sugar

½ cup / 125 ml warm water

Cut a slice off the top and bottom of each orange to reveal the flesh. Stand the fruit upright on a cutting board and, cutting from the top down to the bottom, remove the peel and pith. Set the peel of 1 orange aside. Cut each orange into 5 slices and place them in a bowl. If using tangerines, peel and cut in half.

Fill a large bowl with cold water and ice, and set aside.

In a heavy-bottomed saucepan, add the sugar, then shake the pan so that the sugar forms an even layer. Place over medium heat and cook, shaking the pan from time to time, until the sugar melts. As the sugar melts, gently swirl the pan to mix the sugar granules with the liquid sugar; you can give the mixture a stir to blend in any uncooked sugar. Once all the sugar has turned into liquid caramel, continue to cook until it is a rich, dark caramel color. You will smell the caramel and see it smoking quite a bit.

Remove the pan from the heat and dip the base of the pan into the bowl of cold water to stop the caramel from cooking further. Carefully add the warm water to the caramel, which will spit and splutter. Return the pan to low heat and cook,

CONTINUED

stirring, to dissolve the caramel in the water; this can take up to 10 minutes. When it is dissolved, pour it into a jug and leave to cool.

Meanwhile, cut the peel you set aside into roughly equal rectangles. Remove some of the white pith but not all, then cut the peel into thin matchsticks. Put some water into the pan you used to cook the caramel and bring to a boil over medium heat. This will help remove any traces of caramel in the pan. When boiling, drop in the orange matchsticks, cook for 1 minute, and then drain.

Pour the sauce over the orange slices in the bowl, sprinkle with the orange peel, and chill for several hours before serving. As the oranges sit, their juice mixes into the caramel sauce, turning it into a caramel syrup.

TASTE BUDS EVERYWHERE

As bitterness can signal the presence of toxins, we have more bitter receptors than sweet ones to protect ourselves. What is interesting about our bitter receptors is that they are not restricted to the surface of our tongue, but are found throughout our body. They are in our mouth, at the back of our throat, and on the vagus nerve, which travels from our brain to our internal organs. Bitter receptors are in our airways, digestive tract, intestines, and, most surprisingly, our lungs and (for some of us) our testicles. They all respond to bitter chemicals, but in very different ways.

Our sense of smell and our tongue are the first line of defense against poison, so the bitter receptors in our nasal passages make us sneeze and cough helping us to expel any toxic gases we encounter. The taste buds in our mouth and on our tongue induce the facial response depicted by Brouwer (see page 24) and cause us to spit out bitter-tasting foods. Those at the back of our throat register the bitterness of olive oil, but do not trigger nausea.

The receptors on our vagus nerve and in our digestive tract distinguish a whole range of bitter compounds, deciding what is good and bad. This is important because not everything bitter is poisonous, and many bitter tasting foods are very good for us. These receptors can stimulate our appetite and help us digest food, or trigger nausea to expel toxins from our stomach; in our intestines they can induce diarrhea to rid us of a poison.

Some bitter receptors within our body work in ways that are not yet understood. The taste buds in our lungs do not send any signals to our brain and work contrary to the way the scientists at the University of Maryland School of Medicine in Baltimore, who discovered them, had postulated. They thought that when exposed to bitter compounds these receptors would cause our muscles to tighten, making us cough to expel any bitter poison. Instead, they did the opposite: the bitter taste buds in our lungs relaxed and opened the airways when exposed to bitter gases, making breathing easier. Why they act in this way scientists have no idea, but they were more effective than any available asthma medicine. This discovery has stimulated research into the use of bitter substances, like quinine, to treat chronic lung diseases. As for those bitter receptors in the testicles, that's still a puzzle. Scientists know removing them shrinks the testes and dramatically reduces the mature sperm count, but not why they are there. Clearly, bitter is much more than a taste, and our relationship to it is curious and complicated.

GOLD SPOONS FOR DESSERT

Do you hate plastic cutlery? I do. Sometimes I think I should travel with a fork and knife because plastic is so ubiquitous, especially with street food. I hate paper and plastic cups too. While I rarely drink take-out coffee, sometimes I go to a coffee shop across the street from my Toronto apartment and I take my own cup. I get a discount for bringing a cup and my coffee tastes better—or does it? It is exactly the same coffee. It is not my taste buds and sense of smell that are sending me different signals; it's my emotions and psychology that are influencing me. The materials and design of the cutlery, bowls, cups, and glasses we use for our food and drink affect how it tastes.

Taste and flavor perception is a growing field of research, and there are numerous fascinating studies into how tableware and cutlery modify our appreciation of what we are eating. They show that, like me, most people, when given the same beverage in a real and a paper cup, prefer the taste of the one in the real cup. The weight and feel of the utensil adds substance and an impression of quality. This also happens with wine; you think that it tastes better in a glass than in a plastic cup. Wine glasses are the subject of many studies, and there is much discussion as to the right glass for the right wine. I hate the current trend of drinking wine in upscale glass tumblers, even if they do fit easily in the dishwasher. I prefer a wine glass with a stem. Does the wine taste better from a specific glass? While I'll admit to owning glasses designed for sparkling, white, and two sorts of red wine, I'm not sure, and the research is inconsistent. If the tasters cannot see or touch the glass, they can detect no difference in the wine's aroma, but once they handle the glass, it is a different story.

One thing is certain about glasses: the bigger they are, the more you will drink of any beverage. If you like cocktails and make them using your eye rather than a measure, you should pay close attention to the shape of your glass, not for tradition or taste, but for the amount of alcohol you will consume. It has been shown that everyone, including experienced bartenders, pours more alcohol into short wide glasses than tall thin ones. So the lesson is: drink from tall, thin glasses, or use a measure.

As for bitter, it is cutlery that plays a role. Since we moved from using our fingers, various materials have helped us eat our food: bone, wood, metal, and ceramic. In the West we don't use wood much to eat, just to cook our food or mix it. Most of our cutlery is made from a metal, and the choice of metal can affect the taste of the food. Cutlery has flavor.

A spoon-tasting dinner was held in London in 2012. Seven courses of mildly spiced southwestern Indian food were served with seven different metal spoons: copper, gold, silver, zinc, tin, chrome, and stainless. Spoons were chosen because we are happy to put them in our mouths and lick them, so our tongue has a lot more contact with a spoon than it does with a knife or even a fork. The results were interesting. First, the guests just licked their spoons because, when we eat with a metallic spoon we eat a little of the spoon, too. The zinc and copper spoons made a strong impression with their bitter and metallic taste, the stainless spoon was described as slightly metallic, and the silver spoon, was deemed dull and neutral.

> "We are not just tasting the spoons but actually eating them, because with each lick we consume perhaps a hundred billion atoms." —MARK MIODOWNICK

Then the guests began their meal. The zinc spoon made the black cod taste bad, and the copper one destroyed the taste of the grapefruit. Zinc and copper spoons, bitter when tasted alone, increased the impression of bitterness in the dish by up to 25 percent. However, both these spoons worked with the sour taste of the mango relish. The acidity of the relish stripped off a tiny amount of metal from the spoon and subtly enhanced the dish's flavor. Tin matched well with the pistachio curry, while the gold spoon was the popular choice for the sweet dishes. Of all the metal spoons, gold is the only one with no metallic taste.

And what to do with this information? Well, don't rush out and buy special spoons for specific foods. I can relax about what I serve my wine in as long as it's glass. Instead, it is important to realize that many factors influence our perception of taste. Oh, and also remember not to use copper or zinc cutlery with that chicory salad.

TOBACCO

Probably tobacco isn't the first flavor you think of when creating a dish. Or even the fiftieth. I don't smoke, but now and then I take a puff on my husband's cigar, and I'm familiar with the complex taste of tobacco and its bitter aftertaste. I was aware that chef Thomas Keller made savory foie gras custard infused with tobacco and coffee for celebrity chef Anthony Bourdain, and that molecular chefs were making tobacco foams. I also knew tobacco is related to tomatoes and potatoes, and the plant's leaves are used as a wrapper for cooking. The flavor of dried tobacco leaves is intense, with hints of earth, spice, and wood, depending on where it was grown and how it was dried. Tobacco contains the bitter alkaloid nicotine and numerous tannins, so I thought about sweet dishes, rather than savory, and found it matched with chocolate and cream.

Tobacco is a dangerous substance, and I have no desire to make you addicted to nicotine. It is, however, a very interesting flavor, and the amount of tobacco I use in these recipes is small. You are not inhaling tobacco smoke here; you are eating it, which makes a difference, as nicotine is a strong base that we don't absorb well via the acidic environment of our stomach. These recipes extract the bitterness from the tobacco with little or no toxicity from the nicotine. Because dried tobacco leaves are not that easy to buy and these recipes use only a small amount of tobacco, I chose a cigar, which is pure tobacco. For these recipes it was a Cuban cigar about 5 inches / 13 cm long and ½ inch / 1 cm in diameter, which weighed ⅓ ounce / 10 g. So if you have no kitchen scale, try to get a cigar about this size and use the length measure in the recipe.

This is a mixture of caffeine and nicotine, so I can't really defend it except to say the flavor is surprising and delicious, and not everything can be good for you. Also, it is better to finish a meal with one or two of these truffles than with a cigarette and coffee. These truffles are rich, dark, creamy, and intensely chocolate flavored in your mouth. The tobacco bitterness only hits you when you swallow and it tickles those bitter receptors at the back of your throat. This recipe makes a small number of truffles; if you want more, just double it. If you want to make a bitter nicotine-free truffle, flavor the cream with a large piece of Seville orange rind instead. But living a little dangerously is fun.

TOBACCO CHOCOLATE TRUFFLES / MAKES 24 PIECES

¼ cup / 60 ml whipping (35 percent fat) cream

1-inch / 2.5-cm / 1 g piece of cigar (opposite)

Fine sea salt

3½ ounces / 100 g bittersweet chocolate (70 percent), chopped

3½ tablespoons / 1¾ ounces / 50 g unsalted butter, diced, at room temperature

Cocoa powder

In a small saucepan over medium-low heat, bring the cream to a boil. Break up the cigar and add to the cream with a pinch of salt. Press on the tobacco so the cream soaks into it; cover the pan and let stand for 45 minutes.

Line a 6 by 3-inch / 17 by 7.5-cm loaf pan with plastic wrap. Make a double boiler by filling a large saucepan halfway with water and finding a medium-size metal bowl that will fit into the pan without touching the water. Bring the water in the pan to a boil and place the chocolate in the bowl. Remove the pan from the heat, place the bowl on top, and leave the chocolate to melt.

Strain the cream through a fine-mesh sieve over the melted chocolate, pressing against the cigar to extract all of the flavor and making sure you get all of the cream. Because there is just a small amount of cream, you have to work a little harder. Stir the cream into the chocolate until it comes together. Stir in the butter, piece by piece, until it is incorporated. Pour the mixture into the pan and refrigerate until just set, about 50 minutes.

Using the plastic, remove the chocolate from the pan and cut into 24 squares. It is easier to cut at this point because it is still not hard; use a hot knife. Return the truffles to the refrigerator. When they are firm, toss them in the cocoa powder. Keep the truffles refrigerated, but remove them about 30 minutes before serving so they are at room temperature when you eat them.

Needless to say, this dessert is adult food and should not to be given to children. You can serve the panna cotta plain, but if it is blackberry season, add a few alongside; their acidity matches well with the bitter tobacco and the creaminess of the panna cotta. What I love most about panna cotta is its texture—barely holding itself together—and I prefer to use leaf gelatin for this recipe because it gives a softer set. Use molds that have rounded bases, like custard cups or small glass bowls. It will make turning out the panna cotta easier.

TOBACCO PANNA COTTA / SERVES 6

2 cups / 500 ml whipping (35 percent fat) cream

¼ cup / 1¾ ounces / 50 g sugar

1 vanilla bean, split lengthwise

2 large pieces of lemon zest

1¼-inch / 3-cm / 2.5 g piece of cigar (see page 232)

A pinch of fine sea salt

¼ ounce / 7 g powdered gelatin, or 3 leaves

1 tablespoon cognac

Oil

Fresh blackberries, optional

If you are using powdered gelatin, set ¼ cup / 60 ml of the cream aside in a small saucepan.

Place the remaining cream (all of it if you are using leaf gelatin) and the sugar in a heavy saucepan over medium-low heat and stir to dissolve the sugar. Bring to a simmer, remove from the heat, and add the vanilla bean, lemon zest, cigar, and salt, then cover and let stand for 45 minutes.

For powdered gelatin, sprinkle the gelatin over the reserved ¼ cup / 60 ml cream and let stand for 5 minutes. Heat the cream gently, stirring to dissolve the gelatin, then add to the flavored cream. If you are using leaf gelatin, soak the gelatin in cold water for 5 minutes. Drain and squeeze the gelatin, add to the flavored cream, and stir to dissolve. Strain the cream into a large measuring cup, pressing against the cigar to extract all of the flavor. Stir in the cognac, then pour the mixture into 6 lightly oiled ⅔-cup / 150-ml molds. The mixture will not fill the molds. Refrigerate until set, about 4 hours.

Using a knife, carefully detach the edges of the panna cotta from the mold, then turn out onto the dessert plate with a gentle shake. Add the blackberries.

FENUGREEK

Those of you familiar with fenugreek will think immediately of the small, hard, six-sided, yellowish brown seeds that smell like curry. They are a common ingredient in Indian cookery and commercial curry powders. The seed is bitter, but when ground it has a sweet, almost caramel smell. That is because it contains the compound sotolon, also found in barley, molasses, and hay. Its aroma explains why such a bitter plant finds its way into the manufacture of artificial maple syrup. It is also sold in capsules and a tincture (which I've been told is tongue-curlingly bitter) to help stimulate lactation.

> "This introduces the dangerous topic of bitterness, a characteristic of the greens (methi), and often treated as a threat to American taste buds. I mention it up front to allow those who wish to leave the room to do so now. Those who enjoy bitterness for the way it gives backbone to the mild, counterposes sweetness, cleanses the palate, and heightens the sense of taste may wish to know that tender fenugreek leaves also offer hints of celery, fennel, spinach, and split pea (they are legumes, after all)." —ELIZABETH SCHNEIDER

While fenugreek may seem exotic, this legume, a relative of clover, was once well known in Europe. The ancient Greeks and Romans grew it for animal food, as its botanical name, *Trigonella foenum-graecum*, and common name, Greek hay, reveal. They also used its oddly shaped seeds as a medicine. No doubt the leaves still make good fodder, but they are also delicious to eat. They are very aromatic, with a smell of curry and a mildly bitter taste. Fresh fenugreek leaves can be added raw to a salad, but I prefer them quickly cooked like spinach. I'll call them by their Hindi name, methi, because that's what they call them at my local farmers' market. The bright green, oval-shaped leaves are sold in bunches with roots still attached and are only available in the summer. If your farmers' market doesn't have them, try an Indian or a Pakistani grocery. A bunch usually weighs in around ½ pound / 225 g. Remove and discard the roots and rinse the leaves several times because they are very sandy. Pick the leaves off the thicker stems in sprigs, and you'll end up with about 8 very loosely packed cups / 4¼ ounces / 120 g.

Methi leaves are easy to add to dishes; cook them like spinach and add them to an omelet, a quiche, or a stir-fry. The seeds take more work and you'll find them in the cuisines of the Indian subcontinent, through to Afghanistan and Ethiopia.

I created quite a lot of interest when I bought several bunches of methi leaves in a grocery store in the Indian area of Toronto. The store was filled with half a dozen men buying different ingredients. They couldn't believe that I liked the bitterness of methi, but once I convinced them they all began to tell me their favorite way to cook the fresh leaves. "I always cook them with spinach," one said, and that started me thinking. Some people say spinach is bitter, and while it probably was in the past, it no longer is; however, mixing spinach with methi makes a mildly bitter green. A touch of cream and eggs add richness and make a good breakfast or lunch dish.

METHI AND SPINACH WITH BAKED EGGS

SERVES 2

1 bunch methi leaves, prepared (see page 235)

1 bunch spinach, 14 ounces / 400 g, rinsed and stems removed

2 tablespoons unsalted butter

½ onion, finely chopped

½ cup / 125 ml whipping (35 percent fat) cream

Sea salt and freshly ground black pepper

Freshly grated nutmeg

1 teaspoon freshly squeezed lemon juice

4 eggs

½ teaspoon garam masala, optional

Preheat the oven to 350°F / 180°C.

Place a large saucepan over high heat and, when the pan is hot, add the methi and spinach leaves and stir constantly for 1 minute. Reduce the heat to low, cover, and cook another minute. Tip the leaves into a sieve to drain. When the leaves are cold, squeeze out the excess liquid and chop them.

In a frying pan, melt the butter over medium-low heat. When it begins to foam, add the onion and cook, stirring, until softened and beginning to color, about 5 minutes. Add the chopped leaves and the cream and season well with salt, pepper, and nutmeg. Cook until warmed through, then stir in the lemon juice.

Spread the mixture into 2 individual gratin dishes or a 9-inch / 23-cm ovenproof pie plate or dish, then make evenly spaced depressions in the methi/spinach mixture. Crack an egg into each one, and then spoon 1 tablespoon of the remaining cream over each egg. Bake for 15 minutes or until the whites are just set. Sprinkle with the garam masala, if using, and serve.

This is a good introduction to fenugreek leaves. Adding the leaves to this variation on the classic potatoes sarladaise from my book *Fat* cuts the richness of duck fat–infused potatoes. The fat and the starch of the potatoes in turn mitigate the bitterness of the methi leaves.

POTATOES AND METHI / SERVES 2

2 potatoes

2 tablespoons duck fat

1 bunch methi leaves, prepared (see page 235)

Sea salt and freshly ground black pepper

Peel the potatoes, cut into ¾-inch / 2-cm dice, and place in a colander. Rinse them well with cold water. Drain and pat dry with a clean kitchen towel.

Place the duck fat in a large frying pan over medium-high heat. When the duck fat is very hot and just starting to smoke, add the potatoes. Cook without stirring until the potatoes are golden on one side. Give the pan a shake and turn the potatoes, but do not attempt to turn any potatoes that are still sticking to the pan. Leave them until they detach themselves from the pan.

Continue to cook the potatoes until they are golden on all sides. Lower the heat and cook until soft in the center, about 10 minutes more.

Chop the methi leaves coarsely and add to the potatoes and continue to cook, stirring, until the methi leaves are wilted. Season well with salt and pepper, and serve hot or at room temperature.

This began with a recipe from my friend Naomi's book *Flatbreads and Flavors*. When I chat with Naomi, I know that I live under a rock labeled Eurocentric; she always opens my eyes to something new and she suggested I try the Yemeni Stew recipe in her book.

I played around with the recipe so I doubt that anyone living in Sana'a would recognize this dish but I love the taste of sweet lamb with bitter fenugreek.

FENUGREEK FLAVORED LAMB WITH LIMA BEANS

SERVES 4

1 cup / 6¼ ounces / 180 g lima beans, soaked overnight

¼ cup / 1⅓ ounces / 40 g fenugreek seeds

1 cup / 250 ml boiling water

4 roma tomatoes, peeled, seeded, and chopped

3 cloves garlic, germs removed, finely chopped

1 shallot, finely chopped

½ teaspoon cayenne

Sea salt

1½ pounds / 700 g lamb, cut into 1½-inch / 4-cm pieces

Freshly ground black pepper

3 tablespoons lamb fat or lard

2 onions, sliced

2 cups / 500 ml lamb stock, preferably homemade

1 cup / 15 g fresh mint leaves

Drain the beans, place in a saucepan, and cover with cold water and a lid. Bring slowly to a boil over low heat, then simmer, partially covered, for 10 minutes. Drain and set aside.

Grind the fenugreek seeds in a spice grinder into a coarse powder. Place in a medium bowl and pour over the boiling water; let stand until all the water is absorbed, about 3 hours.

Now add the tomatoes, garlic, shallot, cayenne, and 2 teaspoons salt, stir to mix, cover, and refrigerate.

Preheat the oven to 300°F / 150°C.

Pat the lamb cubes dry and season with salt and pepper. In a heavy flameproof casserole or Dutch oven, melt 2 tablespoons of the fat over medium-high heat and brown the lamb pieces. As they brown, transfer the pieces to a plate. Add the onions to the pan, and the remaining fat if necessary, and cook, stirring from time to time, until the onions soften and color.

Add the lamb stock and bring to a boil, deglazing the pan by scraping up the browned bits from the bottom. Add the browned lamb and blanched beans, and cover with a piece of wet parchment paper and the lid. Transfer to the oven and cook for 1 hour. Then uncover and remove the parchment paper; cook for another hour. Remove the fenugreek mixture from the refrigerator.

Continue to cook until the lamb and the beans are tender. Stir in the fenugreek mixture, taste, and season with salt and pepper. It will probably need a good dose of salt to balance the bitter.

Return to the oven, uncovered, for about 15 minutes or until heated through. Stir in the mint leaves and serve.

SMELLING TASTE

Our sense of smell plays a pivotal role in determining the flavor of a food. Taste and smell are so closely linked in our brain that we don't separate the taste of a food from its odor. Yet, we've all experienced taste without smell. When we have a head cold, our blocked nasal passages impair our ability to smell, and as a result food tastes bland. A food scientist will tell you that your food still had taste; it was the flavor that was lacking. You can test the importance of smell by eating a fruit while holding your nose. The taste buds on your tongue will sense sweetness, but you won't be able to identify the fruit. Odor is essential to the flavor of our food. Only when signals from both our taste buds and our nose meet in our brain can we sense flavor and identify what we are eating.

The receptors on our tongue pick up a limited number of tastes, but our sense of smell is much more sensitive, able to differentiate at least one trillion different odors that, when mixed with signals from our taste buds, give us myriad different flavors.

Our sense of smell works in two distinct ways. We smell food before we place it in our mouth, *orthonasal olfaction*, or what most of us think of as our sense of smell. We sniff our food to tell whether it is good or bad, fresh or stale, ripe or rancid, mild or intensely flavored. This gives us lots of signals about our food and expectations of how it will taste. With familiar foods, it reinforces a desire to eat them: the fragrance of a ripe peach; the meaty smell of frying bacon; or the familiar, welcoming aroma of a long-simmered stew. However, this way of smelling can mislead us, especially with unfamiliar foods. Foods often smell stronger than they taste, making us hesitant to try them. The French cheese Munster has an overpowering odor that makes you expect a very strong tasting cheese; while, in reality its flavor is mild and creamy.

> "A man eats nothing without smelling it more or less consciously, while with unknown foods his nose acts always as the first sentinel, crying out *Who goes there?* When sense of smell is cut off, taste is paralyzed . . . "
> —JEAN-ANTHELME BRILLAT-SAVARIN

We also smell food in our mouth, *retronasal olfaction*, as it mixes with air and moisture in our mouth when we chew it. Our attention is so focused on the oral stimulation that we are unaware of the odor of the food. This retronasal smell combined with the information from our taste buds registers in our brain as a flavor. Smelling food without tasting it, or tasting it without smelling it, results in food with no flavor. To discern flavor we must employ both of these senses.

Despite our ability to distinguish many different odors, we are not very good at identifying them, as the area of our brain where odor is detected is not well connected with our verbal center. We have difficulty in identifying individual flavors within a recipe, and the more complex the recipe, the more difficult it becomes. Most of us, even experienced chefs, have trouble naming more than four.

Information from our taste buds is transmitted to our brain by an indirect route, whereas smell goes directly to our brain, registering in the hippocampus, where we store our emotions and memories, especially memories of places. Odors create primal and long-lasting memories, which is why smell evokes a powerful emotional response. A smell can make us recall a place, a person, an event, or a feeling. Is it possible to discuss the links between food and memory without invoking Marcel Proust's experience with a madeleine that led him to write a very long book? Probably, but it is worth noting that Proust points out that simply seeing a madeleine didn't trigger his memory:

> The sight of the little madeleine had recalled nothing to my mind before I tasted it;
> perhaps because I had so often seen such things in the meantime, without tasting
> them, on the trays in pastry-cooks' windows, that their image had dissociated
> itself from those Combray days to take its place among others more recent . . .

It was only when he smelt the madeleine mixed with the tea did Proust recall his long forgotten childhood at Combray:

> I raised to my lips a spoonful of the tea in which I had soaked a morsel of the cake.
> No sooner had the warm liquid mixed with the crumbs touched my palate than a
> shudder ran through me and I stopped, intent upon the extraordinary thing that
> was happening to me. An exquisite pleasure had invaded my senses . . .

Like Proust, we all have memories, many of which remain buried until we encounter that distinctive odor again. These odor memories don't change the taste of what we eat, but they have a strong emotional power. So while our taste buds can be retrained with repeated exposure, if the smell of the food is linked to a bad or traumatic memory, we may never like the food.

Can a food smell bitter? Burnt toast, caramelizing sugar, roasting coffee, the medicinal odor of bitter alcohols, and the sulfurous, earthy smell of brussels sprouts, all trigger an expectation of bitter in our brain. Taste scientists argue that bitter is simply a taste, but for the cook, bitter also has a smell.

EPILOGUE

Just as I was finishing up this book a colleague contacted me, asking if I would write for a new Internet magazine he was starting. I replied that I couldn't think about anything until I completed the book. Politely he inquired what the subject was, and I told him bitter foods. He excitedly began to tell me how much he loved bitter tastes and that he had cow bile in his freezer. Cow bile? I hadn't considered there might be a bitter flavor I could explore in the animal kingdom. Cow bile is bright green and very bitter, he told me, and is used to flavor *pinapaitan,* a Filipino stew of tripe, intestines, and liver. How could I have not known this? All my experience of bitter had been in the plant kingdom. Next, an email arrived from my editor, telling me about Japanese *mentaiko,* marinated cod's roe that is strongly bitter. So you can see, just as I finish this book I am only beginning my exploration of the world of bitter.

BIBLIOGRAPHY

Abert, Jean-François. *Pierre Gagnaire: Reinventing French Cuisine*, translated by Anthony Roberts. New York: Stewart, Tabori & Chang, 2007.

Alford, Jeffrey, and Naomi Duguid. *Flatbreads & Flavors*. New York: William Morrow, 1995.

———. *Mangoes & Curry Leaves*. New York: Random House, 2005.

Allen, John S. "Why Humans Are Crazy for Crispy." *The Chronicle of Higher Education*, May 27, 2012.

———. *The Omnivorous Mind: Our Evolving Relationship with Food*. Cambridge: Harvard University Press, 2012.

Ayto, John. *The Diner's Dictionary*. Oxford: Oxford University Press, 1993.

Batali, Mario. *Babbo Cookbook*. New York: Clarkson Potter, 2002.

Bayless, Rick, and Dean Groen Bayless. *Authentic Mexican*. New York: William Morrow, 1987.

Beaugé, Bénédict. *Le Gourmand des Quatre Saisons*. Paris: Nil Editions, 1999.

———. *Michel Troisgros et L'Italie*. Paris: Editions Glénat, 2009.

Brillat-Savarin, Jean-Anthelme. *The Physiology of Taste*, translated by M. F. K. Fisher. Washington, DC: Counterpoint, 1994.

Brockway, Lucile H. "Science and Colonial Expansion: The Role of the British Royal Botanic Garden." *American Ethnologist* 6 (3), 1979.

Brown, Deni. *Encyclopedia of Herbs & Their Uses*. Westmount: Reader's Digest Canada, 1995.

Buck, Linda B. *Unraveling the Sense of Smell*. Nobel Lecture, December 8, 2004.

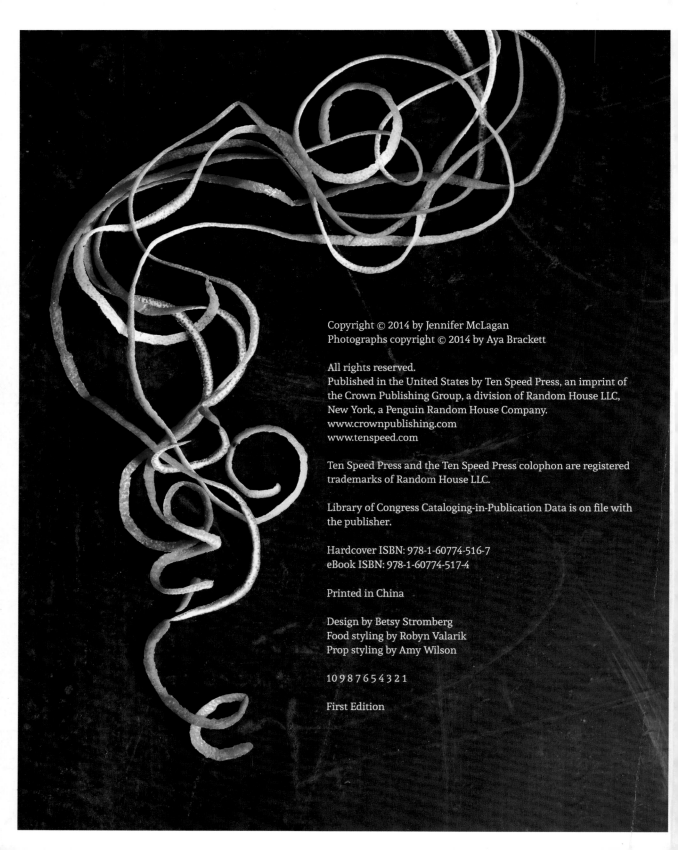

Ten Speed Press and the Ten Speed Press colophon are registered
trademarks of Random House LLC.

Library of Congress Cataloging-in-Publication Data is on file with
the publisher.

Hardcover ISBN: 978-1-60774-516-7
eBook ISBN: 978-1-60774-517-4

Printed in China

Design by Betsy Stromberg
Food styling by Robyn Valarik
Prop styling by Amy Wilson

10 9 8 7 6 5 4 3 2 1

First Edition